Also by Nick Taylor

Sins of the Father:
The True Story of a Family Running from the Mob

Bass Wars:
A Story of Fishing, Fame and Fortune

ORDINARY MIRACLES

Life in a Small Church

BY NICK TAYLOR

SIMON & SCHUSTER

New York London Toronto Sydney Tokyo Singapore

SIMON & SCHUSTER
Simon & Schuster Building
Rockefeller Center
1230 Avenue of the Americas
New York, New York 10020

Designed by Liney Li
Manufactured in the United States of America

10 9 8 7 6 5 4 3 2 1

Library of Congress Cataloging-in-Publication Data
Taylor, Nick, date.
Ordinary miracles : life in a small church / by Nick Taylor.
p. cm.
1. St. Mary's Episcopal Church (Mohegan Lake, N.Y.) 2. Episcopal Church—New York—Mohegan Lake—History—1965– . 3. Anglican Communion—New York—Mohegan Lake—History—20th century. 4. Stelk, Lincoln Frank, 1934– 5. Episcopal Church—New York—Mohegan Lake—Clergy. 6. Small churches—New York—Mohegan Lake. 7. Mohegan Lake (N.Y.)—Church history. I. Title.
BX5980.M564T38 1993
283'.747277—dc20 92-597 CIP
ISBN 0-671-70944-5

ACKNOWLEDGMENTS

I wish to thank the people of St. Mary's, without whom this book would not have been possible. Most especially, Father Lincoln Stelk, who allowed me into his thoughts, his home, his vestry meetings and his church, and so allowed me to witness ordinary miracles, and Ginny Stelk and their daughters Kirsten, Sara and Marla; Judy Salerno, who made it fun; Caryl, Bill and Justin Miller, who made it real; Lily and Harold Van Horne, the Efmans, Obligados, Cousinses, Tuckers, Donovans, Sosos, Munroes, Warneckes, Harrises, Miesches, Deckers, Doyles, Bodekers, Tramontis, Heinemans, Douglases, Ann Marwick, Beverley Taylor, Ed Lumley, John Harbeson, Melanie Bussel, Susan Hafford, Bob Lockhart, David Odell, Marsha McCoy, Jan Faris, Coleman Hill, Eugene Jackson, the Rev. Joanna White, the Rev. Marc Lee and everyone else who shared their hospitality, observations or both.

I wish also to thank the Rt. Rev. Paul Moore, retired diocesan bishop of New York, for his encouragement, George Hernandez, diocesan archivist, for his assistance, and Michael Corney and Jose Malaret of the Episcopal Church Pension Group for help with facts and figures.

Thanks go as well to my good and patient editor, Bob Bender; my always supportive agent, Al Lowman; and to my wife, Barbara Nevins, who is the best.

For Richie

We must try
To love so well the world that we may believe, in the end, in God.

from "Masts at Dawn,"
by Robert Penn Warren

1

Father Lincoln Stelk held out his hands and took the baby and upended him three times into the water. The boy howled. "That's right!" Stelk called out triumphantly. "I baptize you in the name of the Father, and of the Son, and of the Holy Spirit."

The priest turned to the congregation. He raised the blinking boy, now quiet, to his shoulder. Elation shone on Stelk's face. "People of St. Mary's, meet your new son," he cried. Then he stepped down into the aisle and paraded the boy to the back of the small church. Applause from the pews cascaded over them. People craned to see. Stelk turned at the door, where the Stars and Stripes and the Episcopal Church flag hung, and marched back up the aisle in exuberant procession. The boy looked from face to face with bright-eyed curiosity.

That was how Stelk began the second quarter-century of his priesthood.

✢

The day had started in an ungodly welter of confusion. Stelk stepped out into the January cold and hurried across the flagstones from the rectory to the church. He ignored the cold on the bald crown of his head but he noticed, as he always did, the sagging white clapboards of the parish hall.

He had burst into the hall and come face to face with Karin

Efman. She looked up and froze, then fled, trailing excuses while pretending she wasn't carrying something beneath her thick down coat.

Stelk took one step after her, then remembered that he had to find the bishop.

The bishop—or one of the bishops, since there were three in the Episcopal Diocese of New York—usually came in April. But one day Stelk had opened one of the flood of form letters from headquarters to learn that the new diocesan bishop, the Right Reverend Richard F. Grein, was coming to Mohegan Lake in January. It caught him by surprise. He called the diocese office in Manhattan to find out what was going on.

Bishop Grein suggested that Stelk ask the St. Mary's lay people who'd contacted him. Stelk had fumed. He'd worn a collar for twenty-five years, most of that time in small parishes. He'd felt the need, in each, to dictate and control events. He'd been the victim of one parish coup, and the bruises still were tender. Now his own people had contacted the bishop without consulting him, and it didn't seem to matter that it was to celebrate the silver anniversary of his ordination as a priest. Stelk was "less than thrilled . . . a tad upset," as Karin Efman put it.

Stelk had mellowed as the day approached, however. The weeks of Epiphany, between Christmas and Lent, are normally a slow time in the Church, but at St. Mary's they were filled with anticipation. Stelk would enter the church office greeted by sudden, guilty pauses. Whispered ends of sentences wafted from groups of parishioners that he passed. Now and then he'd hear a sudden giggle that would just as quickly stop. When he pressed for details, his wife, Ginny, gave him a Mona Lisa smile.

Before Stelk became a priest he had been a bomber pilot in the Strategic Air Command. That was the look he had at ordination: lean, with dark and piercing eyes, close-cropped hair, a worldly half smile of self-assurance. Now, at fifty-five, he looked more like a priest. His hair, which had receded early, was going white and wisped about his collar. His waistline, once immune to calories, was giving way to an onslaught of desserts. His eyes, still dark, of course, seemed merrier and somehow more forgiving than in his ordination photographs. His hawklike vision now required reading glasses. In those passing years his children had increased from one to three, all daughters, all grown now and away at work or college. The youngest ate no meat; she believed that animals had souls. Other things had changed as well. Lincoln Frank Stelk, trained to deliver history's most destructive weapon, the atomic bomb, had become a pacifist.

The parish hall was busy. Stelk had suspended church school for the bishop's visit. Children scampered as their parents readied the hall to celebrate Stelk's anniversary. He also had canceled the early service and urged everyone to come at ten-thirty to "greet and get to know the good man who is our new episcopal Father-in-God."

Where was the bishop, anyway? Stelk headed toward the sacristy, which connected the church to the parish hall. The pine floor sagged beneath his footsteps, reminding Stelk that the joists needed replacing and there was no money in the budget. The choir was in its corner, practicing amid the hubbub of the parish hall. Twelve blue-robed members sang around an upright piano, played by Carol Obligado, the music director of St. Mary's.

"Anybody seen the bishop?" Stelk asked. The choir sang, "Lift high the cross . . ."

Carol held a chord and pointed toward the door. Stelk went through into the hall outside the sacristy. The narrow space, like every other corner of St. Mary's, had been pressed into use. The acolytes used it as a robing room. They were standing around on the edges of their sneakers, talking, when Stelk hurried in. Four teenage girls and a boy; they all pointed to the sacristy.

Stelk approached the open door. He was eager for the meeting. He was inclined to like the new lead bishop in the diocese from the few things he knew about him. Bishop Grein was, for one thing, a member of the Wheat Field Mafia; he had come from Kansas, where Stelk had been stationed in SAC and where he'd met Ginny all those years ago. Stelk also, in a denomination known for the intensity and vigor of its arguments, agreed with the bishop's emphasis on the theology behind the Church's stands on social issues. Love your neighbor was Jesus talking, it wasn't some council of do-gooders. He agreed with the bishop's emphasis on baptism. He especially agreed—or, the bishop agreed with him, for Stelk was a crusader here—that young people being confirmed should make a serious commitment to church life. He called it a Mature Profession of Faith. Today two young people, the first in the diocese, would be initiated as candidates for the Mature Profession of Faith. Stelk envisioned a pilot program, perhaps a model for a revitalized Church throughout the nation. It was just one of his plans for St. Mary's in the ambitious agenda for the months ahead.

St. Mary's was one hundred and twenty-three years old. It had enjoyed periods of growth and suffered years of stagnation in its life. Now it was growing again. New families appeared almost every Sunday. The cries of the babies interrupted Stelk's sermons, but Stelk heard the voices of new members, a river of them flowing into the future. Where would they go if he had no place to put them, no programs to offer? The church was cramped, the parish hall inadequate. St. Mary's had to expand, Stelk believed, in order to survive. He had a plan for that, too, all ready to promote before the vestry.

Stelk had been eager for new challenges when he had moved his family from Ohio two-and-a-half years earlier. In that time the bitterness of his defeat at Kenyon College had faded into puzzlement. He and Ginny were energized by their proximity to New York City, forty miles away. They enjoyed the theater and the Philharmonic. She played in chamber music groups and he sang in the Taghkanic Chorale. They liked the Westchester County countryside and thought that they'd retire there, if they could manage to afford a house. And now all the reasons for answering the call to St. Mary's and Mohegan Lake, all of the possibilities, were ripening.

Stelk strode into the sacristy to greet the bishop.

+

I had come to St. Mary's looking for a church. I had an author's notion that it would be a good place to find the extraordinariness of ordinary people. The retiring Episcopal bishop of New York, Paul Moore, suggested a church in Ossining. The young rector at St. Paul's-on-the-Hill said he was too busy. It was just as well, because he later resigned from the clergy. Before he did, he suggested I look at the church in Mohegan Lake. "Dynamic rector. Interesting congregation," read his scribbled note.

The voice on the answering machine revealed a sense of humor and a slight impediment that turned *r*'s almost to *w*'s. "Hello, you've reached St. Mary's Episcopal Church, Mohegan Lake, New York . . ." It invited callers to leave a message, ". . . but first, a commercial: Our Sunday services are at eight and ten-thirty, Holy Eucharist, with church school and nursery at ten-thirty."

I drove up from the city for the ten-thirty service the next Sunday.

St. Mary's is a mile or two off the Taconic State Parkway, on Route 6 as it angles east toward Peekskill and the Hudson River. There was a boarded-up stone church on the way, an ungainly van positioned at the roadside to sell hot dogs and then a burst of commerce: a Texaco station, a Volkswagen and Isuzu dealer, Yogi's Steak and Seafood House, a butcher "shoppe," Gary's Penny Pincher, Mohegan Electric Supply. A sign abutting a newly bulldozed tract promised more of the same. STORES, COMING SOON, it said.

What looked like a small English country church sat at the edge of a gravel lot just down the road. I pulled into the lot, and a red-cheeked man, wearing a sweater under his suit jacket, waved me into a parking space. The church was well proportioned, with a steep roof and stucco walls darkened by a winter rain. It had arched stained-glass windows, some demi-buttresses along the walls and a peaked bell tower astride the roof above the entrance. A frame extension ran off the back of the church to another frame building that joined it in an "L." The church bell began to clang. People in robes emerged from a side door and trailed toward the main entrance.

I waited inside the narthex—the church's vestibule—for the opening procession to clear the space behind the pews. The rector had left instructions for another commercial taped to the wall. His neatly printed note read: "Please turn on the outside and narthex lights (far left toggle switches). On a cloudy day, the narthex is dark and uninviting. Besides, it doesn't hurt to advertise." On the table below, next to the visitors' register, a hand-lettered sign on a large wicker basket invited FOOD PANTRY DONATIONS.

The first verse of the processional hymn faded, and an usher swung open the door. He was casually dressed, in blue jeans and a sweater. Inside, the church was simple, graceful and inviting. Whitewashed stucco walls rose to a pitched ceiling of dark wood. Sturdy beams crossed overhead. Memorial plaques studded the walls. A cross, suspended on nearly invisible wires, hung above the altar. High in the wall behind it, backlit in brilliant colors, a stained-glass depiction of a mother cradling an infant—Mary and Jesus, I assumed—and reaching out to three attentive children was set in a triangle with gracefully arched sides.

I counted just eleven rows of pews on each side of a central aisle. Most were full, but I found a seat. The processional hymn ended with a long "Aaah-men." I noticed as I replaced my hymnal in the rack in front of me that the back of the pew had been carved, like a wooden school desk, with names and initials. The carvings were darkened by years and many varnishings.

The priest cleared his throat. He wore his vestments comfortably, the full-length white alb, the cross-embroidered, scarf-like stole that draped his neck and made an X at the center of his chest, the twisted cord cincture, or sash, at his waist that held the tucked ends of the stole. His penumbra of hair made him look like a monk. He gazed at the congregation over black-framed reading glasses. His voice was a strong tenor. He said, "The Lord be with you."

"And also with you," the people answered.

"Let us pray."

Years dissolved, and I was back in church.

✣

I had not attended regularly for almost thirty years. I stopped in my mid-teens, soon after I bore the processional cross into an overhang and dropped it in a clatter on the floor of St. Raphael's Episcopal Church in Ft. Myers Beach, Florida. I gathered from that that God did not intend for me to be an acolyte. Besides, I reckoned church irrelevant.

The world was changing. A rebellious generation was beginning to question all authority—parental, civil, academic. The priests and ministers in their round collars with their pious ways were easy targets.

The Episcopal Church prayer book at the time was all about penance, about atoning for your sins. The Book of Common Prayer, last revised in 1928, was a beautifully written downer. The General Confession seemed to be its central document:

"Almighty God, Father of our Lord Jesus Christ, Maker of all things, Judge of all men; We acknowledge and bewail our manifold sins and wickedness, Which we from time to time most grievously have committed, By thought, word, and deed, Against thy Divine Majesty, Provoking most justly thy wrath and indignation against us. We do earnestly repent, And are heartily sorry for these our misdoings; The remembrance of them is grievous unto us; The burden of them is intolerable. Have mercy upon us, Have mercy upon us, most merciful Father . . ."

I could repeat the General Confession from memory after all my years outside the church.

There was an impatience with all this in the sixties, a restlessness to throw off the traces and go out and set things right. The Episcopal Church in the United States was one of the big losers. An offshoot of the Church of England, it once had been the church of the landed and elite. It was the church of seven of the first fourteen U.S. Presidents, but only four of the last twenty-six, as immigration broadened the American populace. Then, when a wave of fundamentalism swept the Protestant churches and spawned offshoots of its own, the Episcopalians remained "God's frozen chosen," trapped with a liturgy that frowned on spontaneous expression.

Even as many at the local level comprised an overstarched old guard, an avant-garde within the national Church began to take up progressive causes. Episcopal seminarians joined the battles in the South for civil rights. Episcopal priests counseled women seeking abortions before abortions were legal nationwide. The Church ordained women to the priesthood. It quietly ministered to homosexuals, and ordained them, too, as long as they were celibate. (Chaste gays fit the Church's standards for wholesome priestly conduct, according to a resolution of the 1979 General Convention of the Episcopal Church. Practicing homosexuals were placed on a par with straight priests who were sexually active outside marriage, as violating "the traditional teaching of the church on marriage, marital fidelity and sexual chastity as the standard of Christian sexual morality.") The Church was rewarded for these ministries by the loss of nearly a third of its membership in the United States, from 3,615,643 in 1965 to 2,448,712 in 1990. Fewer clergy were needed to shepherd these diminished flocks. In 1965, the year Stelk was ordained a priest, the Episcopal Church had 10,615 active priests and deacons; in 1990 the figure was 8,458.

During that time, however, the liturgy lightened up. The triennial Convention of the Episcopal Church adopted a new Book of Common Prayer in 1979, three years after it had approved the ordination of women. Redemption was the message now, less so propitiation and atonement. The harsh language of the General Confession disappeared from a new Rite Two version of the Holy Eucharist, replaced with a softer Confession of Sin. Even Rite One, more like the old service, made it optional. The new prayer book, with its emphasis on the "good news" of redemption and God's love, carried the potential to broaden the Church's base.

The Church nonetheless continued to lose members. So did most other Protestant denominations. A broad spectrum of people still was finding church irrelevant.

Then the collectivity of the nation seemed to fail. Ordinary civil acts that people had every reason to take for granted disappeared. Ball players stopped signing autographs for kids and started selling them instead. Drivers shot other drivers for changing lanes too fast. Comedians retailed insults, and wealth conveyed celebrity. A new predatory spirit ruled.

Suddenly, church seemed relevant again. For surely, somewhere, people were negotiating these harsh times without losing their humanity. Somewhere the miracles of ordinary life were being done: people raising children, attending to jobs, caring for sick parents and doing a little more besides. Sharing. Acting quietly, with generosity and grace. Tamping down their fear. Rejecting arrogance and greed. These were the true heroic acts. Where did these people find the faith to move forward? Where but in a house of worship were the answers to questions that suddenly were begging for them: How must we live? What shall sustain us? On whom can we rely? Those were the questions that led me to St. Mary's.

I was not prepared for what would happen. That first morning at St. Mary's triggered a powerful nostalgia. The hymns and prayers came rushing back in torrents of familiarity. Then the message—that we must reach outside ourselves to close the circle God has offered us—left me choked with gratitude for the reassurance it implied.

+

Bishop Grein, after meeting Stelk, emerged into the sanctuary. The people were still settling in the pews and hardly noticed him, even in the splendor of his robes. He went to the altar and knelt to pray. He prayed for long moments, his head deeply bowed, so still the drape of his robes seemed carved, as if from marble. The ushers began placing wooden folding chairs along the aisles.

Eugene Jackson stood outside the blue church door, smoking a cigarette. He held a worn Bible stuffed with notes under one arm. He'd forgotten to shave, and he looked grave and distant.

Eugene was the first person I had met at St. Mary's that first day. We were sipping coffee in the parish hall when I noticed his Bible full of notes. He told me he was a preacher and a doctor of religion. He was a tattered man with wild hair and faded clothes, and I was thrilled to meet him. He clearly heard a voice I couldn't hear.

I mentioned this to Stelk. "Ah, Eugene," he said. "Let me show you something." He produced from a file cabinet in the church office a thick envelope of papers Eugene had given him for safekeeping. They were Eugene's notes, hand-written on lined paper.

"The first time he gave me something," Stelk said, "I read it and I thought, maybe he's some kind of a savant, a genius who just can't get it together. I read it about three times." He handed me a paper.

It was titled "Approaches to the Question of Omniscient Almightyness (Supreme Universal) About God." It read: "Renowned personable associations, not incalculably ascertained and the superior, sublime excellence and favoritism's distinctive differential and of existent subsistence's feeling, penetration and influence's natural, essential character and constitution without exaggeration and have inherent property and attribution's ascription and omnipotent characteristics of reliability's substantial character and significant importance and important, valuable permanent, considerable extensions superiorities of God, the Father Creator of universes and in addition higher and greater than Jesus Christ and the Holy Ghost worthy by reasons through aggregation's quantity."

His next subject was "Black Holes Within Space."

Eugene would give the notes only to Stelk. Once, he had entered the church office with a sheaf of papers only to find Stelk absent. The church secretary said she'd be glad to take them. "Are you Episcopalian?" he had asked.

Terry Donaghy attended St. Elizabeth Ann Seton, the Roman Catholic church in nearby Shrub Oak, and said so.

Eugene shrank and held his papers close. "Well, I certainly can't leave these with you, then," he had said. Nonetheless, his writings now filled the better part of a file drawer.

"Big doings today," I said. Eugene, head wreathed in smoke, perked up.

"Yes," he agreed. "The bishop, baptism, confirmation, Eucharist. Is there anything else?"

"Father Stelk. The twenty-fifth anniversary of his ordination."

"Oh, yes," said Eugene. He grinned sweetly, revealing stained and broken teeth.

The church bell clanged and I went inside to find a seat. Eugene stayed behind to smoke his cigarette.

At ten-thirty the church bell clanged again. The bishop finished his prayers and disappeared in the direction of the sacristy. Carol Obligado entered from the way he'd gone and crossed to the organ, genuflecting before the altar. She was tiny, five-feet-and-a-fraction tall, and walked with a vigorous stride. Carol was one of St. Mary's few cradle Episcopalians. Most of St. Mary's members had started life in other churches. Over the years, ex-Baptists, -Methodists, -Presbyterians, -Armenian Apostolics, -Lutherans, -Evangelicals, -Congregationalists, ex-members of the Dutch Reformed Church and the Russian and Eastern Orthodox Churches had gravitated to St. Mary's. The largest collection of defectors were ex-Roman Catholics. But Carol, a Pennsylvania rector's daughter, had been Episcopalian from day one. She was the natural mother of two sons. When she and her husband Fred decided it was time for a daughter, rather than leave it to chance they adopted a three-year-old girl from a Korean orphanage. Susan was in high school now, and both boys were in college. Carol was also the only member of St. Mary's to drive a Mercedes-Benz, a present from Fred on her fortieth birthday.

She sat down at the organ, hiked up the skirt of her black

cassock, placed her square-toed shoes upon the pedals, arranged the music on the stand above the tiered keyboard and began to play: César Franck's *Cantabile.* Carol liked French romantic music for her preludes.

A few minutes later, when it seemed the church could not hold another person, the processional retinue squeezed in at the back among the folding chairs, and Carol struck up the opening hymn. The bishop brought up the rear of the procession. He followed Stelk, who was singing loudly in his serviceable tenor. The bishop looked like a visiting potentate, as indeed he was. His miter, the peaked crown of office, bobbed above the heads of the singing congregation and marked his progress toward the altar. He carried a staff, called a *crozier,* shaped like a shepherd's crook. A little boy near the aisle, squirming in a too-tight suit, watched him, awestruck, as if he might lift off and fly. As the organ music faded, the bishop sat down in a grand thronelike chair that faced the congregation. A heavy gold cross dangled from his neck, outside his vestments. An attending acolyte stood by to hold the crozier.

Bishop Grein had prayed quietly, but he spoke with force. Removing his miter and ascending to the pulpit, he delivered a sermon about faith and service. He pointed, he jabbed the air for emphasis, he knit his hands together and unknit them, opening them like blooming flowers. He talked about the saving grace of sacrifice. He said, "If you will take your life, offer it, give it away, surrender it . . . then you save it. Self-discovery occurs . . . because we give ourselves to others."

The baptismal party sat in front, near the squat plaster font. The words ONE LORD, ONE BAPTISM, ONE FAITH were engraved around its hexagonal rim. The infant to be baptized was asleep in the arms of his mother. She had dressed him in a blue satin jumper.

The vows of baptism had become a central part of the 1979 version of the prayer book. The ceremony once had been private, between the family and the priest. Now it had emerged to be celebrated with the Eucharist. Entire congregations joined in promising to spiritually support the baptized. It was the strongest signal of the Church's new inclusiveness.

Bishop Grein finished his sermon, left the pulpit and beckoned the party to come forward. As the parents and godparents gathered around the font, the father, who now was carrying the baby, leaned over to inspect the few inches of consecrated water in the gilded basin.

Stelk liked to make baptism a celebration. He thought of it as a festival of redemption, and like any festival, the more who came, the merrier. "Any of the children who would like to come up and watch, please do," he invited. "Just come on up. Don't be shy."

A few curious but reluctant children edged into the aisle, urged by their parents. Stelk opened his arms. "Come on. It's okay. This is for you," he said, and they came forward. He distributed them one by one around the font. Bishop Grein led a recitation of the vows:

"Do you renounce Satan and all the spiritual forces of wickedness that rebel against God?

"Do you renounce the evil powers of this world which corrupt and destroy the creatures of God?

"Do you renounce all sinful desires that draw you from the love of God?

"Do you turn to Jesus Christ and accept him as your Savior?

"Do you put your whole trust in his grace and love?

"Do you promise to follow and obey him as your Lord?"

The parents and godparents answered yes to all the questions. The congregation added its support. Then—the moment. Stelk took the sleepy baby from his father's arms and dipped his head into the water and held him up and joyously paraded him, showered with the congregation's warm applause, Stelk the baptist, welcoming another soul into the kingdom.

✢

A parish never wastes a visit by a bishop, and Stelk had given Bishop Grein a full program. The bishop returned to his grand chair, put on his miter and took his crozier from the acolyte. Stelk called on the candidates for confirmation to come forward. A woman in her thirties and three young people just entering their teens came to the center of the chancel and knelt before the bishop. Bishop Grein laid his hands upon their heads and asked the Lord to strengthen and defend them.

The woman was a lesbian and the mother of two children, but it was the three younger people whose confirmation worried Stelk. The woman had attended seminary, and the church was central to her life and her relationship. The teenagers had dawdled through the catechism. They had reddened and stammered when he'd asked who they thought the Messiah was. When that happened Stelk decided, hereafter, to take a different approach to confirmation.

Young Episcopalians before 1973 had to be confirmed before they could receive Holy Communion, the gifts of bread and wine. Confirmation was a rite of passage, the moment when a young person left the children in the pews and joined the adults at the communion rail. The Episcopal General Convention in 1973 made baptism the only requirement for receiving Communion. Priests, Stelk among them, took to placing a wine-dipped finger onto the lips of babes to convey the Sacrament. Confirmation became simply a reaffirmation of baptismal vows. But the ceremony, performed always by a bishop, remained a rite of passage, and the pressure from parents and peers to "make confirmation" could be great.

Stelk objected to such confirmations. The vows that were just a recitation to the kids were lifelong promises to Stelk. "It's a serious commitment," he insisted, waving hands and furrowing his forehead. "You're gonna let your child get married at age twelve? No! It's serious. So is confirmation. So is taking on yourself the responsibility for these promises. These baptismal promises are the center of your life."

The renewal vows did suggest maturity. Renouncing evil and renewing a commitment to Christ were boilerplate, but there was more: loving your neighbor, striving for justice and peace, respecting the dignity of every human being. Stelk said,

"I want them to think about what they're doing and why, not do it just because their friends are doing it."

His solution was the Mature Profession of Faith. He envisioned classes over several months, not for students to spout back the catechism but to consider the conduct of their lives. He was proud that the bishop was accepting the first candidates for this new journey here at St. Mary's. He summoned them forward.

Alice Marwick was a blond eighth-grader who played the trumpet and had an interest in debate. Cynthia Bondi, whose mother was ill with cancer, was a brunette who spent most of her after-school hours working in the office of a dentist. Bishop Grein leaned toward them and placed his hands first upon one bowed head, then the other. Stelk beamed. The congregation, beginning to get restless, stirred. Then the bishop was receiving a new member who had been a Roman Catholic, then installing the new parish officers, and the service moved quickly through the Offertory and into the Communion.

✛

Parishioners poured into the L-shaped parish hall for Stelk's anniversary celebration. Its so-called Green Room, the foot of the L, was a converted carriage house. The Pine Room, the shaft of the L that joined the Green Room to the church, had walls paneled in knotty pine. The Green Room's green walls had long ago been painted over, so hardly anybody at St. Mary's remembered why the room had its name.

A long table dominated the juncture of the rooms. A banner printed on computer paper was strung across the corner. It read HAPPY 25TH ANNIVERSARY!!! Stelk and Ginny and Bishop Grein mingled for a while and then sat down at the table under the banner. People got a second cup of coffee, took an extra brownie and edged toward the table to see what would happen. Some of them had come a long way. Two of Stelk's friends from high school days outside Chicago had made the trip. Suzanne Hartley, who had met the Stelks at his first parish when she was a college freshman, had flown from Ohio. The Stelks' oldest daughter, Kirsten, who worked in New York in software marketing, had driven up from the city for the day. Sara was down from Martha's Vineyard, where she sold advertising for a newspaper on the island. Only Marla, the youngest, wasn't there. Her sisters said Marla didn't buy "the whole church thing." But it was a long trip from Colorado Springs, where she attended Colorado College.

Karin Efman, who also had three daughters, shifted her weight from one solid calf to the other and said, "I can't wait to take my shoes off." The package she had carried earlier, concealed under her coat, now waited among several on the table.

Stelk nodded to the bishop, stood and cleared his throat. He looked around the room and swallowed. He patted the pocket of his black clerical shirt and fished out his reading glasses. He put them on and peered over them, trying to look stern. Ginny folded her hands serenely in her lap. Bishop Grein sat back and crossed his legs.

"Confirmations are normally in April," he said. "I was informed this year's would be in January by a committee of lay people, who already had contacted the bishop."

Carol Obligado stepped out of the crowd. "This was the committee to celebrate the twenty-fifth anniversary of Linc's ordination despite him," she said. Her page-boy bangs brushed the top of her big glasses, which seemed to cover half her face. "We were gonna do it, or die trying."

Stelk smiled. He remembered his ordination as a nightmare of anxiety that had gone out of his control. A huge snowstorm had blown over the Eastern Seaboard. He'd invited Harvey Guthrie down to preach at the service, but Guthrie, Stelk's favorite teacher at the Episcopal Theological Seminary in Cambridge, Massachusetts, had called from Baltimore to say he'd been snowed in. Bishop William Creighton, who was presiding over the ceremony in St. Thomas's Church in Washington, D.C., sang one plainsong prayer while the organist played another. Stelk, used to kneeling himself, had been unnerved when the other priests knelt to receive his priestly blessing. He was glad that tradition had been dropped. He still didn't like losing control. But, by contrast, this thing, twenty-five years later, was a cakewalk.

Stelk took his glasses off and briefly chewed an earpiece. He said, "I faced the anniversary of my ordination with fear and trepidation and anticipation and joy. I can't tell which is which."

He offered the celebration to the baptized baby, the confirmands, the ex-Catholic who had been received as an Episcopalian, the new wardens and vestry members who had been installed. He saved the fondest dedication for his two young candidates for the Mature Profession of Faith. "We don't have the slightest idea what we're doing with them yet," he said. "We know we're beginning something new and God is leading us into something new and if that's the leadership, who can question where we're going? Something good will come of it."

Stelk opened the first package and held up a white sweatshirt. It was traced with the colorful outlines of many small hands, a gift from the Sunday school classes. Childish signatures appeared inside the tracings.

There was a chorus of voices. "Put it on. Put it on."

Stelk pulled the sweatshirt on over his clericals and threw open his arms to show it off. The next package was Karin's. She watched intently as Stelk removed the wrappings and brought out a thick album. "What's this?" he said. He opened it, leafed through it, paused at one page, then another. He seemed to have forgotten the crowd in the parish hall. When he raised his head, he looked overcome and sheepish.

"We stuffed the bulletins two Sundays in a row," Karin said. "We even stuffed the newsletter without you finding out."

Karin had taken months to produce the album that lay in front of Stelk. She had stuffed the bulletins and written letters asking the congregation and Stelk's friends, relatives and church associates for reminiscences and letters of congratulation. She had received, and assembled, an anecdotal tour of Stelk's life as a priest. The album was a well of memories.

"Did anyone tell him about the movie?" someone called.

"I think 'The Missing Linc' is a really good title," Carol said, using Stelk's nickname. There was a stunned silence, followed by groans.

The ceremony wound down. Bishop Grein said he wanted to get home in time for the Super Bowl kickoff and excused himself. Moments later, the parish hall was empty except for a few stragglers and volunteers who stayed behind to tidy up the kitchen. Ginny returned to the rectory to entertain the family's guests. Stelk lingered, saying last goodbyes. Then he gathered up his gifts and started toward the rectory. Pausing at the door, he opened the book of letters to a random page.

His Aunt Mildred's letter began with her familiar nickname for him:

> Dear Linny—
>
> How wonderful that I am given the opportunity to send you my best wishes upon the 25th anniversary of your ordination into the priesthood of our Lord.
>
> Since a thousand miles have separated us thruout our lives we have not been able to make many memories together.
>
> I do remember you as such a sweet little boy with such big, steady eyes. And as a young man, one who loved deeply the music of all the Masters and had loads of their records. It impressed me so much that you knew who were the conductors of all the Symphony Orchestras! It is a wonderful thing to love music.
>
> May God continue to bless you in your ministry to Him, and at St. Mary's. My thoughts and prayers are with you.

2

Aunt Mildred was on the Mobile, Alabama, side of the Stelk family. Stelk's father had been on the Chicago side. That was where the thousand miles had come from. His grandfather, an Illinois judge, had taken a flyer on a land deal around Mobile Bay. The deal came a cropper and the judge went home, but some of the family stayed behind.

We were in Stelk's office, which was full of books and file cabinets and papers stacked on two desks set at right angles to each other. His work space was separated by a bulky sofa from a long conference table where the vestry sometimes met. He'd decorated the room with family photos, cartoons and religious posters. It was late on a weekday afternoon. A sullen rainfall drifted past the window.

"My parents didn't go to church," he said. "But they didn't mind if we did, so my sister and I went with neighbors who invited us. One family were Lutherans and the other Presbyterians. I grew up calling myself a Presbyterian."

This was in Berwyn, Illinois, a Chicago suburb, where Stelk's father worked as a draftsman and his mother kept house and raised the children. His sister, Anne, was four years younger. They both attended J. Sterling Morton High School in neighboring Cicero. School legend claimed Al Capone as a fan of the basketball team.

After high school, Stelk entered Ohio Wesleyan University,

where he became student manager of the basketball team and managing editor of the newspaper, *The Transcript*. He was also in the Air Force ROTC, the Reserve Officer Training Corps. When he graduated in 1956 with a major in political science and a minor in history, the Air Force waited.

"I had a choice of flying B-47s in the Strategic Air Command or entering the Training Command," Stelk said. "I'd been in a B-47 on the ground and swore I'd never get in one of those again. On the other hand, training new pilots presented the opportunity to be killed by somebody who knew even less than I. So I took the SAC."

He trained in Florida and Georgia and got his wings in Laredo, Texas. He moved into B-47s at McConnell Air Force Base in Wichita Falls and took survival training in the mountains, the Sierra Madre, which hung like a distant frown over the prairie.

"I've never liked snow since," he said. "I've never gone snowshoeing again, and I never intend to ski."

Stelk looked out the window. Snow was mixing with the rain now. Darkness was falling, smudging the landscape. Black pools of shadow spread under the pine trees in the backyard, and the picnic tables looked forlorn. Stelk decided the interview should continue in the rectory, over a glass of sherry.

The rattle of the door as we went into the foyer set off a frenzy of barking somewhere upstairs. "Are you here?" Stelk called. Ginny appeared around a corner. She had clear blue eyes and high, firm cheekbones. Her gray-streaked hair was simply cut. She and Stelk had been married nearly thirty years and were very much partners. Ginny was a frequent lay reader on Sundays, and she taught Spanish to seventh- and eighth-graders at the Copper Beech Middle School in Yorktown. "*¡Hola!*" she said cheerfully.

They had met in Salina, Kansas, Stelk said, shedding his black raincoat and folding it over the stair railing. He had emerged from his training a copilot and was sent to Shilling Air Force Base. At about the same time, Virginia Jo Horn was returning home to Salina after dropping out of Bethany College in nearby Lindsborg. Her father had had a heart attack, and she was trying to save on school costs. She enrolled at Marymount College in Salina and took a salesclerk's job at a record store, Jenkins House of Music. One day Stelk showed up looking for *The Kingston Trio at the Hungry i.*

Stelk wriggled gratefully into a comfortable chair in a sitting room just off the kitchen. It had a fireplace and bookshelves that were crowded with record albums and tapes and photo albums from the trips he and Ginny had taken all their married life. Travel mementos decorated the walls. One wall was devoted to primitive weapons: a boomerang, spears, a throwing stick. "I call that my pacifist wall," Ginny said. Her music corner was in the other room, a large room the width of the house. The Stelks used one end for dining; the other was devoted to a grand piano and Ginny's cello, which she used when playing with several informal chamber-music groups. They played for the enjoyment of it, works of Mozart, Beethoven, Gershwin, Borodin and Brahms, among others.

Stelk took a glass of sherry from the tray she offered. Ginny went to the fireplace and took a picture from the mantel. It was a photograph of Stelk as a young copilot in his flight jacket. Even then his close-cropped hair was thinning. "I was flirting with him," she said.

"I was flirting with another girl," Stelk said.

"Well, I got his name and address on the sales slip," Ginny said with a tone of finality. They smiled at one another.

That Christmas in Salina, Stelk was pursuing his love of classical music by singing in two choruses. One was practicing Handel's *Judas Maccabaeus* for a concert at Bethany College, the second Handel's *Messiah* for a concert at Kansas Wesleyan. Ginny Horn was playing cello in both orchestras.

"She was always late for rehearsals," he said, looking sideways to see how she'd react. "She'd be dragging her cello through this group of musicians, and we'd have to stop practice for her. So she was . . . noticeable." Ginny smiled and sipped at her sherry.

They were dating regularly when he was discharged from

the Air Force. Stelk already had taken the State Department's Foreign Service exam and been accepted. He left Kansas for Washington, D.C., to begin a diplomat's career. Ginny stayed behind to complete her degree in Spanish. It was 1959.

Letters flew back and forth between them, sharing dreams of the black-tie drama of overseas diplomacy. They looked forward to exotic postings. They were, at the same time, seeking new forms of religious expression. He had attended Presbyterian services and social affairs in Salina. Ginny's family were Disciples of Christ, but at Catholic Marymount, she said, she "fell in love with liturgy." She attended a ceremony for young women who had decided to enter religious life and become nuns. "It was like a wedding," she said. "I was thrilled at the girls in their wedding gowns, marrying the Church."

"There needs to be an element of ceremony," Stelk agreed. "A couple of hymns and a few prayers, I didn't think that's what worship meant." But neither he nor Ginny could deal with what she called "the infallibility thing." Stelk said, "I liked the Catholic Church, but not its overwhelming authoritarianism and intellectual arrogance. I wasn't willing to check my brains at the door. I needed a place where I could test and debate, decry and deny. The Episcopal Church recommended itself to me."

The Episcopal Church in the United States balances somewhere between Roman Catholic and Protestant, but is not quite either. It considers itself part of the universal, that is, catholic church. Its worship conforms to ancient traditions. But it embraces the laity by making people a part of the service, and it espouses the priesthood of all believers. Stelk had a favorite quote that Anglican Bishop Desmond Tutu used to explain the Anglican Communion's appeal, that it was "peculiar, untidy, but oh so loveable."

"He wrote to tell me he had found this church, St. Thomas's Episcopal, on Dupont Circle," Ginny said. "I wrote back. Our letters were about religion and Corning Ware."

They were married in Ginny's family church in Salina on June 17, 1960. They honeymooned in the Ozarks. Less than three months later, on September 2, 1960, the Stelks were confirmed into the Episcopal Church. Soon Stelk was a lay reader at St. Thomas's. Within a year he was conducting evening prayer.

Ginny got up to refill the sherry glasses. "There was a group, young people from St. Thomas's," she said. "We called ourselves the Third Order. And one night we were sitting in a bar, having a beer, and Linc was talking with a couple of young seminarians from Virginia Theological. And one of them, his name was Walter Neds, leaned over to me and said, 'You're going to be going to seminary.' "

Ginny laughed at the suggestion. The Foreign Service promised glamour and excitement. They had put it on their wedding invitations. They were going to see the world.

The Foreign Service assigned Stelk to Caracas. He plunged into Spanish studies. Ginny, who was teaching high school Spanish, helped him practice. "Then the Caracas post report arrived," Stelk said. "It told all about life in Caracas, everything you'd want to know. It said the Anglican priest came once a month. We found that a jarring thought.

"The Communion was very important to us. And not just once a month, or once a quarter."

He served notice that he was resigning from the Foreign Service. Ginny's first reaction was, "You're kidding." She called her mother with the news. A few days later, an envelope arrived from Salina. "It was a list I'd made, the kind of thing you did in the fifth grade," Ginny said. "You listed the things about the man you were going to marry. It folded up like a rose. I'd written 'clergyman' at the top of the list."

They left Washington in August 1961 for Cambridge, Massachusetts, and the Episcopal Theological Seminary. He said, "I just decided, for reasons that I couldn't articulate and still can't, that this is what I was supposed to do."

I asked him if he'd ever been sorry.

He thought a minute, as sleet peppered the windows. He pressed his fingertips together, nestled his chin on them and pursed his lips. "No," he said. "I've been curious at times, wondering what might have been. I see my own kids wearing crystals and I wonder how effective my witnessing has been. But I've never been sorry."

+

Stelk graduated from ETS in 1964, when many seminarians were accepting calls to aid the civil rights movement in the South. But Ginny was pregnant with Kirsten, and Stelk returned to Washington as curate, an assistant to the rector, at St. Thomas's. He was ordained a deacon that summer. Kirsten was born in November, and Stelk was ordained to the priesthood the following January.

A year later, in 1966, he accepted a call to St. Peter's Church in Delaware, Ohio. The return to the town where he'd attended college was a homecoming for Stelk, and he stayed eleven years. It was a good job and a good town, close enough to Columbus, the capital, for them to enjoy its concerts and plays. Since they were in the middle of the country, it was easy to slake the thirst for travel that both Stelk and Ginny had brought into the marriage. She returned to teaching after Marla was born, and her paycheck went into family vacations with the three girls. But Stelk had given himself an arbitrary rule governing his tenure at a parish: seven years was too short a time to stay, but eleven was too long.

He accepted the chaplaincy at Kenyon College in Gambier, Ohio, in 1977. It was a disastrous move. Stelk was half college chaplain and half rector of the Harcourt Parish Church on campus, the Chapel of the Holy Spirit. Both sides, over time, grew disenchanted. Tracing the beginnings of the disenchantment was impossible. They may have lain in Stelk's disputing the Kenyon endowment's investments in South Africa, or in the antinuclear demonstrations he organized. For whatever reasons, Kenyon's Presbyterian president decided he wanted Stelk to be a less denominational chaplain. Stelk threw his energy into developing the parish church, and the president decided he wanted it to be a less denominational college chapel. Kenyon faculty members among Stelk's congregation didn't want to cross the president. First the college, then the parish, demanded Stelk's resignation.

The parish's demand stung Stelk more, because it was engineered by people he'd considered friends. He fought until he realized it was futile. He resigned as the rector of Harcourt Parish on the last Sunday of Pentecost—the end of the church year—in November 1986. He worked as a substitute teacher and a supply priest, filling in for priests who were vacationing or sick. He considered leaving the priesthood.

"It was a rough couple of years there," said Kirsten, who had graduated from Mount Holyoke and started to work. "But he is who he is, and a priest is who he is."

Stelk sent out feelers. One went to Paul Moore, then the bishop of New York and an old friend. Stelk and Ginny had decided they wanted to be near a city again, for the music and theater they loved and the convenience of airports. He was fifty-two and she was forty-seven. Sara was studying at the University of the South in Tennessee. Kirsten was in Washington, D.C. Marla was still at home, but there was little to keep them in the Midwest. Stelk had an odd desire to be near the sea. He thought it would be nice to be around sea gulls.

St. Mary's, meanwhile, was going through its second search in five years. Its young rector, Marc Lee, had left for a job at the cathedral church in San Francisco. St. Mary's search committee told the diocese that this time they wanted a person of "mature years, preferably between 35 and 55," with parish experience and no health or addiction problems. "Whiskeypalian" was an epithet heard all too often of Episcopal rectors. It would be nice to have someone who could work with youth and grow with the parish. While it waited for a list of candidates, the church installed a homeless family in the rectory. The list that eventually arrived from the diocese contained Stelk's name.

Stelk went looking for his atlas when he received the invitation to an interview. He had never heard of Mohegan Lake. He found it a thumb's length away from New York City after several minutes of squinting through his reading glasses.

He and Ginny arrived to be inspected on a Sunday afternoon in March of 1987.

A car picked them up at LaGuardia Airport. Twilight was falling by the time they turned off the Taconic State Parkway onto westbound Route 6. It was a glum, wet afternoon. Stelk saw the stone church by the roadside through the car's rain-spattered windows. Episcopal churches are stone churches, he thought. That must be it. Then he saw boarded-up windows and weeds groping at the cracks. A quarter-mile west the limo turned in to the lot at St. Mary's.

Stelk was surprised at its simplicity. What Ginny felt at first, when they went inside, was disappointment. She looked around at the white stucco and dark wood, the pews carved with schoolboys' initials, the horsehair stuffed cushions worn to the color of old wine, and missed the elegance of the church in Gambier, with its intricate hand-painted ceiling.

Stelk conducted a service for the search committee. He noted happily that the church used real bread, whole-wheat pita bread. Jesus probably had eaten much the same thing with his disciples at the Last Supper, the institution of the Eucharist. Somewhere along the line churches had started using wafers, thin white stamped-out sacramental wafers. They reminded Stelk of fish food.

Carol and Fred Obligado hosted a buffet dinner afterwards. All the committee members had questions for Stelk. Ed Lumley, one of the lay readers, with a fleshy face and pale, darting eyes, quizzed Stelk about his favorite books of the Bible. Old and New Testaments, please. Discounting the Gospels and Psalms. Isaiah and Acts, Stelk said, which made Ed beam and his eyes cut about as if he were following a pinball game. Carol asked sweetly what Stelk thought about "The Wedding March" at church weddings. He didn't. It was secular music. Carol agreed.

"You'll do," she said.

Ed drove Stelk and Ginny back to their motel at the end of the evening. Several members of the search committee stayed behind to tote up their impressions. They judged the Stelks on a combination of intangibles, a sort of comfort scale. Almost everyone agreed that Stelk was the kind of gentle, accepting priest they wanted.

Stelk and Ginny received their obligatory tour the next day. Carol drove them around Mohegan Lake, with its converted summer cottages. They visited the rectory, tiptoeing because the homeless family's baby was asleep. At Peekskill they admired the gray back of the Hudson River descending toward the sea. They looked at high schools for Marla. They saw farmsteads separated by stone fences and suburban tracts that imposed neatness on the rugged land. Finally, when the tour turned to shopping prospects and entered the parking lot of the Westchester Mall, Stelk was startled to see sea gulls. A flock of them wheeled overhead between the Waldbaum's supermarket and McDonald's, sending their sharp cries down in invitation.

St. Mary's had called him not long afterward, and he and Ginny and Marla arrived that August.

+

Stelk had been hinting almost since his arrival at St. Mary's that the church needed a new parish hall. He'd stood up at last year's parish meeting and said, "We need ways to expand our facilities and activities." The suggestion received the same courteous attention as the Sunday school report.

But Stelk unflaggingly reminded his congregation that God's work took elbowroom. You had to teach, to embrace in Christian fellowship, to serve the community around you. Room for all those things was lacking. The church school classes met within earshot of each other, so that one class could be hearing about God ordering Saul to slay the Philistines while another was learning to turn the other cheek. There wasn't a basketball hoop or a game room to keep a youth group occupied. The kitchen could barely handle Sunday's coffee hour. The food pantry that served the poor was housed in a closet. And, as Stelk was reminded every week as he robed along with the lay readers in the bustle of the sacristy, there was no place to meditate and pray before services.

By January 1990, he'd persuaded the congregation's only

architect to sketch some rough plans. He presented them at the annual meeting with the caution that it would cost some money. He didn't say how much.

The bishop came and went, and by February's vestry meeting Stelk was ready to proceed.

The meeting fell on Shrove Tuesday, the last day before the fasting time of Lent. Down in New Orleans, the Fat Tuesday revels of Mardi Gras were reaching a crescendo. At St. Mary's, Dick Tramonti was frying sausages to go with a pancake supper, $2.50 a plate, served with napkins left over from the 1984 Olympics. The napkins were red, white and blue and urged diners to "Support the 1984 U.S. Olympic team."

Dick was a trim, good-looking man with wavy salt-and-pepper hair, another of the former Roman Catholics at St. Mary's. He and his wife, Miriam, were moderately active in church affairs. They were on one of the counting teams that toted up the offerings after Sunday services, and they also were among the oblations bearers, called presenters, who carried the bread and wine to the altar at the beginning of Communion.

"I'm not a holy guy," he said, responding to a question I had asked. He deftly flipped two sausages. "But people who don't go to church, where do they get their faith?" Dick was a traveling sales manager for General Foods. "Sometimes I'll be driving and just have a talk with God," he said. "A little conversation. I'll say something like, 'Thanks for the day.' It's not a big thing. It's not more than five minutes." He lifted the sausages with a spatula and slipped them onto a plate beside the stove.

I was eating my pancakes among the two dozen or so diners when the door to the parish hall swung open. Two women came in, stopped short and stared. Stelk was pouring syrup on his pancakes. One of the women, after a long moment, said, "We're looking for Appetite Control?"

Stelk dabbed at his mouth with a napkin and stood up, looking embarrassed. Appetite Control was one of St. Mary's tenants. Its members rented space in the parish hall for twice-weekly meetings. "You're upstairs tonight," he said, directing them. "We were having this supper so we gave you the church office." Stelk came back and sat down grumpily. "This is what I mean about a lack of space," he said. "We've got a diet group having to walk through a church supper to get to its meeting. And pancakes and sausage. My God."

✢

The vestry sat around the long table in Stelk's office, across the landing from the church office and Appetite Control, where the women were laughing about encountering the supper.

Nine members and two wardens comprised the vestry. The nine served three-year terms, with three new members elected at the parish meeting every year. Wardens were elected annually. Vestry service was taxing enough that candidates had to be recruited by arm-twisting, and it was a catch-22 at St. Mary's that the only way to get your name off the ballot was to serve. The three newest members were Mary Bohun, a young convenience store cashier whose father, Stuart Wetmore, was the retired suffragan bishop of New York; David Odell, an assistant principal at Carmel High School; and Walt Decker, a deputy director at the American Foundation for the Blind who commuted to work in New York City.

The new vestry members were typical of St. Mary's congregation. It was a cross section of ages, incomes, jobs and races. There were young families, middle-aged parents with grown children, retirees; mostly white, a few black. They were electricians and executives, computer whizzes and telephone linemen, teachers and salespeople and civil servants and people who had trouble finding work at all. One member, Stelk said, revealed his fortunes at the communion rail each week; the man drove an oil truck and when he was working Stelk pressed the bread into hands dark with oil stains, but when he was unemployed, his hands were clean. Some people came to church in suits, others in blue jeans. All shared the overriding characteristic of St. Mary's, which was a modesty in church affairs. The parish budget wasn't $100,000. That defied the popular notion of Episcopalians. "We're different," some members liked to say. "We're not rich."

The other vestry members were John Donovan, a civil engineer; Dwight Douglas, the city planner for the nearby town of Peekskill; Ann Marwick, who directed day care services for the Yorktown School District; John Harbeson, an expert in East African affairs who taught at the Graduate Center of the City University of New York and at City College; Robert Soso, the director of security at White Plains Hospital; and Marilyn Trudeau, who taught high school mathematics. The wardens, whose duties were somewhat more involved, were Gerry Cousins, who repaired and tuned pianos, and Karin Efman, who worked in the office of a dental practice.

The vestry prayed to begin the meeting. Then Stelk tapped on the tabletop with a ballpoint pen and called for order. He was wearing a dark cardigan which, except for the dancing Snoopy pin in one lapel, kept fashion with his somber clericals. There was whimsy in his eyes as well when he looked over his glasses around the table and said he planned a special Eucharist.

"There will be no sermon on that day," he said. "Instead there will be an explanation of the service, of what we do and why, of the robes I wear and so forth." He paused for effect. "I said, no sermon."

"Thank you, Jesus." Gerry Cousins had a jolly burgher's look, prosperous and solid. He had a round pink face, a bristly brown mustache and wore the kinds of clothes one's wife picks out. As the junior warden, he oversaw the upkeep of buildings and grounds.

Stelk let the laughter ripple briefly, then said, "Okay, let's not get out of hand."

The vestry plowed through a mostly boring agenda of housekeeping issues. The work went on under the glare of a long fluorescent light. A forlorn Christ wearing a crown of thorns looked down from one wall; it was a reproduction of a painting whose artist no one could identify that seemed more suited to the Prado than the Louvre for its Castilian gloominess.

On the opposite wall, a poster contended, "There's a difference between being baptized and brainwashed."

The vestry reached: Building Expansion.

Stelk put his reading glasses on and peered over them. "I think we all know we're going to have to get outside money to help pay for what we want to do," he said. He snatched his glasses off and laid them on the table. "The big thing right now is day care. St. Peter's over in Peekskill got federal grant money to open its day care service. They say there's money for that sort of thing."

Dwight Douglas was seated at a corner of the table with his back toward the wall. Dwight wore a dark beard that made him look like one of the Smith brothers on the cough drop box, and his tweedy clothes added a professorial air. He had been a member of St. Mary's for thirty years, since his family moved from Manhattan's Upper West Side to nearby Shrub Oak when he was a teenager. He draped an arm over the back of his chair and said, "There's not much of that kind of money." The way he said it sounded ominous.

"For day care. There's money out there for day care," Stelk insisted.

"I've got a whole booklet on the money that's available for day care," said Ann, brightly. She was slight, with a bouncy mop of hair that at the moment was an attractive ash blond shade. Her eyebrows contained a built-in arch of mild surprise, and she spoke in the West Midlands accent of her native England. Alice, one of the two candidates for the Mature Profession of Faith accepted during the bishop's visitation, was the elder of Ann's two children.

Stelk plunged on. "We've got some decisions to make. Will there be a stage? Can we put in a basketball court?"

"Indoor tennis?" someone said.

"I want to know where the pool is going to be," said Stelk, only half kidding. He was ready to begin. The first step was to ask the congregation what it wanted.

Dwight hadn't moved. He still was sitting with his arm lolling over the chair back. "We need a needs analysis," he said.

"And priorities established. You can't put a gym in, probably. Maybe you can. But you establish some priorities and present some alternatives to the congregation, like a no-build plan, a plan A and a plan B.

"Right now there's not enough information to present."

Stelk had never built a parish hall. His two Ohio parishes had stable memberships and adequate facilities. St. Mary's might have solved Stelk's problem years before. A new church with pews for two hundred eighty worshipers and a parish hall with a gymnasium and auditorium were proposed in 1959, when St. Mary's had five hundred members, but nothing came of the proposal. The church, instead, added a second floor to the Green Room, which was where the vestry members now were meeting. St. Mary's still had five hundred members, more or less, and still needed more space. But what seemed logical and simple was beginning to reveal to Stelk untold complexities.

The vestry dealt with Dwight's suggestion by creating a committee. Stelk was a member. So was Dwight. Its task was to "attempt to formulate specific plans." The straightforward sound of that would prove to be deceptive.

✣

Church parishes rarely agreed, in toto, about anything. Stelk's call to St. Mary's had been a popular choice, but it was not unanimous. His predecessors were, by turns, remote and formal, and while most of the search committee felt that Stelk "fit like an old shoe," as Marilyn Trudeau had put it, two of the fifteen committee members had listed other choices.

Dwight Douglas's top choice was the woman who had led his first Cursillo.

Cursillo, in rough translation from the Spanish, is "little course." In this case it was a course in Christianity that grew out of the Roman Catholic Church in Spain into a full-fledged renewal movement. The Catholic, Episcopal and Protestant churches all had versions of it, offered in intense weekend retreats. Participants—both laity and clergy—would go off for three days of worship, prayer and talk. Their leaders tended to be charismatic. People let the Holy Spirit get hold of them and sang and waved their arms around. *Cursillistas,* as the initiates were called, were supposed to inject their new ideas back into the parishes they came from, but it didn't always work that way. I had heard about Cursillo practically from my moment of arrival at St. Mary's. The opinions were either rapturous or critical.

Dwight and his wife Ann, one of St. Mary's lay readers, were rapturous. They were true believers who were deeply involved in Cursillo. Father David Eylers, the rector of St. Mary's during the seventies, introduced the Douglases to a similar program of weekend retreats when they were feeling the strain of three children under five. Dwight and Ann felt Marriage Encounter had bolstered their relationship. Father Marc Lee, who followed Eylers, arrived in 1982. By then, some members of St. Mary's had been visiting a charismatic congregation in Connecticut. They approached Lee saying they were spiritually starved and needed feeding. They suggested that he attend a Cursillo weekend so that he might bring its manna back to them. He put it off for a year. When Lee finally attended one of the three-day retreats he ranked the experience "four or five on a scale of ten." But he gradually became a supporter. Following his lead, the Douglases attended.

Dwight and Ann embraced Cursillo. It gave them a set of tools to incorporate God into their daily lives, a means to grow spiritually. It also heightened their experience of worship. Ann called it "another dimension." She said, "You can bring it back and enrich what would otherwise maybe be a not particularly deep form of worship."

Before Cursillo, Dwight said, "I had no idea in the Episcopal Church that you could pray through the Virgin Mary to God. I thought that's what those silly Catholics do. But you can do all these things. It's amazing how much more the priests know about prayer that isn't communicated to the average person in the pew."

They became Cursillo's most enthusiastic advocates. Vestry member John Harbeson recalled how Ann "swooped down on me" with an invitation to Cursillo when he began attending St. Mary's in 1986. Harbeson signed up for a retreat, but changed his mind and didn't go. The members who had "made their Cursillos" shared the Douglases' enthusiasm to varying degrees.

Stelk arrived at St. Mary's in August 1987. He had hardly unpacked before he was invited to a Cursillo retreat. Stelk's experience was not at all what the Cursillistas wanted. He returned with the view that Cursillo was "a lot of malarkey." Indeed, he said, it "bordered on utter heresy."

He said, "We went over and prayed to a wafer in a monstrance, actually, I think it was a tabernacle. The leader offered this as a new way of prayer: 'Come and pray to Jesus present in the Blessed Sacrament.' This takes the theology of Christ present in the wafer and takes it out of the context of the Eucharist and makes the wafer itself an object of veneration because Christ is present in there, so you sit there and talk to Christ in the wafer. Now I find that very, very hard to sustain. It tends to distort and destroy the meaning of our gathering as a Christian body."

Stelk found Cursillo to be "a type of brainwashing. You get very little sleep and rest; they rush you into one thing, you have a set period of time, and that ends, you have a talk and the leader then leaves. You never have a chance to enter into any dialogue or questions, because they immediately turn you in to something else, another activity."

He was also uncomfortable with the whole notion of charismatic worship. He preferred traditional ceremony to unfettered spontaneity. "People can raise their hands if they want to," he said. "But if in the midst of the Liturgy someone starts speaking in tongues . . ." Stelk's sole adventure in diocesan politics, when he had run for bishop back in Ohio, had been to head off a charismatic candidate. Stelk hadn't won, but neither had the charismatic.

Stelk's reaction carried seeds of danger. The danger was that St. Mary's would become a house divided. The Cursillo roster listed some of St. Mary's most active members, including Karin Efman and her husband, Richie; Ann Marwick; lay reader

Christine Warnecke; altar guild leader Eleanor Arnold; former vestry members Kathy Munroe and John Weber and Weber's wife, Patty; and church treasurer Bob Lockhart. Stelk could not afford to actively oppose Cursillo, but he refused to actively support it. His indifference crippled Cursillo at the parish level. The so-called Fourth Day, the follow-up meetings, services and suppers designed to help the Cursillistas enlarge on their experiences, foundered. Because of that, some of them felt blocked from their full quotient of empowerment. The Douglases were in the vanguard.

+

The senior warden was the "rector's warden," the rector's administrative surrogate and sounding board. But Karin Efman had turned the position into something more. I found her at a table in the church office one afternoon, folding and sealing the parish newsletters for mailing.

Karin was one of the most accessible members of St. Mary's. She was open, friendly and transparently emotional. The thought of parting with Susan, her oldest daughter, who would leave for college in the fall, already was moving her to tears. The same intense emotion showed up in her worship. She was an enthusiastic Cursillista. She was also an enthusiastic Stelk fan.

"He's a shepherd. He has that kind of father feeling about him. And I think he's a unifier," Karin said, turning from the pile of newsletters. "People have their own agendas, and it's easy for groups to splinter. Every priest that comes to a parish brings a particular thing to it that makes it the way it is. During the David Eylers period, everybody was doing their own thing. But I don't see that now. I think everybody kind of pulls together. That makes St. Mary's the home that it is."

The Efmans were pillars of St. Mary's. Not only was Karin senior warden, but fifteen-year-old Laurie was an acolyte, as Susan had been before her. Krissie, eleven, was the next in line. Karin's husband, Richie, a pharmacist, moonlighted on Sundays. But he faithfully attended the Wednesday morning services, where, as the sole male member of the altar guild, he was responsible for arranging the flowers and laying out the Sacraments.

Karin was a cradle Episcopalian. Richie had been born Jewish, but neither of their families was particularly religious. They met while both were working, he as a pharmacist, she as a nurse, at Montefiore Hospital in the Bronx. They sent each other orange juice and love notes through the hospital's network of pneumatic tubes. They were married in a civil ceremony in October 1970.

A certain religious confusion surfaced when Susan was born. According to tradition, she was given a Hebrew name, Sora Miclah. Eighteen months later, Karin took her to the Second Reformed Church in Tarrytown to be baptized. Laurie, born in December 1974, after the family moved to Mahopac, was baptized at three, in a church Karin found by looking in the Yellow Pages. One day she drove by St. Mary's and decided to attend a service.

"That was it," she said. "I never went anyplace else. I don't know why. It's a feeling. There's just a warmth."

The small church filled a gap in Karin's life. She was close to neither her parents nor her in-laws. "I was reaching out for family," she said. Late in 1978, after Krissie was born and Karin had been hospitalized for unrelated surgery, members of the church brought her food and helped do her Christmas shopping. "These people were my family. That's what St. Mary's is," she said.

Even so, there were cliques. The 1979 prayer book introduced into the Eucharist a moment called the Peace, when the rector and a lay reader passed down the aisle shaking hands and members of the congregation were expected to exchange greetings. Karin said, "You'd sit with people you knew because you didn't want to shake hands with people you didn't know. It was very stiff."

Richie Efman was baptized and confirmed in 1984. He never told his mother about his conversion. "I think she knew, though," Karin said. "A mother's intuition. His sister still thinks it's a phase. She's married to a Roman Catholic."

Karin attended her first Cursillo weekend in 1986. She found it "an eye-opener to just what I could accomplish as a Christian. The importance of Christ in my life. The people there spend the whole time talking about their lives, how they can change, or did change. It's not just the weekend. It's the rest of your life, tools to improve your faith experience, to make it easier to keep the Sunday part in your life the rest of the week."

I asked Karin about the criticisms of Cursillo I had heard, that rather than injecting their spiritual enthusiasm into the parish the Cursillistas kept it among themselves.

"It's not a thing that everybody likes," she admitted. "It's not an elitist group. It's not meant to be."

Karin would not say she felt blocked by Stelk's coolness toward Cursillo. But she felt blocked for other reasons from the level of spirituality she sought. It was evading her, and as the debate over the new parish hall began in earnest it seemed to be vestry politics that most distracted her from worship.

3

"In our intercessions this day," Stelk began, "we offer prayers for Eugene Jackson, a member of the parish, who had a slight heart attack and is still in the hospital . . ."

I realized that I had missed Eugene smoking on the steps and shambling to the altar.

". . . and for the eighty-nine at least who have died in the social club fire in the Bronx last night."

The Happy Land fire, as it was called in the morning headlines and broadcast bulletins, had actually killed eighty-seven, but the bodies still were being counted. The unlicensed club had been doused with gasoline and set on fire by the maddened boyfriend of the coat check woman, and there was only one way out. Even amid the commonplace tragedies of New York City, the Happy Land fire clutched the heart. You wanted to ignore the city's violence and its misery, but Stelk would not. He faced it squarely and placed it before his congregation. For Stelk, New York was more than the theater and the Philharmonic; it was a great, fragile crucible that needed praying for.

The congregation of St. Mary's began praying for AIDS victims and addicts on this same bright morning, with winter sunlight splashing ruby teardrops through the stained-glass windows.

The new Book of Common Prayer had added a series of responsive prayers, the Prayers of the People. The authors had written six versions of the prayers. They tried their best to be inclusive: there were prayers for bishops and clergy, for state and national leaders, for space travelers, for good weather and crops, for prisoners and captives, for the poor, sick and hungry, for refugees and the oppressed, for justice and peace, seekers of God and the departed. But ogreish times had outdone them, leaving local churches to add invocations of their own.

Ginny was the lay reader who led the congregation through a litany of new ills among the old:

"I ask your prayers for the poor, the sick, especially those with AIDS or imprisoned with addictions, the hungry, the homeless, the oppressed, all hostages held anywhere, especially Terry Waite [the Church of England representative who was trying to negotiate a release of hostages when he was himself taken hostage in Lebanon], and their families and for those in prison. Pray for those in any need or trouble."

Whether the prayers worked seemed less important than that they were said. The least the prayers did was relieve the obliviousness of self-obsession. They reconnected the parish to the world, where Eastern Europe was struggling to emerge from Communism, where Nelson Mandela was released after more than twenty-seven years in prison in South Africa, where people were dying of AIDS and men and women had gone dancing at a place called Happy Land and never made it home. Kneeling and remembering all that helped keep things in perspective.

The Prayers of the People led into a Confession of Sin and then the Peace. The reserve that Karin Efman had observed when it was introduced had long since faded at St. Mary's. Stelk's voice boomed out, "The peace of the Lord be always with you," and suddenly people were hugging their spouses and their children and reaching across the pews to shake hands with their neighbors. Stelk and Ginny went down the aisle, pumping hands like politicians.

During the coffee hour after the service, two men approached Stelk in the parish hall. John and Vincent were an inseparable pair. They, like Eugene and choir member Joe De Domenico, a small quiet man with a pulsing vein in his forehead, lived in Mohegan Manor, an adult home about a quarter mile from the church. One hundred and fifty-five men and women lived in the converted motel, which served meals and had a full-time staff. St. Mary's was both convenient to Mohegan Manor and cordial to its pixilated residents.

"That's what a church should be," said Barbara Lang, Mohegan Manor's manager. "They should all accept people's differences, but that's not the way it is a lot of times."

John and Vincent looked alike. Their twin bald spots and rotund forms gave them the inevitable nicknames Tweedledum and Tweedledee. John for some reason repeated the responsive prayers a half-beat late, so that the service always had an echo. He had great, sad, entreating eyes and he was always asking Stelk to pray for him.

John came to an ungainly stop at Stelk's elbow. Vincent caught up behind him. John listed to one side and the other and said, "Father."

"Hello, John." Stelk's voice revealed impatience. He'd been in the middle of a conversation.

John dusted a hand on the leg of his pants, which were an exaggerated houndstooth check, and stuck it into the pocket of his New York Yankees jacket. He pulled out a handful of crucifixes and religious medals, chose one and held it out to Stelk.

"Father, I dropped it on the floor," he said.

"That's okay, John."

"Will you say a prayer for me, Father. I didn't mean to drop it."

"I know, John." Stelk apparently was used to this.

"I just want you to say a prayer because I didn't mean to make it drop on the floor."

"I will, John."

"I didn't mean to drop it."

"I know, John. Okay, John."

Finally satisfied by Stelk's assurances, John turned his sad eyes to the door, then back to Stelk. "Goodbye, Father," he said. Turning again like a ship in a swell, he led Vincent through the door and across the parking lot. They passed from view behind the church.

✣

The weather began softening. On one cool, overcast morning that held a promise of spring, I joined Stelk on a round of visitations.

He put his office work aside with an air of relief when I arrived, and we headed for the car, Stelk walking briskly, his black raincoat flapping around his knees. The car was a brown Ford Tempo that probably had been advertised as bronze. It had a grimy blanket spread over the backseat and dog slobber on the windows. Classical music came on when he turned the key to start the engine.

Stelk followed a series of back roads toward Peekskill Community Hospital. The hilly roads passed ranch houses and once-rural homes that ranged from respectable to tumbledown. Here neat hedges hemmed a yard, there rusted autos sat beneath a carport. The terrain was slashed with juts of rock. It was territory stolen from the Algonquian Indians by Dutch patroons and later occupied by Colonial troops retreating from Manhattan in the Revolutionary War.

When St. Mary's was founded in 1867, Mohegan Lake already had a history. It was the site of Monk's Tavern, a way station on the road to Boston and a rendezvous for Tories. The lake then was known as Fox Pond or Crooked Lake. James Fenimore Cooper's *The Spy* was set in its environs. During the nineteenth century, the area grew to be populated by a mix of farmers, merchants and well-to-do New Yorkers who summered at the lake and hunted in the surrounding hills.

St. Mary's was born in the old tavern, a fact of which the congregation still is proud. Its fourteen founders signed the incorporating documents there on May 19, 1867. Construction on the church began that August.

Two of the founders, brothers Charles D'Urban Morris and the Rev. Adolphus Philipse Morris, already had begun converting the former tavern to a boys' school. The church was an outgrowth of the school. Another founder, William Jones, owned one of the lake's resort hotels, the tall and cool Mt. Pleasant Lodge. Jones was a Welshman who had taught Charles Dickens penmanship. He advertised himself as a "Teacher of Writing, in all the Modern Hands, Stenography, Mensuration, Surveying, Mapping, Geography, with the use of the Globes, Mathematics, Etc.," all this in a florid hand with lots of curlicues. Jones is credited with giving Mohegan Lake its name. James W. Martens was an architect; a centennial church history says he modeled St. Mary's after an English country church he'd seen. Moses Augustus Field, a farmer, had the rare grace to suggest the new church be named after his mother-in-law, Mary Pearsall Bradhurst.

The other founders were William Jones's son Walter, who became a judge; William Roake, David Knapp Conklin and Abraham Hill, all farmers; Peekskill photographer L. C. Laudy; bankers Jonathan B. Currey and Dorlin F. Clapp; Yorktown highway commissioner William J. Horton; and H. M. Bauscher, about whom nothing is known.

St. Mary's was completed in 1872. The church history says a sprig of ivy taken from the Scottish home of Sir Walter Scott was planted by the west wall. Early photographs show the walls covered in ivy.

The new church struggled. Rectors came and quickly went, and no permanent rector served St. Mary's between 1882 and 1903. The Mohegan Lake School for boys founded by the brothers Morris died in the Great Depression of the thirties. The Depression almost killed St. Mary's as well. Then, in 1935, the Rev. Joseph Germeck began what would become a thirty-six-year tenure as rector of St. Mary's.

It was a benevolent autocracy, but between Joe Germeck and the suburbanization of northern Westchester County, St. Mary's survival was assured. Germeck retired in 1971.

The road emerged from a winter filigree of trees and reached an intersection. The groves and stony outcroppings had not surrendered their primal feeling altogether to suburbia. A moment later, Stelk wheeled into the hospital parking lot and found a space.

Eugene was lying in bed in the cardiac unit, an IV tube in his arm. His eyes were closed and his face relaxed and peaceful. A monitor beeped in time with his heart. Stelk placed a hand on his shoulder. Eugene opened his eyes and blinked in surprise.

"How are you feeling, Eugene?"

"Fine, Father. I'm feeling fine."

Eugene said he had been ready to return to Mohegan Manor after his heart attack. "But I don't know what happened. I found myself down on the floor. They told me it was the medication I was on, so they changed it. But I'm still here."

He raised a hand and offered it weakly in greeting. His palm was soft, his grasp gentle. He'd had a shave that morning and a recent haircut. He looked as if the rest had done him good.

Stelk grasped his hand. Eugene closed his eyes as Stelk began to pray, "O God, the strength of the weak and the comfort of sufferers: Mercifully accept our prayers, and grant to your servant Eugene the help of your power, that *his* sickness may be turned into health, and our sorrow into joy; through Jesus Christ our Lord. Amen."

Eugene opened his eyes as the prayer ended. He said, "I was hoping I'd be back in church by Easter. I don't know if I'll make it, though."

"Well, just you worry about getting well. We'll still be there," Stelk said.

"I will, Father."

✢

Stelk left the hospital in a hurry to get to a home Communion. He drove fast, scattering damp leaves along the roadsides. He braked the Tempo to a jerking stop in the driveway of the rectory, rushed through the wooden fence gate and into the parish hall through the back door. In the sacristy, he took a small black box from a cabinet. Its blue velvet lining held a glass flagon and a silver chalice a little larger than a shot glass. The silver needed polishing.

Stelk poured wine—Christian Brothers ruby port, diluted with water—into the flagon. He'd consecrated the wine beforehand, a shortcut that would abbreviate the home Communion services he'd scheduled. "These people are old," he said. "I don't want to overtax them." The case also had a pocket for communion wafers, which Stelk used instead of bread for home Communions. "Another convenience," he said. "It saves me from breaking a whole piece of pita."

He corked the flagon, then wrapped a piece of paper towel around the cork. "It's a nice little set, but it leaks," he said, and snapped the case shut.

I waited while he stopped at the rectory. The mist that had begun the day had thinned and grown luminous. Still, no shadows fell. Presently Stelk emerged behind a straining English sheepdog on a leash. "This is Gwynyd," he called. The shaggy dog yanked him down the kitchen steps and into the garden, where she snuffled among some crocus spears. She squatted, and steam rose.

Stelk sped through Yorktown, pointing out landmarks and muttering about the driving habits of New Yorkers. He drove impatiently, and even riding in a car brought out his more controlling tendencies. His daughter Marla said, "When he's a passenger, he has to tell you everything to do. 'Turn right. Put your foot on the clutch.' I used to hate to get in the car with him. My knuckles would be white. He used to have the perception that a pilot would have. He thinks he still does." A driver signaled a turn in front of him. Stelk drummed his fingers on the steering wheel. "Go on, lady, I'm waiting," he complained.

When we reached Yorktown Heights he turned between two brick posts into a condominium apartment complex, drove uphill among rows of identical buildings and parked near the top of the hill. The landscape stretched away into a blur of grays and browns. Stelk chose a building and knocked at one of its doors. For a long time there was no answer. Then the door opened and a white-haired woman peered out through thick glasses.

"Oh, Father, come in," she said, breaking into a smile. She

pulled the door open wide. "Harold," she called. "It's Father Stelk."

I followed Stelk into a neat, conservatively furnished living room. An old man in a sport shirt and slacks came tottering around a corner, not quite trusting himself on the spongy carpet. He had a full head of white hair and eyes that were as bright as a sparrow's. He, too, wore thick glasses. "Who is it, Lily?" he asked. "Oh, Father Stelk. Come in, come in."

The Van Hornes were a parish treasure, almost a lucky charm to the congregation of St. Mary's. They were clucked over, worried about and catered to, and loved for their humor and spark and devotion to each other. Lillian, or Lily as the parish knew her, was eighty-seven and Harold was ninety-one. They'd been married for sixty years, and you could see in them what one rarely saw: a prospect that enduring happiness was possible.

They came from vastly different backgrounds. Lily's parents were French-speaking Swiss. Her father, Louis Bichsel, had founded the French YMCA in New York City and served as its secretary. The family lived a few doors from the French Evangelical Church at 126 West Sixteenth Street in Manhattan, which they attended every Sunday. Lily's mother, Lena, played the church organ; Lily and her sisters pumped the bellows from behind a curtain to give the organ breath. French was spoken in the Bichsel household. Lily learned English in school and then worked as a translator at the French consulate general.

Harold had a tin ear for languages. He tried four years of French in high school and got nowhere. "The last year I went in there, the teacher—I'll never forget it—said, 'What, are you here again?' " he recalled with a rueful paroxysm of a laugh.

"I don't know why he didn't learn French," Lily said. "He said he couldn't get it."

So when Lily met Harold she had to speak English. He responded with a Gallic chivalry if not the tongue. They fell in love and, over her father's thunderous objections, were married —in both French and English—at the church on West Sixteenth Street on February 20, 1930.

The Van Hornes joined St. Mary's in 1970, when they retired and moved to Yorktown Heights from Tuckahoe, near Yonkers. Joan Ruedi, one of their two daughters, also was a member. They'd been active, volunteering, serving on committees, even attending a Cursillo. But age was slowing them. Lily had a cane that she refused to use. She and Harold both followed the hymns and prayers in large-print versions. Harold's recent heart attack had kept them homebound and prompted this visit from Stelk.

"Parts wear out," Harold explained. "Like an old car that gets to be a clunker."

Stelk handed out copies of the service entitled Communion under Special Circumstances. Harold took the sheet of paper to the window and bent over it, squinting in the diffused gray light streaming through the scrim of mist. He looked up helplessly. Lily guided him to an end of the sofa, where a lamp cast a gentler light. Stelk began the abbreviated service:

"Jesus said, 'Abide in me, as I in you. As the branch cannot bear fruit by itself, unless it abides in the vine, neither can you, unless you abide in me. I am the vine, you are the branches. By this my Father is glorified, that you bear much fruit, and so prove to be my disciples. As the Father has loved me, so have I loved you; abide in my love. . . .' "

They accepted the Sacraments with closed eyes and trembling lips.

Stelk was closing his home communion kit when Harold sat up and blurted, "It's so hard to feel that you're just sitting here and the rest of the world goes by. Things are moving on, everything's happening, and we just sit and watch it."

Lily laughed. "Well, when you get old, darling, that's what happens."

"I know. That's what happens."

"We helped a little when we first moved up here. We were able to do things," Lily said. She stood up and left the room in short, shuffling steps. She returned a moment later with some printed prayer sheets. "I still do these," she said. "I mail them. To the shut-ins. Every week. There's only three of them now. I read them, too. This is a nice one. It's one little job. It's so little." She seemed to be apologizing.

"It's time that you gave somebody else a chance to do it, too," Stelk said gently. "It's nice to share."

His words were kind. But what comfort could anyone, even a priest, provide in such a case? I knew something about old people. So did Stelk. My mother was in a nursing home in Florida, and my father was struggling with her absence. Stelk's parents both were dead and Ginny's mother, a widow, was speechless in a nursing home after suffering a stroke. They had brought her with them from Ohio to Mohegan Lake, and Stelk had seen her still-bright mind struggling to express itself. I knew, as Stelk must have, that every soothing word, every patiently offered tidbit of advice, seemed gratuitous against the anger of the old, their rage when their infirmities betrayed their experience and their intentions.

Harold brought out his ninetieth birthday card, a present from St. Mary's church school classes. The outsized card was covered with signatures. "I bet you've never seen a card like that before," he said proudly. The talk turned to the Van Hornes' family. They had six great-grandsons, they said, and one great-granddaughter, whose mother was Jewish.

Lily's face wrinkled with a vague concern. "We wonder, is she going to be raised up Jewish, do you think, like the mother? We haven't asked."

"You can't go wrong, converting them," Harold declared. His jaw set hard as a fish's.

"You have a very nice great-granddaughter, so you can be happy with that, right?" said Stelk.

"Yes. So long as she's well," Lily said.

Stelk said his goodbyes then. Lily and Harold followed us to the door. Harold looked as if he might plunge into the carpet. "I really am weak," he said. "I've got to lie down after this."

✛

Stelk drove back toward Mohegan Lake for his second home Communion. The damp chill had left the air, and the mist was reduced to a few pockets. He pulled into the rising driveway of an old summer house on the south end of the lake. It was part of the original summer colony, set on the hillsides above the lakeshore.

Two women sat on the enclosed back porch. One rose slowly to answer Stelk's *rap-rap* on the jalousie pane. Helen Pepys was ninety-one, her cousin Binky, older; she wouldn't say how much. Helen wore slacks and a comfortable blue sweater, Binky, a sweater and a dress.

"We've always lived within a house or two of one another, even when we were little girls growing up in Brooklyn," Helen said. "Now we're all the way up here and Binky lives just there." She pointed out the window, where you could see the backs of other summer houses, discreetly spaced among pine trees and big showy rocks and one tree-sized rhododendron.

"Our mothers were sisters," Helen added. "We always liked to say that one mother wasn't enough, because we didn't always get the right answer." That set off a little burst of giggles.

They had been coming to Mohegan Lake since 1923.

The enclosed porch was the room that Helen lived in. It was bright, with comfortable chairs and a big sturdy table arrayed with books and plants—a Boston fern, aloe, African violets, forced daffodils and lilies—and an amethyst crystal on a little wooden stand.

Stelk celebrated Communion at the table. The women leaned over the prayer books he had brought for them. Helen read along, one eye tearing as she strained over the words. Stelk handed them communion wafers and passed the small silver chalice.

"It's a great comfort right now, for you to give me Communion," Binky said.

As we left, stepping along flagstones, Helen pointed out the spots where tulips and daffodils were pushing up through the wet earth.

✛

As the weather warmed, Stelk quickened the pace of his expansion campaign.

"Dear People of St. Mary's," began the letter from the vestry's planning committee to members of the congregation. "It has become painfully obvious that the Pine Room and the Parish Hall are not sufficient in space or function for our needs."

A list of the insufficiencies followed:

"—The Church School classes meet in what could be considered common space because we have no formal classrooms and our room dividers have long since seen the day when they closed.

"—The choir robes and practices on Sundays among the children and teachers assembling for Church School.

"—The sacristy also serves as a vesting room, and the acolytes dress in the hallway. There is no quiet place for our Rector to reflect and pray before services.

"—Our church office is up a steep flight of stairs, making it inaccessible to the handicapped and difficult for the elderly.

"—Our Community Food Pantry, a large and successful part of our mission and community outreach, is housed in a closet which also stores cleaning supplies, tenants' equipment and a safe for our valuables."

The letter went on to say that the kitchen was too small for a church supper, the meeting space was inadequate for the outside groups that wanted to use it, reducing rental income, and that the crawl space under the Pine Room's floor was home to unidentified but bothersome and potentially unsanitary "critters," probably raccoons.

The punch line came on page two: an estimated cost for the needed improvements of between $750,000 and $1 million.

"This is a major financial undertaking," the letter pointed out. "Without the support of the congregation, we cannot even consider it." It went on to suggest that 1992, the one hundred and twenty-fifth anniversary of the founding of St. Mary's, would be a wonderful time to open a new parish hall.

"Please consider all this prayerfully and respond as soon as you can so we know whether to proceed.

"Faithfully yours, Kathy Munroe for the Committee."

Stelk posted the architectural sketches on the parish hall bulletin board. The sketches showed a new two-story building off the existing parish hall. One floor was drawn as classrooms, the other as a single large "community room," with a larger kitchen, additional toilets and more storage space. The new space freed the old for the choir, food pantry, sacristy and offices.

"I hope you'll look at these," Stelk urged during the announcements at services. "We need your comments and suggestions."

John Harbeson, one of the vestry members taking a particular interest in the expansion proposal, stood to one side as the congregation browsed the drawings. People studied them with the mild interest of museum-goers, standing back and rubbing their chins and murmuring. "It's funny," John said. "Everybody's talking about this as something 'they' are doing. What 'they'? It should be 'we.' "

He was right. The comments I heard went along these lines:

"I thought they were going to make the church bigger."

"They're not going to do anything inside the church."

"I guess they couldn't."

I also heard an underlying disappointment that the plans were not somehow more grandiose, as if the congregation wanted some glitter for the money they were being asked to consider spending.

"There's no room for a gym," someone said.

"Where is the stage?"

"Where's the hot tub?"

Stelk mentioned the drawings at every Sunday's service and set an Easter deadline for responses.

✢

Stelk held healing services each Tuesday night during Lent. One couple that attended regularly were Bill and Caryl Miller.

Stelk was wary of the Millers. They'd shown up suddenly last fall to have their picture taken for the parish directory. Stelk had never seen them before, a long-haired, bespectacled man with an angular nose, a woman with brown hair, gentle eyes and a quick smile, and a gangly twelve-year-old son who wore his hair long in the back in a tail; all the boys were doing it. Stelk bridled at the father's long hair, which fell to his shoulders. "I couldn't believe it," he said. "They looked like sixties hippies in the eighties."

Then the boy turned out to be a case. His father tried to make him attend Sunday school, but the boy refused. Justin would bolt for the parking lot. White-bearded Frank Doyle, the church school superintendent, would stand at the door and watch him ducking from one car to the next, the tail at the nape of his neck bouncing like a horse's mane. He'd crawl into the family's Ford Bronco, turn the radio on and try to stay down out of sight.

Stelk was convinced the Millers had come to St. Mary's because it was time for Justin's confirmation. It was the kind of thing, this bald campaigning to get a child confirmed, that made him want to strengthen confirmation into a Mature Profession of Faith.

The Millers actually had been members of St. Mary's since 1982. They'd moved the year before from New York City to a ranch house in a tree-lined neighborhood between Mohegan Lake and Peekskill. Bill was raised in Mott Haven, a tough part of the Bronx, near St. Ann's Episcopal Church. He was "a hell-raising kid," but the church youth group and a priest's advice kept him off the streets, and he had been an Episcopalian ever since. Caryl's maiden name was Pisano. She was born and raised in Little Italy but rebelled against her Catholic upbringing. She liked St. Mary's the first time they attended it. "It was friendly and open," she said. "Unlike my church. I hadn't been a practicing Catholic for some time."

"It's a special place, St. Mary's," said Bill. "It's more special as you get to know people more."

Caryl had been the first to stop getting up on Sunday

mornings. "Bill always kind of kept going," she said. "But you lose your . . . not faith. I was working, sometimes I had to go in on Sundays, and I got out of the habit."

"I always had the feeling I wanted to go," Bill said, "but I couldn't get Caryl and Justin to go. She didn't like to get up. Justin didn't like to get up. I don't like to get up, either. So we stopped. We didn't go for a long time."

Then they received a notice about pictures for the parish directory.

Caryl had decided by then that Justin needed religion. "Everyone needs a foundation of religion, growing up," she said. "Then they can choose it or not when they do grow up."

Bill said, "I was counting one sin after another. No big sins. Just . . . things."

There was a need that far surpassed those, however. It had nothing to do with forming values, or Bill's little sins, or even, as Stelk suspected, Justin's confirmation. The Miller family had a sudden need for miracles.

Their lives had been all but perfect, the kind of suburban idyll that is one version of the American Dream. Caryl was working at G. Wizz, a gift and novelty store at the Jefferson Valley Mall, on Route 6 east of the Taconic Parkway. Bill worked for American Express in New York City, where he reviewed the work of credit managers. They owned two cars. Justin played in a backyard tree house. They bought property in the Adirondacks, and planned to build a cabin there. Caryl was promoted to manager. Then, in the summer of 1989, she started having trouble using the stick shift in her car.

"They told me I had something called Epstein-Barr virus—it makes you extremely tired and affects the extremities," she said. "Then they left me alone. For a while."

The Millers showed up for the directory photographs. Winter came. The worrisome weakness in Caryl's hands grew worse, and then she started falling. She forced herself to work through Christmas, then resigned.

Finally, in January, the doctors made a diagnosis. Caryl had amyotrophic lateral sclerosis. Most people know it as Lou Gehrig's disease. The dictionary paints a dry picture of what the Millers faced: "a rare progressive degenerative fatal disease affecting the spinal cord, usually beginning in middle age, and characterized especially by increasing and spreading muscular weakness."

Caryl was forty-one, and she was dying. Justin was turning thirteen with his world gone out of control. His defiance masked confusion, embarrassment and fear.

✢

Stelk expected no one at the healing services to throw away their crutches, but he wouldn't rule it out. "I have no idea what physiological reactions there are," he said. "But I know there is a close connection between psychological predilections for wellness and healing and being well and healed.

"At a minimum, it's reassurance. At a maximum, who knows what can happen?"

The services played to small houses. I arrived one Tuesday evening to find the entire congregation seated in the choir stalls. Three of them were Cursillistas who came to church at every opportunity. They were tiny Eleanor Arnold with her crinkly smile, Ann Douglas, who was tall and wore her sandy hair short in tight waves, and John Weber. Weber was a rangy telephone lineman with short black hair. Dressed in blue jeans, heavy shoes and a red sweatshirt, he looked as if he'd come from work. The rest of the group were Ed Lumley, conservative in Wall Street gray, vestry secretary Frances Armstrong and Caryl Miller, who was wearing a ski jacket and pink tights. Dusk was bleeding the light from the windows, and the warm lights inside the church felt comforting.

Stelk entered from the back with the night's lay reader, Ann Marwick. He wore an alb, and his cincture was purple, the color of Lent.

He began the service with opening prayers and then delivered a homily. He paced stiff-legged in the middle of the chancel as he spoke, and he seemed to have something on his mind. He drew his text from Mark 11:15, in which Jesus drives the moneychangers from the temple:

"He was protesting . . . the commercialization of religion, the use of religion for purposes beyond . . . the worship of God.

"He was a threat. He was a threat to the pandering of religion. He was a threat to the primary commandment of the time, 'Thou shalt not threaten the cash registers.' He was the kind of threat, whether he was in the Soviet Union or the U.S.A., he would still be crucified [today]. Because he was one who refused to accept this secondary nature of religion. Religion was purposeful of itself. One did not sell it off.

"Often we find religion being used to bless the most irreligious actions. We find people finding excuses to perpetuate poverty and hunger and homelessness in the richest country in the world. It is obscene. It is obscene to have homeless people in this country. It is absolutely irreligious."

I had not heard a sermon in which Stelk was so impassioned. His Sunday sermons were articulate, but blander. A car passed on Route 6 as the church door opened. Bill Miller entered, blinking to adjust to the dim light. He moved to the front, took a seat in the first pew and smiled at Caryl in the back row of the choir stalls.

"The cleansing of the temple is a highly significant action," Stelk continued. "Yet we don't get ourselves challenged by the challenge of Christ to set aright the priorities of human life in our own lives and the lives of the people that we deal with. We find ourselves so easily calmed . . . by quietness and peace . . . into backing off a little bit . . . making excuses."

Stelk's voice dropped. He seemed for a moment to be talking to himself. The windows were dark now, and the sanctuary was like a lighted clearing in dark woods. Stelk said he had known someone who accepted the challenge. His name was Jonathan Daniels, a classmate at the Episcopal Theological Seminary. Daniels had joined the march on Selma and stayed on in Alabama, where he was killed.

"He was shotgunned down by an Episcopalian . . . who was

freed by an Episcopal judge . . . because Jonathan was obviously a rabble-rouser. He was dealing with blacks . . . They called him a white nigger . . ." Stelk's voice was edged with pain.

"[But] Christianity should confront the status quo. It's dangerous, but it's the only way to live." The church was utterly quiet.

Then Stelk turned to healing. The Litany of Healing is contained in the Book of Occasional Services, those held too infrequently to be included in the Book of Common Prayer. The congregation first names aloud the people for whom prayers are offered. Eleanor Arnold closed her eyes and offered up a stream of names. The rest of us spoke in murmurs. Ann Marwick led the litany:

"Lord, grant your healing grace to all who are sick, injured, or disabled, that they may be made whole;"

"Hear us, O Lord of life."

"Grant to all who seek your guidance, and to all who are lonely, anxious or despondent, a knowledge of your will and an awareness of your presence;"

"Hear us, O Lord of life."

"Mend broken relationships, and restore those in emotional distress to soundness of mind and serenity of spirit;"

"Hear us, O Lord of life."

"Bless physicians and nurses, and all others who minister to the suffering, granting them wisdom and skill, sympathy and patience;"

"Hear us, O Lord of life."

"Grant to the dying, peace and a holy death, and uphold by the grace and consolation of your Holy Spirit those who are bereaved;"

"Hear us, O Lord of life."

"Restore to wholeness whatever is broken by human sin, in our lives, in our nation, and in the world;"

"Hear us, O Lord of life."

I touched Caryl's hand during the Peace; it felt gnarled. She pulled it away quickly.

The group moved to the altar to receive anointing and the

laying on of hands. Stelk dipped his thumb in chrism—consecrated oil—and moved along the altar rail, placing his hand on each head, forming the cross on each forehead with his thumb. A warmth flowed from his fingertips. He conveyed a gentle strength.

Stelk had celebrated Communion and the service was nearing an end when Ann Douglas suddenly broke into song. She tilted her head back and closed her eyes and raised the palms of her hands as if in supplication. She sang, "Father, we adore you . . . Lay our lives before you . . . How we love you . . ." Some of the others haltingly joined in.

Ann said Cursillo had given her spirituality expression. She had not attended church as a child in England, in part because her mother was brought up in a strict Calvinist orphanage and never wanted to set foot in church again, while her father casually "tipped his hat to the C of E." She met Dwight in Canada, where she was raised. They returned to Mohegan Lake after they were married, and it was the family life at St. Mary's that drew her to the church. She was baptized and confirmed when she was pregnant with their second child, kneeling "in all my hugeness" to receive the bishop's laying on of hands. Her spirituality grew, and she became a lay reader. The Marriage Encounter weekends she attended with Dwight taught her to incorporate God into her life. Now she could sing, quite naturally, to God.

The anthem died and the service ended and the small congregation left the church and headed for their cars. Bill and Caryl walked close together. He touched her elbow to steady her. Then they were gone into the night.

4

The approach of Easter produced in Stelk a mood of jubilation. He always felt the season's special joy. The closer the celebration of Christ's Resurrection, the more animated, even playful, he became. "I love the old tunes . . . plainsong, Gregorian chants, gospel," he began his sermon on the second Sunday before Easter. He looked slyly over his glasses to see who was listening. The congregation was just settling in for the usual fifteen minutes.

"Dem bones, dem bones, dem . . . dry bones," he sang in demonstration. "Dem bones, dem bones, dem . . . dry bones," he repeated, giving his tenor a little working room. The third time he sang still louder and waved his arms like a conductor and the people began to sing along.

Soon Stelk was leading a laughing songfest from the pulpit. "Let's connect them bones, dem . . . dry bones . . . Dem bones, dem bones, gonna . . . walk around . . . Now hear the word of the Lord."

The Lesson from Ezekiel, the Epistle from Romans and the Gospel from John, all had focused on death in sin versus life in God. Now Stelk spoke of the same affirmation, of eternal life. "Is it true?" he asked. "If it is true, we are empowered in ways we can hardly imagine. Then indeed we are living a life that the grave will have absolutely no effect upon, and we are living a life with the risen Christ of history and involved with God in a way far beyond our understanding and expectation . . ."

Stelk the preacher was not an orator. Soaring rhetoric and insistent cadences were not his thing, nor the pregnant pause, nor the pounding fist upon the pulpit. Issues of the day were unlikely to intrude. The fire of his healing service homily about Jonathan Daniels was something he apparently held in deep reserve. People were more likely to leave St. Mary's reflecting on their own lives than fired up to change the world.

He most often was a reassuring preacher. A parishioner named Jan Faris had written, for Stelk's book of reminiscences, that she and her family had come to St. Mary's after another preacher's sermon on nuclear war, fire and brimstone frightened her two young children. Stelk, by contrast, liked to say he only preached one sermon "because there is only one sermon to be preached, and that is that God loves you."

The message came back to him sometimes in unusual ways and faraway places. Two years earlier Stelk and Ginny had been vacationing with their daughter Marla in Australia. They were exploring the Great Barrier Reef from a boat moored to a diving platform when suddenly two women burst from the water, flung open their sleek wet arms and told Stelk, "We love you *this* much!" Stelk was nonplussed. Then the women introduced themselves. They had belonged to a youth group at Stelk's church in Delaware, Ohio.

"They recognized him because he hasn't changed much in twenty years," said Marla. She was the daughter who looked most like Stelk, with a face that hinted at some secret source of laughter. "And they were remembering one of his sermons. It was one of the ones he uses at Christmas. He has three of them."

Stelk had stopped preparing his sermons long ago. He didn't write them out and read them. He rarely spoke from notes. He used no props. He could find the inspiration for a sermon in an old song on the radio, a movie he'd seen long ago or the comic pages of the Sunday paper.

He said, "I guess I try to give some kind of personal affirmation. I try to be supportive within the context of the text. I let the text speak to me instead of me speaking to the text."

He was best at tapping the impulse that was central to religion, the need to keep uncertainty and fear at bay with faith:

"We live in a time which hungers for meaning in life. We live in a time in which thousands of people have given up on any sense of meaning in life and existence and are finding meaning in drugs. We live in a time in which people have turned away from the God of Abraham, Isaac and Jacob, the God and Father of our Lord Jesus Christ, and are trying all kinds of new ways, which are really old ways, of trying to find some meaning in their lives.

"There was a song not too long ago . . . well, longer than I care to recall . . . that asked the question, 'Is that all there is?' How many people spend time on psychiatrists' couches these days trying to find out, 'Isn't there more to life?'

"We have a society in which we honor more the prophet of the marketplace than the prophet of God. Society elevates consumption for the sake of consumption. What kind of meaning does that give in life? Even the most successful describe it as a rat race. We double, we triple, we quintuple our speed, but we shatter our nerves in the process."

The balm, he said, is the discovery of being loved and the ascendency of some purpose in your life. "To be known and loved, and to have a purpose.

"God knows our names. And God knows our purposes, far beyond any purpose that we can imagine for ourselves . . . And for those who are still searching for that purpose, the search itself is a recognition of something, a meaning in life beyond the meaninglessness and the absurdity which is pushed at us from other quarters. It is an assertion of meaningfulness in human existence, in human life, in your life and in mine. We are loved . . . and we have a purpose for our existence."

Stelk's was usually a quiet affirmation, but sometimes his reassurances were zingy and exuberant: "The Law was meant to be liberating, to help people live in such a way that they might live and have life.

"You are the light of the world, and if you don't shine forth in the darkness, who is going to? It is not only a privilege and a responsibility, it is a joy. In the midst of all that says that we are negated and we are put down, Jesus says, 'You are affirmed.' You are yes, not no. You are the salt of the earth. Be salty. You are the light of the world. Shine forth."

Nor was he beyond an occasional hallelujah shout. Easter brought out that impulse in him, and brought a resounding close to his dry bones sermon:

" 'Dem bones, dem bones, them dry bones . . . Dem bones gonna walk around . . . Now hear the word of the Lord.' That's the word! Amen."

✣

Holy Week began with palm fronds waving and children jangling bells, triangles, castanets and tambourines. The cacophony was part of Palm Sunday tradition at St. Mary's. Blood red drapes shrouded the altar and processional crosses to symbolize Christ's passion. Stelk's red cincture made an almost jaunty slash across his vestments. Bleak events lay ahead in Christ's suffering and death, but Stelk, looking beyond to resurrection and redemption, entered Holy Week in his ebullient Easter mood. By the end of the week, he was transformed.

"In the darkness, fire is kindled."

So begins the Great Vigil of Easter in the new Book of Common Prayer. The fire at St. Mary's was kindled in a square red barbeque grill set just inside the parish hall door, where it sent a thin plume of smoke to the ceiling. I took one of the lighted candles the acolytes were passing among the congregation.

"Put them out when you enter the church," Stelk called. "Our fire insurance is paid up, but we don't want to pick up on it."

The parish hall was unusually crowded, for three priests and parts of three congregations were on hand. The Great Vigil rotated among St. Mary's, the Episcopal Church of the Good

Shepherd in Granite Springs to the east, and Grace Lutheran Church of Yorktown. The 1979 Book of Common Prayer had reclaimed the disused Easter Eve service as the Church's most solemn liturgical observance. Leading to the joy of Easter, it was also the most striking triumph of redemption over propitiation and atonement that the new prayer book had to offer. Tonight Father Tim Kennedy of Grace Lutheran was the preacher and Father Robert Dresser of Good Shepherd the deacon, or assistant. Stelk, the host priest, would celebrate the Eucharist.

Carol Obligado waved a hand in the direction of the choir, and singers from the three churches began the Kyrie: "Lord have mercy upon us . . . Christ have mercy upon us . . ."

In dots of candlelight and threads of song, the procession moved slowly from the parish hall to the church. Dresser led, carrying the large, elaborate paschal candle lit at the beginning of Easter to symbolize Christ's Resurrection. The line of worshipers stretched behind him, parents holding onto children as they tried to keep their places in the Kyrie and shielding their candle flames. Traffic slowed along Route 6 as drivers rubbernecked.

The church was bright with Easter finery. Pots of pink and yellow tulips, daffodils and iris formed a path across the chancel to the altar. Sprays of Easter lilies decorated the windowsills and the corners of the alcove behind the altar. In the acolytes' seats opposite the choir, a small girl leaned back and tilted her head to smell the Easter lilies in the window.

Brand-new organ pipes gleamed overhead. They were the bequest of a parishioner who had loved the organ works of Handel, and Carol was excited about debuting them. They stood in two shimmering ranks atop an oak sound box mounted on a platform over the rear door between the flags. A small extension held the Zimbelstern. It looked like a fanciful anemometer, a doll-sized carousel made from clock parts that spun like the workings of a music box and produced the sound of silver bells. The pipes and chiming Zimbelstern had been installed three weeks earlier by a young man named Dean Christian, who Carol described as being "in very good physical shape." She had practiced long hours for tonight's inauguration.

The notes the pipes produced were big and vigorous, even in the plaintive Kyrie. They had a breathy throatiness that made the old church vibrate. Carol was all motion at the console, somehow finding switches and keys and the long, slatlike wooden pedals as she directed the choir and flipped the pages of her music. The music sheets were lit by an old-fashioned pharmacy lamp standing on two thick, old and unread books. One was a journal of the 1967 Episcopal General Convention (held in Seattle), the other a Reader's Digest tome entitled *How to Live on Your Income.* The congregation filled the church and sang the last words of the Kyrie: "Lord, have mercy upon us."

Stelk began the Liturgy of the Word: "Let us hear the record of God's saving deeds in history, how he saved his people in ages past; and let us pray that our God will bring each of us to the fullness of redemption."

The stories were told in song and prose, in psalms and Scripture. Verses of Genesis recounted the creation, the flood and Abraham's sacrifice of Isaac; of Exodus, the deliverance of Israel at the Red Sea; of Isaiah, the presence of God in a renewed Israel and the salvation offered freely to all. The storytelling resembled the Jewish feast of Passover, the Seder.

Kennedy put his glasses on to deliver the sermon. He was young and intense and an alliterative writer:

"Jesus turned to the thief on his right with the Edict of Eden . . . The soldiers thought this . . . a counterfeit kingdom offered by a counterfeit Christ . . . For the disciples, if Friday was black, Saturday was blue, blah . . . If Friday was black, then Sunday was bleak . . ."

✢

Across the aisle, opposite me, a row of Middle Eastern faces endured the sermon stoically. The men were stifling yawns. Their dark hair and heavy mustaches might have been found in a scene from a mosque. The women, in the row behind them, looked as if they belonged in chadors. But they were at St. Mary's for a baptism.

Sultan and Elaine Jabbour had been married at St. Mary's on Valentine's Day 1988. It was an accident. Elaine was Russian Orthodox, Sultan an Eastern Orthodox Jordanian. The Russian Orthodox Church they attended wouldn't marry them on the date they'd chosen, which was a Sunday. They had paid for a reception hall and couldn't get their money back. Someone suggested that they try St. Mary's. They had been attending ever since.

"In my opinion, I was glad," said Sultan, who was twenty-six and a civilian pharmacist with the U.S. Navy. This was on the day he and Elaine had dropped by the church office to go over the baptism ceremony with Stelk. Sultan had a flat, heavy, friendly face. His eyes had a basset hound's droopy expressiveness. Elaine, twenty-four, was a dark blonde with a cupid's bow mouth. They asked if Stelk minded a videotape camera. "I don't mind, I don't mind," he said a little brusquely. "But I don't want to get into one of these big productions." Stelk was impatient with all new technology.

Nicholas Alexander, their son, was three months old. He had slept through the procession, but as Kennedy finished his sermon, the baby awoke and looked around brightly at the candle flames.

Stelk called the baptismal party forward. Sultan and Elaine and the godparents moved to the font. One of the men aimed the video camera from the side aisle.

Stelk immersed the boy three times, and great smiles broke out among the stoic faces. Then the priest held the boy aloft. "Let me introduce you to your new son, who is a gem," he said to the congregation, which was packed into every pew and corner. He moved down the aisle with the boy, blinking, head damp, raised on his shoulder, as the people applauded. Suddenly, unexpectedly, a primitive cry arose. It ripped through the church like a sharp gust of wind. A woman with a desert face and coarse salt-and-pepper hair, wearing a green dress and big faux pearls under a black coat, whooped, "Ayyyyehyehyehyeh!" Then she tilted her chin up and looked around with an expression of fierce pride.

Sultan's mother, Nada, had unleashed the ancient cheer of joy. It was joy as pure and radiant as the smile that lit Stelk's face when he said, at the beginning of the Eucharist, "Alleluia. Christ is risen."

And the congregation responded, for the first of many times during the seven weeks of Easter, "The Lord is risen indeed. Alleluia."

+

"It's all the twice-a-year Christians," Fred Obligado whispered the next morning. Easter had dawned mild and damp, with a mist that verged on rain. The church door was open to relieve the closeness of the overcrowded church. Fred and the rest of the ushers had set out as many folding chairs as they could fit into the aisles and the back of the church. Now there was standing room only. A fire marshal would have cleared the place.

"Alleluia, Christ is risen," Stelk called from the back of the church.

"The Lord is risen indeed. Alleluia."

Despite the long Easter Vigil service of the night before, Stelk's voice was filled with energy. He seemed to feel like shouting the news. After all his exultant expectation leading up to Easter, now he embodied the breathless discovery of the Resurrection. He was transformed. You could hear it and see it in his face, in his triumphant smile and shining eyes.

He preached about the Resurrection, dismissing skepticism that said the rebirth of Christ was too good to be true. His voice rose as he proclaimed, "Each of the Apostles was executed except John, who died in exile. For a made-up story?"

The open door let in the sounds of passing cars on rain-slick Route 6. A mother carried out a crying baby.

"Something happened. The most significant event in human history.

"It is this that is too good to be true. But it is too true not to be believed."

Stelk's energy carried through to the announcements. He talked about the "different sound, the different feeling" produced by the organ pipes. He told of giving the newly baptized Nicholas Alexander Jabbour his first Communion and laughed recounting how the boy had wrinkled his face at the wine he'd tasted on Stelk's little finger. And he made a last, optimistic pitch for responses to the expansion plans. The vestry was meeting Thursday night, he said.

✛

Stelk opened the meeting with a green pencil for a gavel and a yellow box of cough drops next to his right hand. His pace during Holy Week and Easter had caught up with him, and he was fighting a spring cold. A chapter of Alcoholics Anonymous, another of the groups to which St. Mary's rented space, was meeting downstairs. Sounds of laughter and the smells of cigarette smoke and coffee drifted through the office door. Stelk offered a prayer of thanksgiving for Harold and Lily Van Horne. He said, "I went by to give them home Communion and learned they'd gone out to Bible study. I thought that deserved a prayer."

Karin Efman burst in, puffing. She chaired a committee on parish social life in addition to her senior warden's duties. She announced she was planning a game night to raise money.

"A casino night?" asked David Odell.

"Trump is not our name," Ann Marwick said.

"I am not Ivana," Karin answered.

"You should be Marla," somebody said.

John Donovan, the chairman of the planning and development committee, had a red Irish face and worry lines across his forehead. Both color and lines deepened when Stelk asked for his report.

"We're getting close to crunch time on a lot of questions," Donovan said. "What's going to be in the building? What's it going to look like? How are we going to raise money? With all that, we feel we need the vestry's blessing to go on the way we're going."

"Do we continue, or not?" Stelk condensed the question. "At least up to the point where we have to make a major expenditure of money?"

"Architectural and engineering fees will probably run $75,000 to $90,000," said Donovan.

Dwight Douglas sat back and draped an arm over the back of his chair. "It's unclear that we've determined what we want," he said. "We had a packed house for the Easter service. Are we trying to build a bigger church?"

"I thought all that was clear," Stelk said. "The church school can't continue to operate. The choir has no place to dress and practice. AA needs room to continue to operate. There are other community needs."

"What are they, the other community needs?"

Stelk began rapping his knuckles on the table edge.

Dwight continued, "We have some ideas. But I don't know if they have been placed into a statement of goals. We want better space for the choir. How does that compare against our church school needs?"

Dwight's questions sounded logical to me. They were a planner's questions. How did the vestry know Mohegan Lake needed a new day care center, and how did a day care center further St. Mary's mission? As a planner, Dwight wanted a logic in the process and a truckload of facts. But the questions clearly frustrated Stelk, who saw the church's needs as a given. The sound of applause drifted up from the AA meeting. Stelk rested his chin in his hands. He said, "Why is it important to prioritize at this stage?"

"If you aren't sure of what you want, you'll never get it," Dwight said. He unleashed a burst of planner's jargon, words like "consensus . . . input . . . organized . . . evaluated . . . prioritized."

Gerry Cousins said, "We've been talking about this for the last six years."

"Typical Episcopalians," said Karin.

"Maybe we ought to have a meeting about the process," Harbeson said. "Maybe we ought to define the process. So that we can see what decision has to be made at which stage. Would that help you?" He gestured as he spoke, holding blocks of air between his hands and setting them firmly on the table, moving them from side to side, using his hands to part the air in front of him.

Here was another issue Stelk had not anticipated. Harbeson's concern with procedure seemed to flow from his academic background. John was a fifty-year-old former Congregationalist. He sang tenor in St. Mary's choir and played the organ in Carol Obligado's absence. He was tall and gawky and looked like a professor. Where Dwight's black hair and beard were neatly trimmed, John's grizzled beard and his sandy, graying hair wanted to spring out in all directions. Dwight wore a dark suit and a button-down shirt with a rose-colored tie knotted neatly at the collar. John wore a faded polo shirt with two pens and a comb stuffed into a plastic sleeve in the breast pocket. He spoke in the same rapid-fire delivery he used for lectures to his students, clipping words and leaving them in fragments.

Stelk looked incredulous. "Does the vestry feel that this place"—he swept an arm around to indicate the parish hall—"is adequate? What I think was being asked for tonight is simply the official sanction of the vestry that says we've got to explore expanding this place."

Dwight said, "It isn't so simple to say 'The vestry's in favor of expansion.' I mean, expansion to do what?"

Harbeson began to interrupt, and Dwight barked, "Let me finish. I mean, we all come to church for a particular reason. We have our spiritual lives that we come to St. Mary's to feed. And we have a sense of a St. Mary's that has a history and a purpose in the community. What is our reason to be? Why St. Mary's at all? You have to step back and look and say, 'Where do I want to be? What is there else? What's missing in my life now at St. Mary's that I want added in here?' That may translate into a physical need or it may not."

"We ought to define the process," Harbeson insisted. "We ought to know the steps in the process." He formed a block of air and set it on the tabletop. After more discussion, he offered a complicated resolution that the vestry begin a "four-part exploration" into purposes and long-term goals, specific needs and physical improvements. Frances Armstrong, the vestry secretary, wrote it all down with a pained expression on her face.

"Where does this motion leave the committee?" Gerry wanted to know.

"I would say discharged," Stelk said bitterly.

David Odell listened to the ensuing hubbub and finally cleared his throat. He was tall, lanky, with an ordinary face and neatly combed gunmetal gray hair. He was dressed, as usual, in a sweater, slacks and penny loafers. His wife was a Roman Catholic, and he always came to church alone. He'd seen chaos in his high school administrator's job and was used to dealing with it. He said, "We're diverted from course here, okay? I don't see that we need to reinvent the wheel.

"It was a simple request, and it was blown all out of proportion. I think we're talking ourselves to death."

He sat back and knit his fingers together.

Harbeson said, "I don't think anybody really doubts that expansion is in the cards. But we want to do it right. We can't start laying bricks and mortar until we see where the shoe doesn't fit."

"We're a hell of a long way from bricks and mortar," David said.

Harbeson's resolution passed, and it was it almost midnight when the vestry finished the rest of its agenda. Frustrated and exhausted, the members joined hands in a closing prayer.

Karin said, "Thanks be to God," when it was over.

Stelk went home to the rectory in a funk. He thought he had let the meeting get away from him and he could see months added to the process as the vestry debated what the church was all about. "We don't have that kind of time to waste," he said. The business pages already were forecasting an economic downturn that would make raising money difficult.

+

Karin drove home in a daze, went to sleep thinking and woke up disturbed. She got on the telephone. By Sunday she thought she had a quorum.

The morning's services continued the Easter celebration. "Alleluia, Christ is risen," Stelk greeted the ten-thirty congregation.

"The Lord is risen indeed. Alleluia."

The service was a folk mass. Carol Obligado left the organ bench for the small upright piano in the chancel, and Gerry Cousins played the guitar. The Van Hornes were in church for the first time in several weeks. Eugene also had returned. Sultan and Elaine Jabbour were there with their son, who'd been baptized at the Easter Vigil. John and Vincent were in their accustomed places at the front. Bill Miller sat alone on the aisle.

Toward the end of the service, Carol handed out cymbals, tambourines, triangles and castanets to accompany the communion hymns. When Stelk said, "Let us pray," the whole place tinkled and chimed and then laughed at the noise it was making. The recessional hymn, "Lord of the Dance," set to a Shaker melody entitled "Simple Gifts," was springlike in its clack and jangle.

The noise had hardly died when Stelk convened a vestry quorum in the church office. Karin, David Odell, Gerry Cousins, John Harbeson, Mary Bohun and Marilyn Trudeau—Stelk was the seventh—sat around a table munching Girl Scout cookies. Gerry's daughters Tricia and Terry had sold them to half the congregation. Waving a half-eaten cookie, Stelk said, "There has been some concern about what we did Thursday night in the wee hours. It was the longest vestry meeting I have ever attended, and I hope we do not repeat it."

He said the parish did not need to redefine its goals as Harbeson's resolution called for. "Your search committee that called me here did that," he said. "They produced a parish profile. Christian education and the music program were the two highest priorities. There was a concern for ministry in the immediate area, which is why you have the AA groups here, and the food pantry, and why you were housing homeless people in the rectory, which is one of the reasons I came here . . .

"And then I came and we started talking about needs and everybody that I spoke to talked about the need for more space. So what do we do to keep the momentum we have before it falls on its face and we have to re-resurrect it again?"

Stelk sat back, placed his glasses on the table and popped the rest of the cookie in his mouth.

"Can we throw this thing out?" Karin said, meaning Harbeson's resolution. She had a fretful look. She had told me again that vestry debates were distracting her from worship. "I was very confused. There must be some way we can expedite this and get it over with. We've done all of this stuff. It just needs to be written."

John sat up and pushed his glasses from his nose up into his thatch of hair. "Bottom line. This is not a question of whether. It's a question of how. I am committed to building. Let the record state, put it in the minutes. I have talked to Dwight, Dwight is committed. Now . . ."

Now lasted for some time. John said the process he envisioned was "a question of crystallizing and fine-tuning, dotting the *i*'s and crossing the *t*'s." He formed his blocks of air and set them down. He said, "If our purpose is the same as it was a few years ago, this will take five minutes. If we have changed, then we'd better find out about it now."

Everyone but John saw his resolution as demanding a sequence of actions that only a statement of goals could begin.

"No," said John.

"No?" Gerry was amazed.

"John, look at the resolution." Stelk was pleading.

"Look at the resolution," Gerry said.

"If you want to put more language into the resolution, I'll be happy to do that," John offered.

David stretched his long legs out beneath the table. He tapped his fingers together. "We're getting mired in words," he said. "We are getting mind-boggled with semantics. Here is this great cloud, this goals statement, which I don't think is that difficult to create. Why don't we create a committee—God so loved the world that he did *not* send a committee—to do this, a goal statement?"

"Would you do that, John?" Stelk asked. "You and Dwight, get together with anybody else you want."

"To do what?" John was hunched forward in his chair, his paisley tie crumpled on the tabletop. Gerry removed his cardigan sweater and draped it over his seat back. A blue jay flitted by outside the window, and the sound of utensils being washed rose from the kitchen.

"To redefine the purposes and long-term goals of the parish, to explore specific needs relative to these goals . . . and then explore how these items relate to the physical structure." Stelk was using the language of John's resolution.

"You want me to do that?"

"You and Dwight."

John said, "This is a collective process that should involve the entire vestry and perhaps others as well. That's the way it's done."

"Jo-ohn!" Karin sounded as if someone had stepped on her foot.

"I'm sorry, it's not necessarily the way it's done. It's one way of doing it." Stelk's voice was heavy with exasperation.

John was insistent. "It's not a one-person job. And I don't guarantee it can be done in a month. If I'm asked to do this, I will write every member of the congregation. I will poll . . ."

Yelps of protest drowned him out.

"What you're saying, then," Gerry said, "is you're not really convinced that the needs of this parish—"

"That is not what I said. I will not have you put words in my mouth."

"You don't know if we need a building yet. That's what it sounds like to me."

"Gerry, you are not only putting words in my mouth, you're changing what I've already said. I will not put up with that." John took his glasses off and put them on again.

"Let's back off a minute," Stelk said. He looked at John. "Are you asking that the whole congregation do this? This is not a Congregational church. Why can't we accept the fact that this has already been done and trust the people who did it?"

"If I'm going to do this, this is how I'm going to do it," John insisted. He drummed his fingertips on the table. "And if you don't like the way I'm going to do it, then somebody else can do it."

Weary sighs sounded up and down the table. Mary Bohun took off her glasses and rubbed her eyes. She put her head down on her hands for a few seconds. Karin reached for a Girl Scout cookie, and looked as if she wanted to fling it in John's face.

Stelk worried the rim of a paper coffee cup, bending it back and forth between his fingers. "In that case, John, I won't ask you to do it."

"I don't think you need to write books on it," David said.

Stelk said, "If we can just get a purpose statement as a starting point, maybe we can begin to see how the other things fall into place . . ."

Somehow, those words turned a key. Harbeson said he could write a purpose statement without starting from scratch. He wouldn't even have to poll the congregation. Then, when Stelk declared he wanted the vestry to commit itself to build a building, John said he was all for that, too.

A new resolution finally reached a vote. It charged the planning committee with stating the parish's purposes and long-term goals, exploring the needs that grew out of them and whether those needs required a new parish hall. The committee was to report its findings to the vestry.

"Are we clear on what the motion is?" Stelk asked. "Any further discussion?" He barely paused. "All in favor say aye." There were no nays.

"Then it's carried."

It had been a dizzying exercise in parish governance. Karin headed straight to Kathy Munroe's house to tell her all about it.

✣

Harbeson's stubbornness unleashed the furies, and his turnaround at the end of the meeting failed to rein them in. Four of the vestry members launched a telephone campaign to remove him.

Stelk also was furious. "I don't mind being opposed, but I don't like being blindsided," he said.

But he had also admonished those who wanted to remove Harbeson, and by week's end the campaign had petered out. Harbeson, meanwhile, was chastened by the force of the reaction. He went around soliciting advice from members of the congregation and the vestry, mending his fences.

The next Sunday found him at the organ. Carol Obligado had gone off with Fred to be a baseball groupie. Ted, their oldest son, played first base for Bucknell, and they enjoyed taking a spring weekend now and then to watch him play. They had been in Lynchburg, Virginia, for a game against Liberty Baptist when Ted hit a grand slam home run with Jerry Falwell in the stands. It seemed to Carol that the wind toward the outfield on that day was the act of a discerning God.

John reminded me of Picasso's Don Quixote as he played. He was gaunt, all joints and angles. He was over six feet tall, but he wore Carol's cassock since he played the organ too seldom to have one of his own. It was far too small for him. His bony wrists protruded from its loose black sleeves, and he'd flipped its skirt over the back of the bench to free his lanky legs to work the pedals. He played with a fierce, transcending concentration, as if the sacred music and the organ's throaty tones had the power of balm. If any bitterness remained from the dispute within the vestry, John didn't show it as he played.

5

The Westchester countryside hung out gold friezes of forsythia. The tulips bloomed in the rectory garden, and the azaleas at the church door swelled toward bursting in another month. Stelk put away the black wool cape he wore outside on cold mornings to greet worshipers at the end of services. It was during this time of life's renewal that Shirley McCord told Stelk she had decided to return to work full time.

Shirley was a lifelong member of St. Mary's. Her part-time job left her free on Friday mornings. For the last three years she'd spent her Friday mornings at St. Mary's, distributing groceries from the church's Community Food Pantry to two dozen or so families that couldn't afford enough to eat. She had the help of a few regular volunteers, but none of them was going to be able to step in if Shirley found her full-time job.

The food pantry was the heart of St. Mary's local ministry. It was begun in 1981. Before it was created, the mission committee of the vestry had organized deliveries of Thanksgiving and Christmas baskets to a handful of people on the lists of local charities. Then God spoke to three members of St. Mary's.

"We were standing around one day after the service," said Frank Doyle, the church school superintendent. "Chris, Fred and I. And each of us had a story about hungry people or poverty we'd seen that week. It was as if God was telling us to do something."

Chris was Christine Warnecke, one of the lay readers. Fred Bodeker sang in the choir. All three served on the mission committee. They went to the vestry to suggest that St. Mary's set up some kind of food distribution program.

"It wasn't easy to convince them," said Frank. "We were a middle-class community with no obvious signs of hardship. You had to look, but it was there. Eventually, they came around."

St. Mary's was too small to support a food program on its own, so Frank and Chris solicited other churches. Two area Lutheran churches joined in, and so, eventually, did St. Elizabeth Ann Seton, the Catholic church in nearby Shrub Oak where St. Mary's secretary Terry Donaghy was a member. Each of the churches donated some food and some money to buy more.

Fred sold insurance for a living. Because he made calls at night and could arrange his days, he became the food pantry's shopper.

Fred was a large man with a broad, waggish face, a onetime Missouri Synod Lutheran who, with his Presbyterian wife, Noelle, had joined St. Mary's because they found it "warm and caring." Noelle taught the church school's first- and second-graders. Fred played a bass trumpet in addition to singing in the choir. Hardly anybody played a bass trumpet anymore, but the instrument fit Fred's conservative streak. He liked the contrariness implied by the outmoded instrument, and he and his older son, Billy, a high school freshman and an acolyte, who played a conventional trumpet, performed Christmas anthems together at the church. The two of them, husky father and lanky son, were also members of the Greenwich, Connecticut, American Legion Drum Corps, a venerable outfit that suited Fred in the same way the bass trumpet did.

Fred went to the Westchester County offices in White Plains and found some old civil defense pamphlets about how to stock bomb shelters. He began haunting the Shop Rite on Route 6, shopping the sales, buying food in case lots. "I buy from the basic food groups," he said. "Canned tuna, canned meats, peanut butter, spaghetti, canned fruits, applesauce. Nothing perishable, no breakfast cereal, no coffee, no tea."

Government surplus stores provided the balance of the food, agricultural commodities like flour, cornmeal and rice, American cheese in five-pound blocks. "And honey," said Fred. "We've gotten box after box of honey. It sits and crystallizes. People can only eat so many pancakes."

The need the vestry had questioned was clear once the pantry opened. Forty or fifty families were showing up each week, exhausting supplies. The volunteers who gave out the groceries started checking addresses and learned that half the people they were supplying came from Peekskill, which had food programs of its own. Since then the average Friday saw between twenty and two dozen people at the door. A few had children, but most were couples. Some were young and down on their luck, others elderly and trying to stretch small fixed incomes. They all had one thing besides poverty in common: they were sick of powdered milk.

"That's another thing we get from the government, powdered milk," Fred said. He was standing at the door of the pantry, peering in, wondering where to put the morning's donations from the basket in the narthex. I had followed him, carrying a bag of canned goods from the basket. Every shelf in the tiny room looked full. "What are we going to do with eight hundred pounds of powdered milk?" he asked. "Maybe we could turn it into chocolate pudding. There would be enough to fill a swimming pool."

"What are we going to do with eight hundred pounds of chocolate pudding?" demanded Diane Cousins. Gerry's wife was tall and blond and sharp tongued. She favored jersey dresses that fell below the knee.

"Maybe it's not eight hundred pounds. Maybe it's less," Fred ventured. He assessed the large boxes that took up two full pantry shelves. "I bet it's eighty pounds, though."

Diane turned on her heel and went off in pursuit of her two pale, blond daughters, who were dancing like sprites around the parish hall.

The pantry was a jumble of boxes and cans. Hand-lettered cards set off sections: Soup, Canned Vegetables, Tuna Fish, Peanut Butter, Baby Food. Pasta and tomato sauces were stacked under Italian, an assortment of chow meins under Chinese. Odd cans and jars took up the end of one shelf: smoked oysters, tiny aubergines, artichoke hearts in olive oil, sardines in tomato sauce, gefilte fish, several small boxes of Scottish shortbread cookies. This was marked, Weird Stuff.

"We get that stuff around holiday time," Fred said. "I usually can set up a whole German cookie section. And candied yams. We always have a ton of candied yams."

Stelk stuck his head in the door. "Anything yet?" he asked.

"Not yet," Fred answered. "You want some powdered milk?"

"Ha," said Stelk, and fled. He'd been trying to keep up with Shirley's job hunt. So far he'd been unable to find a replacement for her for the Friday morning distributions, and he worried that the food pantry soon would be without a vital part.

✢

"If we don't grow, we stagnate. If we stagnate, we die." Stelk slapped his palm emphatically upon the tabletop, setting off veiled glances between the members of the planning and development committee.

Earlier, he'd handed them twelve pages of material prepared by the search committee that had called him to St. Mary's. He contended they set out parish goals, the first of which was to solve a lack of space.

"Wait a minute," John Harbeson had said. He was wearing a blue windbreaker over a faded T-shirt. It was a warm night in early May, and Stelk had shifted to his summer wardrobe of short-sleeved clericals. "At what level are we talking about goals? Are we talking about goals in terms of the size of the choir room? Are we talking about goals in terms of whether we are going to expand the community outreach?" He made a shaping movement with his hands.

That was when Stelk had lost his patience. "I'm past those

things," he said. "I think the goals are self-evident. If we need them written down, write them down. But let's get this other stuff done."

"If they're self-evident, what are they?" Walt Decker, the vestry's jowly foundation executive, demanded.

"Expansion of our facilities for the ministry within this congregation. How can we provide our church school with a place in which a Christian education can take place. That's the primary goal. The music in our worship. This is one of the best musical small congregations in the whole country, I'll bet."

"What is the goal?" Walt interrupted.

"The goal is to provide the choir with some space where they can function without being underfoot," Stelk snapped.

"Expand the choir?"

"To support its operation and to provide for its expansion if possible."

"You're on a roll, Father," said David Odell.

"This is a growing congregation and it's going to grow even more in the future. We cannot handle it. Unless we commit suicide, we cannot go back."

"What's the goal?" This time it was Kathy Munroe. Kathy was Karin Efman's friend and a devoted Cursillista. She had one short leg, the result of childhood osteomyelitis, but built-up shoes concealed her limp. What you noticed instead was her wry smile and attractive oval face, framed by short brown hair.

"To offer this to more people," Stelk said. "And it's not so we can get more money." He spaced his words for emphasis. "It's because we . . . need . . . to grow . . . to be healthy. If we don't grow, we stagnate. If we stagnate, we die." He slapped the table. "The growth is necessary for life, for the vitality of this congregation."

"Are you saying that we've stagnated?" asked Walt.

"All I know," Stelk said, still speaking forcefully, "is that it's overwhelming when the church school comes in, forty or forty-five kids and teachers, into a sanctuary that seats a hundred and already has seventy in it." He was talking about the moment during the offertory hymn when the children streamed in from the parish hall to join their parents for Communion. One of the acolytes would open the door and they would spill into the church like minnows entering a pond, some darting gay and bright, some shy, some sauntering and self-important. It was always the loveliest moment of the service.

"And that is a very strange occurrence in this day and age at most churches," David said. "Churches are losing their people. It's almost an anti-Christian period that you're going through."

"Yes, it is," Stelk agreed.

"It's not a religious period that we live in."

"Christendom is dead and gone," Stelk said. "We're in a period between the periods, a time between the times. That's why this church is phenomenal."

He paused and sighed. "Unfortunately, we can't expand the worship space. We can't go toward the street, we can't go out to the side. If we moved the chancel back, the ceiling might collapse. The only thing we could do is add a service." He grinned suddenly, and his voice lost its edge. He seemed to relax. "In Ohio, the families came to a nine-fifteen service, and we had an eleven o'clock service for older, traditional people. As far as they were concerned, that is when God worships."

"God likes to sleep in," David said.

The committee was through with serious business for the evening. Walt and David started talking about how expansion might affect the acolytes. "An acolyte training room," Walt suggested. "A substitute altar, candles that switch on."

"And a place to put their sneakers."

"Lockers."

"Odor-proof lockers."

But as the meeting broke up, a question David had asked earlier hung in the air. "I'm confused about the beginning point," he had said. "What is the first thing we have to do?" All the talk of goals had failed to answer that.

✢

Stelk plunged ahead regardless. One day I accompanied him and John Donovan to a meeting with Naomi Tor. Mrs. Tor was the Town of Yorktown planning director. The township included Mohegan Lake, and Stelk and Donovan wanted to know about the local review requirements for building a new parish hall. They also wanted to gauge Mrs. Tor, to get a feel for the strictness of the review process and maybe to soften her up a little. Stelk wore his clericals with that in mind.

He drove the Tempo, occasionally remarking about other drivers on the road. We talked about new cars, and Stelk declared that he was "constitutionally incapable of buying a car made in Japan." The Yorktown offices were in a converted elementary school. Mrs. Tor, who occupied a narrow office on the second floor, turned out to have a lively, elfin quality. She was a native of Sweden who had lived in Israel before coming to the United States.

She said the project would be reviewed by the town's conservation board, its engineering board and its architectural review board, as well as a building inspector. She asked if any wetlands were affected. Stelk said, "The only wetlands we have are in my basement."

"In your basement. No, that doesn't count. But you should get that fixed," she said. "Mildew." Then she turned to the parish hall sketches, leafed through the code books and said, "I don't see anything here that's outrageous."

Suddenly she vented a giggle that came out of nowhere. Stelk and Donovan looked at each other. "Oh," she said. "I just read Russell Baker in the *Times* this morning, about how overused is 'outrageous.'

"So, when are you ready?" she asked. "You can probably get on the next agenda. Too early? July? August? Just call me when you think you are ready."

"That's a relief," Stelk said when we had left the office and were back at his car. "But the big problem's going to be what it always has been. Which is, the money."

Stelk returned to the church, where Donovan headed off to another appointment. Gerry Cousins's red Mustang was parked in the short driveway that looped by the church steps. Gerry was hunkered down by a large chunk of granite in the grass under an oak tree. A toolbox was open on the ground, and a large bronze plaque leaned against the rock. Gerry heaved the plaque into place on the face of the granite and started to insert bolts at the corners.

I'd never noticed the plaque before. It was inscribed, BOYS OF THE MOHEGAN LAKE SCHOOL WHO MADE THE SUPREME SACRIFICE FOR THEIR COUNTRY DURING THE WORLD WAR. Gerry, in his junior warden's role, had sent it off for restoration. Now the bronze looked new, as if it could not have been cast at a time when the world had known only one great war.

Gerry seated the last bolt and mopped his brow. May had continued warm, and the sun came on a deep slant from the west. Stelk spied the vanity plate on Gerry's car: 88NOTES. "I thought it was eighty-eight keys," he said.

"It is," said Gerry. "I couldn't get that one. I applied for it, but they told me it was assigned to Liberace. Apparently he had a car registered in New York."

"But . . ."

"Yeah, I know. He's dead. I'm next in line, but it's supposed to take a couple of years to clear the system."

Gerry was more than a piano tuner. He designed pianos. "But the manufacturers don't want designers," he said. "They want glorified shop hands." So he had gone into business tuning and repairing. Diane, whom he had met as a music student at Shenandoah College and Conservatory of Music in Virginia, where she was studying to be a medical technician, handled his billing and appointments. She also held a part-time job as a medical secretary for a Pleasantville physician.

Gerry closed his toolbox and stood up, revealing a heavy brass belt buckle in the shape of a grand piano. His company's name, emblazoned on the Mustang's door, was T.H.E. Best

Piano Services, not The Best. "You can't make false claims," he said. "I am the best. But how are you going to prove it? T.H.E.? It stands for Total Harmonic Euphoria."

He waved goodbye and left for his last service appointment of the day.

+

Stelk also had a final call to make. We climbed back into the Tempo and headed in the direction of Peekskill Hospital. At the reception desk inside the entrance, he riffled through the denominational preference cards placed there for visiting clergy. He found a room number and bounded up the stairs without waiting for the elevator.

Harold Van Horne was in a second-floor room. A urinary tract infection had put him back into the hospital. His spindly legs were outlined by the covers and his thin arms were bruised and bandaged where IV tubes had been dripping antibiotics into him. His white hair was rumpled by the pillow and his weakened eyes distorted by his thick bifocals.

"I can write but I can't read," he said. His eyes turned upward to the television set suspended from the wall on a metal stalk. "And the television, oh, what's that?" He struggled to push himself into a sitting position. "They told me I need these tubes another day, then I can take pills. It's getting better, but I hurt last night."

He paused to rest from the effort of lifting himself. "Father, I'm glad you're here," he said. "I need to walk. I'm weak. I'm just so weak. I can walk with a walker, but not without a nurse." He said he hoped to be home by the weekend. "I'm looking forward to being back in church again," he said.

"And you, you old son of a gun." He greeted me as if I were a lifelong friend. His smile was both brilliant and shaky from the effort. "How are you doing?"

Stelk took Harold's hand and offered a prayer for his recovery. An attendant entered with a meal cart. It was suppertime. "I'll come back and help you walk with your walker," Stelk promised.

The late sun oozed through the dog-nuzzled windows of the Tempo as we left the hospital. Stelk turned south, away from the church, and drove in the direction of the Hudson River. We rode along a back road into a rural part of Cortlandt township. He slowed at a junction and pointed out a triangle of property shaded by towering hardwoods. A small frame house, its white paint faded, was visible through the foliage. Stelk pulled into the gravel driveway.

"I've made an offer on this house," he said. "It's a restoration project. But Ginny and I have decided we'd like to retire here. Around here somewhere. I've got to be looking forward to that now. A place like this, we can take a few years to fix it up and have it ready when the day comes. Maybe rent it in the meantime. And if anything happened to me, she'd have a place to go."

A stir of evening breeze bent the treetops and churned the leaves like sea foam. A woodpecker drummed somewhere overhead; we turned our faces upward.

Stelk searched the trees in vain, then looked back fondly at the house. Vines rose above the windowsills. A rank garden spread in a rectangle between the house and a freestanding garage. The chimney seemed to lean, and the screen door at the back hung askew. Stelk saw it tidied and cozy.

"It'll be a lot of work," he said, only for a moment looking doubtful. "But everything around here is so expensive."

✢

By the third Sunday in May, John Harbeson and Walt Decker had hammered out a goals and mission statement. It took them two morning commutes to Manhattan on the Metro North Railroad and two lunch hours in the city. They established St. Mary's overarching goal as, "To be, and to be known as, a spiritual oasis of Christian love and commitment to serving those in need."

They called for a wholesale expansion of facilities: the parish hall, the parking lot, even the church.

It was Rogation Sunday, a day for prayers for plantings,

crops and harvests. Freshly turned earth at the edge of the church parking lot marked a Boy Scout landscaping project Stelk planned to dedicate today. Spring rains had left puddles in the muddy lot and more rain threatened. Stelk had called the planning and development committee to an early breakfast in the parish hall. The damp had aggravated his arthritis. He sat at a peculiar angle.

"You look like you're in agony," Walt said.

"Close to it," said Stelk, sounding martyred.

The committee reviewed the nine-page document, but the issue on everybody's mind was money. It was as if the exercise of putting goals on paper had rendered them in stone, no longer a matter for discussion. Now the committee worried about how to sell expansion to the congregation as the national economy got worse and worse. John Donovan cleared his throat and described a conversation he'd had with a parishioner. Donovan had a smoker's voice, deep and harsh. The parishioner had asked Donovan how much the expansion was likely to cost. "I said the estimate was about one million, and I thought he was going to fall out of his chair," Donovan said.

"I really hope people don't get hung up on a million-dollar figure at this point," Stelk said fretfully. Ginny was sick in bed with a cold and her own bout of arthritis. Her headache had forced them to leave a New York Philharmonic concert last night at intermission. Stelk had looked in on her after the eight o'clock service, but he missed his customary Sunday breakfast with her in the rectory: refrigerator cinnamon rolls, one hard-boiled egg, orange juice and coffee. He leaned forward stiffly and picked an apple Danish from a serving plate. "Because that is just so ballparkish. It may cost less." On the other hand, he said, "It may cost more."

"It won't cost the parish a million dollars," Walt said.

"I told him that," said Donovan. "I told him we were trying to get grants. But if our portion of it comes to too much, we'll have to look at it again."

"But to buy a house in this area, you're going to pay well over two hundred thousand dollars," said Kathy Munroe.

"We're talking about a gathering place for many families, for maybe four times the cost. I don't think we're going to sell this by saying we need more room so we can have more AA meetings and day care."

Walt spoke with a just-awake slowness. "It has to be something that everybody can get pumped up about. And relate to in one way or another."

"Our mission is to increase the spiritual life within this congregation," said Stelk. "If we are not stronger internally, we are weakened in external outreach."

"I agree," said Kathy. "But there are some people who are going to be hearing mission as outreach and not addressing our own needs."

"When we talk about mission, it's not us doing good for somebody else. It is the total growth of God's work within us, which affects others and ourselves." Stelk spoke in his pulpit rhythms.

Somebody said, "Hear, hear."

People began arriving for the ten-thirty service. Ann Marwick came in and went into the kitchen to set up the coffee service. Frank Doyle arranged chairs for the church school classes. Each swing of the parish hall door added to the bustle and confusion. Towheaded little Jonathan Miesch marched in chanting, "Roses, roses, blooming. Roses, roses, blooming." He was followed by his parents and younger brother. The choir robed and started warming up in its corner outside the door to the sacristy. Children darted back and forth.

Stelk excused himself to check on Ginny and get into his vestments for the service.

✢

Judy Salerno had chosen this morning to get up and go to church for the first time in years. Her husband, Dan, told her she was crazy. Judy set her feet on the cold floor and agreed with him. But she got up anyway and left him tossing grumpily in bed.

Judy thought of St. Mary's as the white church with the

horrible blue door that she passed twice a day on Route 6, as opposed to the stone church with the red door, the Methodist church in Shrub Oak, which she also passed. The door could have been Delft blue, or Dresden, but it was this chalky blue that couldn't make up its mind what kind of blue to be. Judy once had been a Roman Catholic. Lately she'd been feeling called to return to church.

"From what I'd heard of Episcopalians, they weren't disgusting," she said after I had gotten to know her. "They didn't have a pope. They didn't have Cardinal O'Connor. Other than that it sounded pretty much like the Catholic Church."

She'd read that St. Mary's had a food pantry, which sounded like an outlet for her surplus coupon bargains. And it was close to home. She decided to inquire.

Stelk had answered the phone himself. "St. Mary's Church."

Judy asked, "Do you think that this church might be a viable alternative for someone who was Catholic?"

Stelk said, "Yes, it would."

Something in his voice made her relax. "You would say that, you know," she said.

He laughed. "Yes, I would," he confessed.

She had made an appointment to talk with Stelk on Monday. But on Sunday morning she grew suspicious that the priest would put on his best behavior for their meeting and she wouldn't see what he was really like. She decided to get up and go to church.

Judy was forty-three and had been away from church as long as I had. She was raised in Floral Park, a neighborhood in the outer reaches of the New York City Borough of Queens, near the Nassau County line. Her memories of her Catholic youth were mostly traumatic. She hated confession, since she seemed always to have something to confess from a long and dreary list of sins. And she had the indelible, horrifying memory of gagging at her first Communion. She was the most religious member of her family, but she had dropped out and not looked back.

In the meantime she had lived in Manhattan, worked in advertising, overbought on her credit cards, kicked the shopping habit and moved to the country with Dan, whom she had later married. They lived in Putnam Valley, on a rocky hillside above a stream, in a farmhouse built about the same time as St. Mary's. Dan taught school and Judy learned that by clipping coupons and sending off for refunds, she could shop practically for free. The rest of the time, she pursued lost causes, like trying to close Con Edison's nuclear generating plant at Indian Point, on the Hudson River below Peekskill.

"I was a hermit," she said.

Sitting toward the back of the church, she wondered if it had been worth getting out of bed. A baby was squalling behind her. The balding priest, whose sideburns were a little long, had just taken a sip of water and was settling in at the pulpit.

"Happy Mother's Day," Stelk began. "I know what the calendar says, but this is not an error. I am wishing you a Happy Mother's Day on Rogation Sunday because this is the Church's Earth Day. I want to talk with you this day about our Mother Earth."

Judy was tall and tended to slump to be less conspicuous. The prospect that the priest would preach on the environment made her sit a little straighter.

Stelk said the Church had "a large sense of and concern about environmental issues." He went on to talk about the history of Rogation Day, how it emerged from a pagan holiday, the Church's adoption of it "to proclaim the presence of the real God" and the Elizabethan practice of beating the bounds.

"You went out and walked the bounds of your parish, praying for God's blessing, praying for the fields, the plantings and the seeds. I don't know how we would beat the bounds of this parish. It would take a long litany for us to make it all the way around. In most places it's come down to walking the edge of the church property. We aren't going to do even that today. But we are going out to bless the plantings that the Scouts have been putting in out here. If it's pouring rain, it's all off. But it won't do that."

The congregation laughed lightly at Stelk's assurances.

"We are celebrating today our understanding of the relationship between God and creation," Stelk continued. "Between us as part of that creation and God. Did God give us a throwaway society? It gives Mother Earth a kick in the teeth when we throw bottles and cans away. It is, basically, un-Christian. The issue is responsibility. Recycling a can takes only five percent of the amount of energy it takes to make a can from scratch.

"We are part of this created universe. We cycle through it. We are born, we live, we die and we are part of this continual recycling process."

Stelk's brief for recycling was backed up by three large garbage cans in an alcove of the parish hall, one each for plastic, glass and aluminum. St. Mary's asked its church school children to bring in redeemable cans and bottles, and Frank Doyle turned them in for money at the supermarket. The five-cent New York State deposits helped support the church school and its mission fund.

Stelk closed with a prayer of thanksgiving:

"We give you thanks, most gracious God, for the beauty of earth and sky and sea, for the richness of mountains, plains and rivers, for the songs of birds and the loveliness of flowers. We praise you for the good gifts, and pray that we may safeguard them for our posterity. Grant that we may grow in our grateful enjoyment of your abundant creation . . . Help us to be sure that no one may suffer from our abuse of the resources of nature, and that generations yet to come may continue to praise you for your bounty."

At that point, Judy said, "I thought, 'So far, so good.' "

She was charmed when the children entered the sanctuary during the offertory hymn. Today they all were carrying spring flowers, small bunches of daffodils, irises and lilies, as they joined their parents with smiles and hugs and laughter. Despite the trauma of her first Communion, accepting the Sacraments was Judy's favorite part of the service. She took the bread and wine with reverence. She watched two fathers carry their infant children to the altar rail and accept the Host with one hand while they held the babies with the other. Stelk leaned down to fuss over the babes and touch their foreheads with a blessing.

The service ended with a hymn based on St. Francis of Assisi's "Canticle to the Sun." It was a fond poem to the natural world:

> Dear mother earth, you day by day
> unfold your blessings on our way,
> O praise him, Alleluia!
> All flowers and fruits that in you grow,
> let them his glory also show:
> O praise him, O praise him,
> Alleluia, alleluia, alleluia!

Stelk led the congregation, singing the final verses, outside to the freshly planted plot of earth. The plot was backed by a low stone wall and bordered by railroad ties. One of the acolytes, Matt Harris, and his Boy Scout Troop 165 from Yorktown Heights had transformed a weed-dotted strip of mud into an attractive swatch of crabapple trees, holly and juniper shrubs and a variety of perennials.

Stelk climbed with a hitch in his step onto the cross-tie border. The overcast had thinned. The children still held their flowers. The choir stood to one side, robes hitched up above the puddles. A father held two dozing children, one in the crook of each arm. A car with a pounding stereo passed along Route 6. The congregation bowed their heads, and Stelk asked for blessings on the plants and flowers.

Judy decided she was looking forward to tomorrow's appointment with this Father Stelk.

✛

"Lincoln Stelk," he said, shaking her hand when she arrived at his office the next morning. "I thought that was you yesterday morning."

She was a large woman, taller than Stelk, dressed in black

jeans and a loose purple sweater. She wore her gray-streaked black hair pulled straight back in a ponytail that she'd fastened with a purple band. Her oval face had a soft, neglected beauty.

"Well, I thought you might be on your best behavior today, so I should check you out," she told him.

"Well?"

"I liked your sermon. And everything was so relaxed. It was like you; you made a mistake and nobody cared, you just went back.

"I made a mistake?" Stelk arched an eyebrow.

"Well. And the children came running in. That was nice. Afterwards there were all these people in the parish hall. They were friendly. That was nice, too. It was nice."

Judy looked about the book-lined office, with its stacks of papers. She noticed several small crucifixes on the walls, and lines from the Psalms transposed to greeting cards. She also noticed the framed epigram, "There's a difference between being baptized and brainwashed."

"You said you were Catholic," Stelk ventured.

"I haven't felt like a Roman Catholic for thirty years, or twenty years, as ever long as it's been. I haven't considered myself Catholic for years."

She described, as she did to me later, a childhood in which she'd attended church reluctantly. "Going to church was the same thing to me as going to school," she said. "I didn't want to do it. I was doing it because I was made to do it, and it didn't pay me no never mind if I pretended I had a stomachache to get out of school or get out of church. I didn't want to go. It was something you had to do."

Judy was not alone in dropping out. So did most of her family, her friends and acquaintances and, as she was to find out later, her husband. Unlike them, she retained a yearning.

"When I try to think it through, I think it was so traumatic for them that they just threw the baby out with the bathwater," she said. "I was turned off by the church, but I wasn't turned off by God per se and Jesus specifically, the teachings of Jesus being fairly important in my life in terms of doing unto others and turning the other cheek. I thought those were really, really important things. Even if I was saying motherfucker seven hundred and forty times a day, I wasn't killing, raping, stabbing or trying to, you know, be cruel to people."

What had prompted her return to church was simple. She was a good person who felt that she had lost her goodness, and she didn't like it.

She said, "I was at a point where I could not speak a sentence without saying, 'Fuck this,' and, 'Fuck that,' a hundred and seventeen times. I mean, if I ended up in a room with my niece or nephew I would literally have to stop and think about some of the words that I said, because it was either, 'Fucking good,' or 'Fucking bad,' or 'You fucking idiot,' or, 'You fucking asshole,' or 'You fucking driver,' or, 'You fucking checker.' And I couldn't stand being that. I mean, Who am I? Why am I being this way? It was something that I didn't have control over, and I didn't like not having control over it. And it just had kind of crept in. You don't start out calling everyone a motherfucker. You work up to that. You call them an idiot, you call them a moron, you call them an asshole, you call them a shithead, and then you work up to everyone being a motherfucker. I thought, 'Where is this coming from and why am I doing it?' "

She and Stelk talked for two hours. "I came in with guns blazing," she said. She asked Stelk about abortion, divorce, birth control, women's rights, gay rights, civil rights, war and gun control, issues on which she was an unabashed liberal.

In the end they differed on one point. He didn't believe the Church should marry homosexuals. Stelk was no arbiter of lifestyles. The Episcopal Church ministered to gays and lesbians, and Stelk agreed with that. He had no problem with the Church's acceptance of gay priests. He was rather proud that St. Mary's had welcomed a lesbian couple and their two children into the church six months earlier. He felt that embracing the family was a proper exercise of Christian love. But he believed that homosexual marriage was different from heterosexual marriage no matter how you looked at it, and that the Church shouldn't place them on a par.

"I came looking for the catch," Judy said after that first meeting and two more that totaled six hours. "Aside from that, there wasn't one."

They talked about the food pantry, too. Stelk wanted to know if Judy was free on Fridays. She said she'd think about it.

6

The vestry gathered, somewhat warily, for its May meeting. The agenda was loaded with land mines, the biggest the goals and mission statement John Harbeson and Walt Decker had produced. It set out a step-by-step rationale for building, but it was not clear how the full vestry would react.

A cold front had brought crisp air and a promise of bright stars. Bob Soso was wearing a colorful sweatshirt from Van Cortlandtville Elementary, his daughter's school. It sported a mascot wildcat with such a gaping snarl its tonsils showed. Bob was one of the few members of St. Mary's who always wore a suit to services, and they were well-cut Italian models. His family dressed well, too; Jenna was a picture-book little girl in her Sunday dresses, with her hair in braids; Bob Jr. in his blazer had a prep school look and Bob's wife, Pat, wore the only full-length mink coat seen at St. Mary's. Bob said that when he was a boy growing up on the island of St. Vincent, his mother had taught him to always look his best at church. Stelk, who had already changed to short-sleeved clericals, had fished a V-neck sweater from his winter wardrobe.

Money proved to be on the vestry's mind, as it had been on the planning committee's. Gerry Cousins had fired the church sexton, who had been cheap but lazy, and hired a cleaning service to replace him. "Where is the money going to come from?" Harbeson demanded.

Stelk was in an edgy mood. He reacted testily. "Well, it's going to come from where everything else is going to come from, from the general income."

St. Mary's budget, five months into the year, was out of balance but not terribly. Generous Easter offerings had brought income, which included plate offerings, pledges, rentals of the parish hall and interest on St. Mary's small endowment, to within $1,500 of expenses. Heating oil had cost more than expected, but the boiler was off now. Office expenses had been driven up by a one-time copier repair. The real problems lay farther down the monthly budget printout, under headings like "Repairs to Prop. & Equip." and "Major Prop. Improvements."

Ann Marwick rushed in, just in time to receive a copied list from Gerry Cousins. It was a summary of an engineer's inspection of the parish buildings. An ominous subheading read, "Corrective measures needed."

The rectory, church and parish hall all needed work, some of it major. "Repair water infiltration in the bell tower" was just one example. The church bell had been still since March, when the new organ pipes were installed and the bell rope, which often was soaked with rainwater down to the bell ringer's fingers, was tied off awaiting repairs to the tower. Beams needed to be shored up, paint stripped, roof tiles replaced. Gerry was trying to make up for years in which St. Mary's had balanced its budget by deferring maintenance.

"Our planning for capital repairs has been very weak," Dwight Douglas said.

"But this is common among churches," Stelk said.

"Universal," intoned Harbeson.

". . . because vestries tend to focus on immediate concerns." Stelk paused a moment. "We're doing the same thing on the Diocesan Budget Committee," he confessed. "There was no money set aside for the election of Bishop Grein. It cost over half a million dollars: the election, Bishop Grein's installation plus the farewell for Bishop Moore."

"That's where the real money went," somebody said. The retired Bishop Moore was as well known as a social lion who loved a good party as for leading the Episcopal Church in New York in vigorous ministries to the poor, homosexuals and racial minorities.

"They had a heck of a party," Stelk said.

Karin announced that her casino night had died for lack of interest, and shortly, Mary Bohun gathered her sleepy young daughter and said she had to leave.

"I'm sleepy, too. Can I go home?" Walt Decker asked facetiously. The goals and mission statement loomed next on the agenda. Copies of the document lay before each member.

Walt and Harbeson had set out a coherent case for expansion. The problem was that, as a cornerstone of everything that followed, the document had to carry the weight of competing priorities. Harbeson the academic had wanted to give it rationale and logic. Dwight the worshiper wanted a spiritual imperative, but Dwight the planner wanted facts and figures. Stelk just wanted to get on with it.

"We may have to find some way to structure in an assistant," he said. "It's difficult for me to do anything with the church school if I'm in the services. And the youth program has not had the attention that it needs."

Dwight shifted in his chair. He was professorial in a bottle green corduroy sport coat with leather elbow patches. Harbeson, across the table, was wearing faded jeans and T-shirt. Dwight said, "If we want an assistant priest, there's office space, there's activities that might require space. How do those things weave together? That's what I was talking about last time.

"That's one thing," he said. "The other thing is . . ." He said growth at St. Mary's seemed limited by the size of the church building. "You could go back twenty years and see the same number of members, despite the fact that this area has doubled in population, and despite the fact that we have wonderful people here doing terrific ministry," he said. "That building somehow dictated what we were. You wonder about how you could get around that problem . . ."

Dwight was suggesting that adding a supermarket parish hall made no sense as long as the parish worshiped in a boutique church.

"One of the first suggestions I made when I came here was to build a new church," Stelk said. "That went about two inches before it got shot down.

"The only other approach, Bishop Moore told me, 'Hire a curate and hold extra services.' I told him about the Saturday night services. [Marc Lee, Stelk's predecessor at St. Mary's, had tried to reduce Sunday overcrowding by initiating a Saturday night service, but the people who attended came back on Sunday anyway.] He said that does not work for Episcopalians. It works for Roman Catholics. But Episcopalians just don't worship on Saturday night."

"They party Saturday night," somebody said, setting off laughter.

"We can't really work on this building; it won't take any alteration," Stelk continued. "The only option we have is to build a new church, and that is not something this congregation is going to accept. Three services on Sunday morning will provide a lot more space. That's another reason we would need an assistant. That is the only approach that I can see."

Dwight tapped a finger on his copy of the mission statement. "I think this is a very good step. But to me there are still a lot of questions. Three services on Sunday would have some impact, but it will not be the same as having a church that is twice the size. All those things need to be quantified to enable you to look at where you really are going."

Stelk heaved a loud sigh. "It seems like you could spend the next ten years going over this and still be stuck with the situation that we need to expand now."

Donovan cleared his throat impatiently. "This whole thing was brought up because we wanted to get the vestry's backing. We can analyze flow and usage and everything till it comes out our ears."

Dwight waited a few minutes before he spoke again. "If I was being asked tonight to vote on a resolution that this vestry explore a building addition, I could vote for that. If it was to vote on a building addition, I could not vote for it. I don't have the data."

"Nobody's asking you to vote on a building addition," Stelk said.

"Are we in support of a building addition? I could not vote for that, either. There is enough information to say that we ought to go and find out about financing, and about planning, for a building addition."

"That's exactly what we're doing."

"I keep hearing the words, 'support for a building expansion,' " Dwight insisted.

Ann Marwick broke in. "We can all move on or we can sit and talk about it again. I am not going to sit and talk about it. We have to make a move at some point."

"We're leaving at ten o'clock," Stelk said.

Walt said, "I envision that at some point down the road, the vestry will have in front of it a physical plan represented by architectural drawings, a spiritual plan . . ."

"Illustrated by laser light," said Karin.

". . . in some form or another, and a financial plan. And that's what the vestry will have to approve or not, based on whether it answers all of these intermingled questions."

"Excellent. Fine. No problem," Stelk said sharply. "But we can't even proceed if there's no authorization."

"I move that we support the work of the planning and development committee in the development of the physical plan, financial plan and spiritual plan," Walt offered.

"That's fine. Yes," said Stelk.

"Moved and seconded," said Harbeson.

Stelk asked if there was any more discussion. Karin's voice rose above the others. "No. And if anybody opens their mouth . . ."

The motion passed, giving the planning and development committee authorization to proceed.

✛

Dwight thought a new parish hall was probably a good idea. But he said the basic question remained, for him, unanswered. Expand for what?

Dwight had had what he called "intensive church raising," he told me one Sunday after church. This was later, after the expansion drama had concluded. We were sitting in his comfortable living room in Peekskill, and Ann was brewing tea. Dwight and his brother, two years older, first sang in the choir at St. Stephen's Episcopal Church on Manhattan's Upper West Side. Dwight was eight when the two of them became choirboys at the Cathedral of St. John the Divine. They rehearsed twice a day, sang at two services, studied Latin and took courses in religion. He was thirteen when the family moved to Shrub Oak and joined the congregation of St. Mary's.

When he returned to St. Mary's as an adult, after he and Ann were married, Dwight obeyed an instinctive aversion to church politics. Ann said she "did the normal kinds of things that women did in the church then." She worked in the nursery, taught church school, managed the junior choir. St. Mary's, for her, "was this whole wonderfully accepting world where you could pray and praise and be accepted for who you were."

David Eylers was Joe Germeck's hand-picked successor as rector. Germeck was a big, charming man who looked like an Irish beat cop and ran the parish like a principality. Eylers lacked Germeck's charm. He was ponderous and formal, "the equal of Nembutal in the service," according to one parishioner who was close to him. He and his wife became parents when they were no longer young. They lost one child, then another. Their sorrow struck them dumb; they could not communicate their anguish, and the parish could not see how to help them. Eylers grew isolated from all but a hard core of supporters, and when a call came from a church in Beacon, both Eylers and St. Mary's were glad to say goodbye to one another. He left saying, "I hope you'll invite the new rector to dinner."

Dwight and Ann stayed on the sidelines while Eylers twisted in the wind. But they were grateful to him for introducing them to Marriage Encounter, the retreats that had strengthened their relationship. They determined to be more active in church affairs. There was no new rector for two years. The congregation ran the parish.

"It was good and bad," Dwight said. "The more you get involved in your spiritual life, the better. The more you get involved in church, it looks like it would be good, but it doesn't have to be."

Still, they sang in the choir, did their turns on the vestry and watched their children serve as acolytes. Ann became the parish's second female lay reader. Then Marc Lee came to St. Mary's. The Douglases found Cursillo, and their spiritual lives began to require more attention.

"We're stuck out here in the suburbs," Dwight explained. "We've got our jobs, got our kids. If you're not careful, you go to church on Sundays and when Lent rolls around you take a little extra effort, and that's it. That, to me, is very static. To deepen your prayer life, to get in the better habit of reading the Bible, or reading religious works, it's not that easy . . ."

When Stelk did not embrace Cursillo, Dwight turned to him directly. He desired the priests' secrets of prayer, the path to God that was hidden to all but the initiates. That spring he had gone to Stelk to ask for help. He wanted spiritual counseling.

When I asked Stelk about this, he said, "I'm not sure priests know more about prayer than anyone else." But he had met with Dwight. Stelk had recommended some reading, including *Prayer and Personal Religion,* by the Right Reverend John B. Coburn. Then Stelk couldn't make it, or Dwight couldn't make it, and the sessions stopped.

As Stelk pressed the parish hall expansion, Dwight grew more frustrated. He saw Stelk festooned with administrative burdens that he gave himself. "It's not easy for him to delegate, and a lot of this stuff just hangs on him," Dwight said. Spiritual growth was the answer. "That's the main issue. If you're practicing your religion better, the administrative tasks become minor issues."

The vestry, too, was blindly focused on administrative issues. Dwight thought it was trying to build first and plan later, but every time he tried to say so he met impatience and hostility. "I just get negative responses," he said. "I don't feel capable of input."

By the time the vestry voted to support the planning committee's explorations, Dwight felt isolated from the other members and from Stelk. They were like travelers who spoke different languages, all trying to get to the same place but unable to give each other directions. And the gap, he felt, was widening.

+

Sara Stelk called from Martha's Vineyard early in June to tell her parents to expect her for a weekend. She was coming down to pick up some furniture from Kirsten. That was how Stelk found out his eldest daughter was moving in with Joe.

"So you're going to live with him," he said to Kirsten when she got around to calling. He tried to keep the coldness from his voice. Ginny used to tell him he could hurt the children just by looking at them.

Stelk and Ginny still hadn't met Joe Byrne. Kit—the name her parents and her sisters called her—had met the Irishman in a tavern near Madison Square Garden early in 1988. She worked for the Institute of Electrical and Electronic Engineers then and had spent all day at a booth at a trade show at the Penta Hotel. He was a union carpenter working on a renovation at the Woolworth's on Thirty-third Street. She stopped at the Blarney Rock on Seventh Avenue to have a drink.

"I sat down next to this guy," she said. "He looked at me and said, 'You're not old enough to be here.'

"I told him, 'I'm free, white and twenty-one. The bartender's not carding me. Why should you?' "

Kirsten was then actually twenty-three, but looked younger. She used hardly any makeup and wore her straight hair in a ponytail and bangs. The red-faced, gray-haired man with the

Groucho Marx eyebrows on the next stool was forty-three. She loved his accent, and he made her laugh. "I stayed there until eight o'clock that night," she said. "There must have been something."

They met at the Blarney Rock twice more. He took her to the St. Patrick's Day parade while she played hookey from work. They discovered they both liked comedies and old musicals like *The King and I,* and old romantic movies that made them cry. Eventually she told her parents about him.

"They thought it was a bizarre friendship at first," Kirsten said. "When it lasted, they realized there must be something more."

There were more differences than similarities between the two. Kirsten enjoyed classical music and played the viola and violin. She performed with the Tri-State Philharmonic Orchestra, which practiced at the State University of New York at Purchase. Joe liked golden oldies from the sixties. Kirsten graduated from Mount Holyoke with a degree in political science and religion. Joe dropped out of school in Ireland at fourteen to learn his father's trade. She was a dove, he was a hawk. She favored civil rights, he disliked black people.

Beyond all of that, Joe Byrne was married with four children.

The marriage didn't work, hadn't worked for some time. Joe and his wife lived separately but, as Irish Catholics, they hadn't divorced. Then Ann Byrne contracted cancer, and Joe felt obliged to move back in to help with the children. Kirsten withdrew for a time. She said, "I just thought I didn't need to be there. There was too much going on."

When Ann Byrne died in the fall of 1989, Joe and Kirsten resumed their relationship, and her parents renewed their concern. Ginny thought the age and class differences would be too much to overcome.

Joe must have had a similar suspicion. He wanted to ask Kirsten to marry him but was afraid she'd say no. Kirsten sensed this and waited. One day in a park by the water near the Throgs

Neck Bridge, a romantic day with small fat clouds like cherubs high in the sky and the sun glinting, she said, "Why don't you ask me?"

He did, and she said yes. It was just before Memorial Day.

And not long after that, Kirsten called to tell Sara she was moving from her place in Richmond Hill, Queens, to Joe's house in Throgs Neck, the Bronx. Did Sara need any furniture?

Kirsten purposely put off telling her parents. The priest's daughter in her knew Stelk wouldn't like her moving in with Joe. She had always felt "this clerical aspect hanging over me," she said. Stelk had thrown a long shadow when she was growing up; pictures in the paper in his clericals and vestments, church on Sundays, Daddy's work always following him home in the form of some altar guild or vestry member. But moving in with Joe was simply practical. She said, "We wanted to pay for most of the wedding ourselves, and it didn't make sense to be paying for two houses. We were always at one place or the other anyway."

Stelk sometimes felt that he was very old. He held outmoded views. Later, when television's teenage doctor, Doogie Howser, went to bed with his girlfriend, Stelk would preach a sermon of complaint, and Alice Marwick, who was by then fourteen and no longer a candidate for the Mature Profession of Faith, would attack him for promoting censorship. He couldn't seriously have expected Kirsten to ask his permission before moving in with Joe.

"She knew what I would have said," he told me.

When he learned about the move, he had to think about it.

He thought about Jesus' words in the Gospel of Matthew: "He who loves father or mother more than me is not worthy of me; and he who loves son or daughter more than me is not worthy of me." He wondered if, by accepting what Kirsten was doing, he was being an unworthy servant of the Lord. He did love Kirsten. He was against her living with Joe and afraid for her happiness. But she was an adult, she knew her mind and he respected her. Stelk didn't want to tear his family apart. He decided to put a lid on his objections.

✣

My mother had had a painful, humiliating year, beginning with the series of strokes that put her in a nursing home. Her left side dragged, with a useless leg and arm. "It's been noodle-ized," she said, lifting the arm into her lap with her right hand to keep it from tangling in the spokes of her wheelchair. Mom had always soldiered on.

She, more than my father, had erected the guideposts for my life. She had been the one who trooped me off to church on Sunday mornings. She worked as a reporter, earning pay that was shamefully low even by the standards of the day, and when I got married for the second time she took my wife aside and said, "Encourage him to write."

Now, at eighty, she endured the trials of physical therapy, trying to learn to walk again, using a walker or struggling between a set of rails. She had to page a nurse or an attendant to help her to the bathroom, and she couldn't understand why they kept raising the bars at the sides of her bed.

I became a frequent flyer, shuttling between New York and Ft. Myers, Florida, where my parents lived. I went as often as I could. I had no idea, when I got there, what to do. Still, I found moments to be treasured. I would sit by Mom's bedside and read to her from the *News-Press,* the paper where she'd worked. Now and then a piece would interest her or make her laugh. I rubbed lotion on her skin to ease the itch of rashes that erupted on her legs and shoulders. Her mind for distant times was clear, and we talked about old memories. The present, though, was cloudy. We'd sit under a shade tree in the courtyard, and she would look up and ask if that was our apartment. She wanted to know why we didn't tip the "waitress" in the dining room. I began finding her in diapers.

Slowly she stopped trying. She didn't see the sense in it. She stayed in bed, even for meals. The attendants couldn't get her up, couldn't make her try to walk. "Why don't they just let me die?" she cried. My father found it impossible to comfort her.

Then she had another stroke, and I received a call telling me that she was in a coma.

I didn't ask Stelk to put her on the prayer list, but he did it anyway after I told him once why I'd be away that weekend. The list appeared in the Sunday bulletins, and the lay reader at the Wednesday morning service read it in its entirety. New names were added weekly and acknowledged in Sunday's intercessions before the Prayers of the People. I prayed for my mother the only way I knew, which is to say, I thought of her with love and wished her pain would ease. Among the kneeling congregation, at the words, "Let us pray for our own needs and those of others," I would say her name. For myself, an only child, I asked for strength and forbearance and the intelligence to make the right decisions for her and for my father.

The effect of the prayers—I saw them as kindly, vague collective thoughts rising from the congregation like mist over a lake, though the altar guild's Eleanor Arnold prayed specifically for everybody on the list and probably others did, too—was to comfort me. It was my assurance of communal sympathy, that sorrow may be shared, as well as joy, and therefore lightened. I did not believe that God would cure my mother. What God would do was link human beings with one another and provide them, provide me, with a rationale for the suffering of someone deeply loved.

✛

I doubt my father believed in prayer. Perhaps he did before he became embittered and again when fear began to press on him. He wanted only an uncomplicated life. His hope was so strong it amounted to faith.

He lived alone for almost a year after my mother entered the nursing home. It was a great relief to him at first, for he had been unable to care properly for her. He took to eating breakfast every morning with a group of chatty older women at the Woolworth's lunch counter, went swimming every afternoon and visited Mom, on his good days, in between. But he was eighty-three, they had been married for forty-eight years and her absence seemed, over time, to drain him. He grew weaker. He stopped going out for meals. He rose in the night for spectral wanderings. His thigh began to bother him, which his doctor took at first to be arthritis.

My mother was still in the hospital when he was admitted for tests. They showed prostate cancer that had metastasized. The CAT scan showed its ominous phosphorescence sprinkled in his bones.

My wife, Barbara, came with me on my next trip to Florida. Dad was in a dimly lighted room on the oncology wing. He was weak and gloomy. He'd lost the smile that had always been his ticket, that he'd at first turned on the nurses when he thought that they could send him home.

"I guess it's going to be a long road for me," he said.

"Long road to what?" I asked.

"Till I get any peace and comfort. When am I going to go home?"

Mom stabilized and was discharged to the nursing home, where she lay, apparently senseless, in a four-bed room, a feeding tube dripping milky-colored nourishment into her body. She would have turned it down if it had been her choice. She'd signed a living will, but in Florida a feeding tube inserted in the stomach was not considered an extraordinary means of keeping one alive. Now my prayers requested dignity and knowledge: my mother's knowledge that she was not alone. I prayed she knew that Barbara and I were there with her.

We divided our time between the hospital and nursing home. We badgered Dad to get up out of bed and walk around, to keep the habit if for nothing else. He could manage a turn around the ward, wobbling between us, clutching our arms, and then flop onto the bed, exhausted. All we could do for Mom was talk to her.

The time came to return to New York. We stopped at the bank on the way to make our final visits. Barbara waited, reading with the car door open, while I did whatever dreary business was required. When we reached the hospital, Barbara discovered she was missing one shoe. We returned to the bank and found it sitting primly in the parking lot. We saw Dad at the hospital and then went next door to the nursing home.

Mom was lying as she had each time we'd seen her, huddled, vaguely fetal, breathing in little shallow breaths. I brushed her hair off her forehead and kissed her. We told her about the missing shoe.

"Hi, Mom," I said. "We would have been here earlier, but Barbara left her sandal in the parking lot outside the bank."

"I was reading. I forgot it," Barbara added.

"So we had to go back to get it."

"But it was still there. Nobody had run over it or anything. You know me, Clare. I'm still scatterbrained."

We were holding hands and laughing, chattering and silly with this trivia, when my mother's eyes blinked open and made an anguished reconnaissance across the ceiling. My heart stopped. "Mom?" I said. Barbara's hand tightened on mine. My mother's eyes closed and opened again. This happened several times before the lids lowered and stayed closed and she breathed on into her extended sleep.

We were at home in New York when the call came that night to say that she had died.

We held a small memorial service for her at St. Hilary's Episcopal Church in Ft. Myers. Old friends gathered on short notice. The priest who'd been the rector at St. Raphael's when we attended there still lived in the area, and he officiated. He didn't remember me slamming the cross into the overhang. I read from Jorge Amado, one of Mom's favorite authors: "We all know how Time rushes by when we are happy." I said I thought that time at last was passing for my mother very fast indeed. Dad was too weak to attend.

"In our intercessions this week we remember Clare Taylor, mother of Nick Taylor, who has died," Stelk said that Sunday. I received a few cards of sympathy from members of St. Mary's. It helped, a common uplifting.

What helped more was the conclusion I allowed myself to draw from her reaction—surely it was that and not coincidence—to our silly tale of the forgotten sandal: that Mom heard or perceived us and, reassured that we were well and happy, allowed herself to die. She satisfied her love for us and then released herself. In her shapeless gown and sagging flesh, she achieved the dignity of choice. Her divinity lay in that choice, just as Christ's lay in his choosing to proceed to Jerusalem and death. The divinity of all of us lies in the kind of choice my mother made.

In all of this, I found myself sustained by my connection to St. Mary's. It was not just the way the people of the church reacted, but a faith that I was redeveloping that I saw St. Mary's people shared, a faith that accepted death even as life remained worthwhile.

7

June was half over when I returned to St. Mary's. Stelk had changed his stole to the green of Pentecost, the long and uneventful season of the church year that lasts through November. Summer had arrived in earnest. The stained-glass windows of the sanctuary were tilted open. Men sat in shirt sleeves, and women fanned themselves with the morning bulletins. Frank Doyle was conducting Sunday school in shorts.

My mother's name was off the prayer list and my father's had been added.

Stelk preached on the "oddness" of Christianity. His sermon revealed a metaphysical side that seemed of a piece with his favorite reading, the moral science fiction of Robert Heinlein and Isaac Asimov. This side had emerged before, when he had spoken at the vestry of living "in a time between the times." This time he sounded as if he expected Armageddon.

"I've said before I think we are in a crucial time in the history of the human race, one of these important, crucial moments when there is a change impending," he said, taking off his glasses and chewing on an earpiece. "None of us will ever see it. Probably our children won't see it. Maybe our grandchildren will. But we see aspects of it all around us. The monolith of Communism has disappeared. The Cold War is over.

"But before we start cheering for our side, look at us. What was the most powerful and richest nation in the world ten years ago is now the biggest debtor nation in the world. Crack and cocaine and alcohol and other drugs are wracking our culture. We can't even find ways to provide housing and food and health care and clothing for a large segment of our populace. We, too, have our problems."

Christ also lived in uncertain times, Stelk said. Christ's oddness was that he ministered not only to people close to him, but to "people who were outside the pale—tax collectors, lepers and women. That's one of the reasons he got crucified."

Stelk suggested that such oddness, the duality of being involved in the world but not of it, is essential to a Christian life.

"We do not pull away from the world about us. We recognize our involvement in this world and in the people who are of this world. God's world and God's people. We find from these odd actions of ours the strength and the courage to continue. To preach, and to teach, and to heal, as Jesus did, and as he sent his disciples out to do.

"And what are the disciples' names? John, Mary . . . Peter, David . . . Kathy, Karin . . . Lincoln . . . Put your own name there. For all of us are sent to raise the dead, to heal the lepers, to cleanse those who are unclean, to bring health and restoration to a world sorely in need of it."

St. Mary's also seemed to be in a time between the times, a moment of waiting, with endings coming and beginnings that were impossible to see. A fund-raising campaign was the next step toward parish hall expansion. The school year was almost over, meaning the church's families would scatter for the summer. The national economy was fraying at the seams. There was, at the beginning of summer, a sense of exhaustion, of a need to pause and take stock.

Another week deepened the heat wave. The church's two small ceiling fans whirred futilely, high overhead. Stelk warned that walking to the altar could be dangerous. "With this humidity the carpet wrinkles," he said, sighting down the center aisle. "It looks like the Red Sea. So be careful going back and forth."

John and Vincent tottered in during the Epistle, and Stelk preached about things not going right:

"I'm sure you've had the kind of day where you get up in the morning and come down to find the cat has thrown up on the kitchen floor, that the dog has spent the night teething on the coffee table in the living room, that the newspaper has been delivered into the biggest bramble bush you have in the front yard. And it's the first day of vacation and the kids are home."

Everybody laughed but Karin Efman. Stelk had his calendar correct. The school year was over, and Susan, her oldest, would graduate from Lakeland High that afternoon.

Susan Efman, at eighteen, was a typical suburban teenager. She was ordinarily attractive, with high cheekbones, a strong nose, blue eyes and brows that were darker than the blond, wavy hair she wore pulled back with a barrette. Knee problems had ended a youthful interest in ballet. Now, her mother said—and Sue didn't disagree—her favorite sport was shopping. After a Sunday morning service as an acolyte, Sue would leave the parish hall to the adults, make straight for the family car and sit impatiently behind the wheel, listening to the radio while she waited for Karin, occasionally dashing in to urge, "Mother, come *on!*" Susan had been accepted at Oswego State, a branch of the New York state university system three hundred miles away, on Lake Ontario. Karin was devastated by the prospect of her leaving. She'd been crying at the thought of it for months.

"I just can't help it. I'm a mother," Karin would say, dabbing at her reddened eyes.

Harold Van Horne looked frail and weary. He nodded in the heat, and Lily leaned to him at the end of the sermon and asked if he was all right. He made it to the altar for Communion, but allowed an acolyte to help him back.

He and Lily seemed so bound, so mutually dependent on each other that when one partner died, the other would surely die of grief. I thought of my lonely father, in the middle of a lunch he seemed to be enjoying, blurting out, "I miss her."

✛

The vestry met late in June, eager to hurry through its business. "There's not much to do and we ought to be out of here soon," Stelk said. The agenda was free of parish hall expansion business. Dwight Douglas, in any case, was absent. Dwight, too, gave the sense of something ending.

"There's something you need to add to parish life," he insisted. "Something that's external but comes back into the parish and helps the parish. It doesn't have to be Cursillo. But if Cursillo's not it, then what *are* we doing? What will be the pathways that are provided for spiritual growth? What are the tools to help us grow spiritually?

"What I find difficult is that there isn't a driving need for growth."

Stelk disagreed. He said the Cursillistas "tend to be upset when others don't respond the way they have. There are other ways of stretching and growing, like involvement in social concerns, being involved with groups that reach outside of themselves to serve others and find Christ in others.

"I'd love to see the parish be a place where there is a very active spiritual growth group, such as the Douglases and some of the others are looking for. At the same time have a group of people active in community concerns and helping those in need. Find a way to take seriously the need for Bible study, theological reflection, to think through and live out more fully the faith that we profess.

"But if I do all these things, it's not the same as the parish doing them. Other people have got to get involved."

Stelk and Dwight were saying the same things, but couldn't hear each other. Dwight and Ann told me they were quietly looking for another church.

Stelk didn't know this at the time, and he was in a bubbly mood. His vacation was approaching. He told the vestry he and Ginny were planning to attend an international conference of reading teachers—tax deductible, since Ginny taught—and then join a tramp steamer making calls along the coast of Norway.

As happy as that announcement seemed to make him, Stelk

said he had still better news. He said his prayers for a food pantry volunteer had been answered.

"Her name's Judy Salerno. She's a new member. She's also a coupon clipper," Stelk said. "She shops where they take double coupons. So if orange juice is ninety-nine cents and she has a fifty-cent coupon, with double coupons she gets it free. She'll teach us how to shop."

"She doesn't work, does she?" said Ann, a trifle cattily.

"With her kind of expertise, I think we could expand the food pantry," Stelk continued. "She was out of the church for ten or fifteen years. She thought it was time to get back. She didn't know why. She says she can't believe she found a place that was nonsexist, nonracist, nonhomophobic. I think it's really a blessing that she came here."

John Harbeson gave a report of the parish's insurance coverage that was very brief, prompting a flurry of congratulations.

"Very nice," said Ann Marwick.

"Excellent report," chimed in Gerry Cousins.

"Short," Ann added.

John bowed from the waist to the table.

Gerry recited some estimates for stone work on the church's front steps and foundation, replacement of slate roof tiles on the rectory and inspection of the bell tower. He said there was a need to exterminate some carpenter bees that had moved into the rectory.

"We also have honey bees in the attic," Stelk announced. "The reason I know this is that the honey drops down from the hive into my study next to the bedroom."

"Oh, well, why don't we sell it?" suggested Mary Bohun.

"We could call it Holy Honey," said Walt Decker.

✢

A Friday night choir party at Carol and Fred Obligado's was another harbinger of summer. Carol invited everyone to bring a dish for the buffet. Then a late thunderstorm passed, leaving the air steamy and the grass wet. Carol and Fred moved inside with the plates and utensils and the cooler full of wine.

I arrived as the party was getting under way. People were sampling the buffet, grouping in the kitchen, dining room and living room and talking about anything except church business.

Barbara Miesch, who taught remedial reading at a New York City high school, said she had been unhappy as a teacher.

"That was when I saw it as a job," she said. "But then I decided it was a mission, a ministry, and my attitude changed. I asked for the remedial assignment." Barbara was part of a lesbian couple, a handsome woman with closely cut gray hair and pale, appraising eyes, and deeply religious. She was one of the laypeople who read the Lessons and Epistles. When Barbara strode to the lectern in her slacks and tweed jackets, the congregation could expect a recitation heavy with religious fervor. She was saying that some of her fourteen- and fifteen-year-old students came to her classes unable to read. Then she would become a missionary and put her beliefs to work.

"I look for motivating factors," she said. "I suggest the Bible as reading. I tell the kids I'll pay for it. I slip a little religion in when I can."

Melanie Bussel was saying that she never looked forward to the summer because the choir didn't sing. "I'd rather sing than eat," she said. Melanie was compact and brunette; she set her short dark hair and olive skin off against bright silk dresses. She was the choir's strongest soprano, and she liked to let her voice soar above the others. Even on Normal People Sunday, the once-a-month service at St. Mary's during which the choir didn't sing, Melanie's soprano rose in unrestrained celebration from the pews. She said she had moved to New York from Memphis, Tennessee.

"This was years ago," she told a group around the kitchen table. "And I kept seeing old women with all these shopping bags. Nobody was helping them and I couldn't understand why. So I tried, you know, to help. And they looked at me like I was crazy. Nobody told me about bag ladies." She looked from face to face and blinked behind thick glasses.

In those days, Melanie said, she lived on Central Park West. Her mother was a hard-smoking, champagne-drinking Italian immigrant who'd covered trials and written detective stories for men's magazines, and became the editor-in-chief during the fifties, of both *True Detective* and *Master Detective* magazines.

"Of course, she wasn't Renée Buse. She was R. F. Buse. The readers couldn't have stood it, knowing those magazines had a woman editor. They would have died," Melanie said proudly.

The relaxed atmosphere produced a side of personalities I'd never seen on Sunday mornings or at vestry meetings. Gerry Cousins appeared in a flamboyant Hawaiian shirt, Diane in bright red shorts and socks. Stelk had left his clericals hanging in the closet in favor of an open-necked sport shirt and tan slacks, but he still wore his requisite black shoes. He sat in the living room and let the party flow around him.

John Harbeson, wearing a tie-dyed and embroidered shirt in the style of an African dashiki, stood in a corner of the living room, waving his arms at Bob Lockhart, the parish treasurer. They were arguing about Nelson Mandela. Bob was an ex-captain in the Marines and an archconservative politically. He was telling John that Mandela, whose African National Congress had had Soviet support, was a puppet of Soviet Russia, never mind that the Soviet empire was crumbling. Any mention of the Soviets made Bob squint suspiciously. You couldn't turn your back on them, he said.

John said, "Bob, Bob, Bob. The Cold War is over."

Bob, eyes narrowed, insisted, "The Russians still have the ability to make a lot of nuisance if they want to."

John said, "Oh, come on."

Then sheets of song lyrics were passing from hand to hand, and Carol sat down at the piano in the living room. She started playing "Good Night, Irene," and submerged the discussion of the New World Order.

Stelk sang and waved his arms like a conductor. Ginny came in from the kitchen and sat next to him. They sang "Forever and Ever" and "Have I Told You Lately That I Love You" and other songs hoary with age. And when the singing ended, Stelk clamped a hand to his breast theatrically. "That touches, that touches," he said. Then he leaned over and kissed Ginny on the cheek.

The singers moved through the old favorites, took a turn at some Kingston Trio numbers, tried some Christmas carols on the theory (mistaken) that it would make them feel cooler, and at last settled into hymns and spirituals. John took over at the piano and pounded out, "A Mighty Fortress Is Our God," and the party sang on into the summer night.

✣

St. Mary's switched to its summer schedule at the beginning of July. The single service, held at nine-thirty, was designed to beat the heat. A second service wasn't needed, because summer attendance was light. As a result, parishioners who rarely saw each other came together. The rest of the year, with few exceptions, the eight-o'clockers and the ten-thirty faithful never mixed.

Stelk reflected on the deaths of three parishioners in the month just past.

Robert Skae, a retired policeman, and Vera Colbeck and Frances Schmidt, both elderly widows, "spoke far more than most theologians have ever read, about what it means to live out the Christian faith, quietly, personally, within their own lives," Stelk said. He read a note Skae, who died of cancer, had written his granddaughter before he died: "Do not be disturbed that my chapter in life is ending, because the book of our family goes on."

Then Stelk announced, "I'm off duty as of noon today." The congregation had begun to clap warmly when one of the Miesch boys yelled, "Yay!" and everyone broke into laughter.

Coleman Hill's was one of the faces I hadn't seen before. He was an eight-o'clocker, and I normally attended at ten-thirty. Coleman was the oil truck driver whose open hands at the communion rail, Stelk had told me, revealed whether he'd been working. Lately they'd been clean.

The first thing Coleman did after the service was stop in the parking lot to light a cigarette, which gave me a chance to catch up and introduce myself. He cocked his head and squinted as if the smoke had gotten in one eye, scratched his arm above his rolled-up shirt sleeve and then said he'd have some time one afternoon that week to talk about St. Mary's.

He lived in a section called Van Cortlandtville, toward the end of a street of modest homes. I found the one with the yellow shingles he'd described and parked in the descending driveway, safely away from the barking German shepherd straining at its tether. Wash hung on the line beside an above-ground swimming pool.

Coleman came to the door in jeans and a T-shirt. He had a short blond mustache grizzled with white, and his wavy white hair was still damp from the shower. He said that he normally would not have been home at five-thirty.

"Been raining, though. Can't get the work in when it rains."

Coleman said he was trying his hand at painting and small contracting. He gestured at the walls and said he'd painted the house himself, inside and out, to get a break on the rent. He preferred the work of delivering home heating oil, but said the work wasn't what it used to be.

The small entrance hall beside the stairs was piled with high-topped, fat-tongued sneakers. Coleman had a son and two daughters at home. In the dining room, to the left, a single dish remained from supper. Family snapshots were grouped in a frame above the sideboard, along with a pair of cat figurines that had twins in the living room window. Coleman took the dish to the kitchen and came back and sat down at the table. His wife, Florence, brought dark, sweetened iced tea and disappeared. Coleman lit a cigarette, and again it appeared the smoke had gotten in an eye.

"Nope. Been blind in that eye since I was eleven, nineteen fifty-two," Coleman said. "Dog died, is what happened."

He launched into a bizarre and tragic story. He'd been attached to the dog and was angry when it died. Alone after school, he started throwing the family kitchen knives into the floor, one by one. His aim was good until the last one. The big carving knife struck the floor oddly and sprang back at him; the blade struck him square in the left eye.

"This all happened about two weeks after I stood up in the Baptist church and said I accept Jesus as my Savior," he said.

Later, Coleman said he'd fallen into a corner of the kitchen cabinet, but everybody knew it was a lie. He lay in Peekskill Hospital with a sandbag on each side of his head to keep him from moving it and further damaging the optic nerve. At the end of three weeks, he yelled that he could see colors again in his good eye. He didn't remember being able to see only black and white, only the surprise of seeing colors once again, so glorious it made him call out and bring people running.

Coleman was confirmed at St. Mary's in 1953 and later sang in the choir. While he was growing up, the Hills also attended the Baptist church in Peekskill and St. George's, the stone Catholic church on Route 6 that had since been replaced by St. Elizabeth Ann Seton. Coleman's father was a Peekskill wedding photographer who'd shot atomic tests in New Mexico during World War II. That got him a job at Edgewood Arsenal in Maryland, taking pictures of goats being shot with military rifles so Korean War surgeons would be familiar with the wounds. The family spent a year in Maryland.

Coleman dropped out of high school three months short of graduation because he wanted to open a garage. He dropped out of church at the same time. He got into carousing and drinking. He worked in garages but never got it together to open one of his own. Along the way, Coleman found his calling. He liked driving home heating oil delivery trucks. Over the years, church stayed in the back of his mind.

"Used to be in the Baptist Church," he said, leaning toward the ashtray and picking up his cigarette, "we had Communion once every third week. Somebody misses, he goes the next week and finds out, no, he has to come back in two weeks. I think Communion should be there whenever anybody wants it. Every week. I feel that way with baptism, too. It shouldn't be once or twice a year. If parents come and say, 'I'd like to have this child baptized,' why's it got to be next July or something? Same thing with confirmation. When they're moved to go, hey, that's the time to do it."

Coleman was saying the church should be at the disposal of the worshiper. Access to Communion was central to the way he viewed a church.

"That's one of my biggest things for St. Mary's," he said. "I like where it says on there"—he raised his hands to shape the invitational paragraph that appeared in St. Mary's bulletin each week—"anybody who's baptized is welcome to receive Communion. I believe in that. Baptized and believe. So that's my Number One for St. Mary's. It's right there."

I asked what Communion meant to him.

"Same thing the reverend says. Being invited to the feast."

Coleman said he preferred the more traditional Rite One of the Eucharist, which Stelk generally used at the eight o'clock service. "You know, where it says, 'We do not presume to come to this thy Table . . .' "

The prayer was a powerful example of the Church's old Liturgy. It continued, ". . . O merciful Lord, trusting in our own righteousness, but in thy manifold and great mercies. We are not worthy so much as to gather up the crumbs under thy Table. But thou are the same Lord whose property is always to have mercy. Grant us therefore, gracious Lord, so to eat the flesh of thy dear Son Jesus Christ, and to drink his blood, that we may evermore dwell in him, and he in us."

The more modern Rite Two was an invitation to celebrate the redemption of mankind. Coleman came to the altar as a sinner. He received a sinner's sense of comfort from the act of worship that roused him in the mornings. "When Sunday rolls around," he said, "I'm getting up. Even if I don't set the clock, I tell myself, it's time to get going.

"But if I didn't, I don't see any difference," he said. Coleman believed people should get to church "whenever they're moved to go." He quickly added that they should be moved to go on Easter. "That's when everybody should get there. Then Christmas. And then whenever."

+

Coleman appeared regularly at the nine-thirty service with his mother. They sat near the front of the church on the right, opposite the pew that John and Vincent usually took.

Coleman might have claimed his pew as a birthright if he had cared about such things. Walter Jones, his great-great-grandfather, was one of the founders of St. Mary's. Coleman's mother, Rosalind Hill Tandy, a sturdy, white-haired woman, kept the family scrolls. Her name went back three generations, to Rosalinda Monk, the tavern owner's daughter who married Walter Jones. Rosalind Tandy could take you back a whole lot further, too, all the way to William Bradford, who as every school child used to know, came to America aboard the *Mayflower* and was governor of the Plymouth Colony. William Bradford was Coleman's seventh-great-grandfather. Rosalind had a copy of the family tree. She would stand in St. Mary's parking lot after the service and point down Route 6 toward some forgotten landmark and describe its role in local history, along with the roles of the various Hill ancestors. Coleman would shift from foot to foot while this went on, smoking and squinting off into the distance, scratching his arms above his rolled-up sleeves.

Coleman told me he was having trouble making ends meet with his small-contracting business. It wasn't replacing the money he made driving.

When Coleman started making oil deliveries, he said he was virtually guaranteed ten months of work a year. "The only time off was July and August. Then it got to be eight months. Then with that shortage in the seventies, it was six months. Now it's a four- or five-month season. It just keeps cutting down. You don't start really to get busy until December, then it's January, February, March. April they start topping the tanks off already. It's all over."

He'd been laid off the year before, he said, and spent the winter making service calls for another oil company in a truck he was afraid to drive on icy roads. "You didn't make no money anyway. When May came, I decided to try C & C and see if it's for real." The initials stood for Coleman and Coleman, he and his son, Coleman III, called Coey, the two of them working together.

The economics of the work hinged upon insurance. Coleman said he needed to paint entire houses to make any money, but he needed expensive insurance since he and Coey were going to be working up on ladders. "Can't afford the insurance, you're stuck with little jobs, can't make no money," he said. A man needed money to make money.

"When you only average about four hundred a week, it don't do it," he said.

Sometimes, when he needed money, Coleman had called upon the church. "They've helped me a few times," he said. "A few hundred here and there." He rubbed his face and looked uncomfortable.

In return, Coleman did frequent service as an "outside usher" at the ten-thirty service, directing drivers in the parking lot. He gave money when he could. "Five or ten, I try," he said.

Coleman said he had seen a miracle happen at St. Mary's.

His daughter Rachel had been four or five years old, and David Eylers had been the rector at St. Mary's. "She's twenty now, so it would have been, what, 1975? She'd wake up in the night with blood pumping from her ears. Blood would just pump out her ears. Pump!" Coleman held out his left hand a good distance from his ear. "We'd take her to the doctor, the emergency room, and they said, no, it don't pump. It don't do nothing. There's nothing wrong with her."

He paused to consider the Parliament balanced on the ashtray rim. "I took her over to Reverend Eylers. We prayed at the altar, and it stopped. It was just the three of us."

I asked what he thought had happened.

"He heard the prayers."

There was a long pause. Coleman narrowed his eyes against the curling smoke from his cigarette. The television in the living room sounded a long way off. The clock on the sideboard chimed at quarter past the hour. He sighed. "The doctors in the hospital, they'd see the blood all caked in her ears. But they didn't see it running, you know. They didn't see it pump." He held up his hand again to demonstrate.

"Was it a miracle?" I asked.

"To me," he said.

+

St. Mary's people began opening their mailboxes to find postcards of spectacular fjords overhung by snow-rimmed cliffs. They learned Stelk and Ginny had had a fine time at the International Reading Association convention and now were exploring the rugged Norwegian coast.

"Linc's still in a time warp," John Harbeson said the Sunday after they returned, when Stelk failed to appear on time for the service. Carol Obligado ran out of preludes and searched her *Organ Book No. 1,* from C. H. Trevor, for filler material.

Stelk finally appeared at quarter to ten. He was wearing a vivid green stole from Guatemala that Ginny had given him for his fifty-sixth birthday two days earlier. The traditional green of Pentecost that draped the altar and the pulpit was dull compared to his new stole. He was in a jaunty mood. He preached about the need to work for peace and freedom and justice and human dignity while waiting with hope "in this time between the coming and the coming again."

The clear air of the fjords had refreshed Stelk. He was ready to get back to business. He told me he was looking forward to a meeting with Bob Pierpont.

"He's a professional fund-raiser and a member of the church," Stelk said. "He's agreed to help us out."

Pierpont came to the parish hall on a warm night. Men from the regular AA group were lounging outside the door and smoking between intermittent episodes of rain. He nodded to them and walked smartly up the stairs to the church office.

Stelk sat in his accustomed place at the corner of the table. He was dressed for gardening, in a loose white shirt and a shapeless pair of cotton pants. All he needed was a pair of work gloves and a trowel. Pierpont wore a dark gray pinstripe suit, a white shirt with a button-down collar and a striped burgundy tie. His black tasseled loafers gleamed. A white handkerchief peeked from the breast pocket of his coat. He was a tall man, with gray hair going to white and a face full of creases and sharp angles.

Stelk introduced him around to the vestry and planning committee members. Pierpont smiled a brittle smile and got to the point: "Why don't you tell me what you're doing?"

Stelk reprised the case for a larger parish hall as Pierpont listened, all attention, like a mouser waiting for a mouse. Down the table, the planning committee chairman, John Donovan, tested the hairs of his new mustache with his tongue. Walt Decker leaned back and clasped his hands atop his head.

"Things aren't quite as bleak as they seem," said David Odell when Stelk was finished. "We have an endowment."

The late L. Palmer Brown, the congregation's Handel-loving benefactor, had strong ties to St. Mary's. He was the last owner and headmaster of the Mohegan Lake School. Money left him by his father, a Yorktown judge, supported his career of teaching and music, and when he died the estate was still substantial. He had left not only the price—$22,000—of St. Mary's new organ pipes and Zimbelstern, but $210,000 besides. The will provided that the principal remain intact, and St. Mary's had invested the money conservatively, in certificates of deposit, corporate bonds and money market funds.

Pierpont pounced on the endowment. "What other endowment do you have?" he asked.

Stelk described St. Mary's sole disposable asset. It was a house in the northeastern Westchester town of Somers that had been left to St. Mary's and Grace Episcopal Church in White Plains. John Baynard, a young medical supplies salesman who had had friends at both churches, had left the house to be used for retreats. But St. Mary's vestry hoped to sell its share to Grace Church and use the money as the foundation of a building fund. "It's probably worth around two hundred thousand dollars," Stelk said.

"So you've got, what, a hundred thousand to St. Mary's in a split?" said Pierpont. "What are your offerings?"

"We've budgeted sixty-two thousand in annual pledges and another nine in plate offerings," Stelk said. "We get another eight thousand in usage fees from groups like Appetite Control and AA, party rentals and things."

"You're thinking of day care," Pierpont continued. "Know anything about it? What kind of rental could you expect? A thousand a month? Five hundred?"

Pierpont's questions were refreshingly direct. They had the effect of removing the fog of pipe dreams from the parish hall expansion plan and revealing the reality. He asked about the church's growth, the health of the local economy and the possibility—now an almost daily topic in the media—of a recession. A thin smile flickered as he listened to the answers. Finally, he asked, "Has anyone here been through this before?" He looked at Stelk. "Have you built a church before?"

"No," Stelk said without apology. "But I've acquired a couple of organs."

Pierpont's smile played around the corners of his mouth. "I'd guess you have four hundred thousand of sheer fund-raising to do," he said after thinking for a moment. "And I'd guess you could raise another four hundred thousand from all sources; I'm talking grants, loans, selling that house. You'll have to scale back from a million dollars. But with some creative number crunching, I think you're on the right track."

"Bingo," said Walt Decker.

"Make it basic at first. You can always make it fancy later. That's part of being a church." Pierpont's voice took on motivational tones. "That's part of striving and growing. We're not Harvard or Princeton or Yale. We're not talking about a billion dollars.

"Are any of the great families still around, whose names are on the plaques in there?" he asked. "No? That's too bad. But you'll still get some real surprises," he predicted. "Some people will say, 'We're in our eighties, our children are well taken care of, what are we going to do with it? Let's give a real blockbuster and pledge twenty-five thousand over five years." He sounded as if he were talking about Lily and Harold Van Horne.

Somebody said, "We'll have to do a lot of arm-twisting."

"You won't be arm-twisting," Pierpont corrected. "You'll be teaching stewardship, the joy of giving. You'll be teaching paid-up stock certificates and life insurance." He suggested seeking two twenty-thousand-dollar gifts, six of ten thousand and ten of five thousand.

"In what kind of forums?" Gerry Cousins asked.

"Multiple. You'll preach about it. You'll pray about it. You'll hold conversations. Somebody ought to be putting together a prospect research file. After assessing it, you may decide you want a six-hundred-thousand-dollar building. On the other hand, I wouldn't advise you to be too fainthearted."

The meeting slowed. The vestry had heard what it wanted to hear from Pierpont, and Pierpont had run out of questions. The fund-raiser told a joke. Then he arose suddenly, smoothed down his lapels and said, "Have we done what we can do? Can I get out of here?"

When the door closed behind him, Stelk looked around the room and said, "What do we do?"

The group assigned several tasks among its members. They would approach Grace Church about buying St. Mary's interest in the house in Somers. They would talk to Bill Bujarski, the architect, about scaling back the plans he'd drawn. They would explore with the Episcopal Church Building Fund, the Church Foundation and Trinity Church, the wealthy Wall Street Episcopal parish, the possibility of grants and loans. They agreed to meet again in early August.

The smell of coffee and cigarettes hung in the parish hall as the vestry members left. A few AA members lingered in the parking lot, talking and laughing, clinging to their camaraderie of self-denial.

8

August arrived in a torrent of rain. It brought Stelk visitors, the Coti-Curras family from Barcelona, Spain, and a headache.

"I'm going out of my mind," he said. Sebastian and Milagros Coti-Curras, whose elder daughter had spent a year as an exchange student with the Stelks in Ohio, spoke no English, and Stelk's Foreign Service Spanish had lapsed badly. Sara was hosting Julia, the exchange student, and her sister Mary Elaine, on Martha's Vineyard. Ginny was chattering happily away *en español.* Stelk felt like a fifth wheel. He laid down his pencil and massaged his temples.

Stelk had been playing with Bujarski's sketches of the parish hall, trying to fit in a day care center. He still believed, he told me, that day care remained the best hope for obtaining grant money for the parish hall. David Odell, the assistant high school principal, had emerged as the vestry's primary backer of the expansion plan. He had written a letter urging Stelk to appoint a standing committee on expansion and establish a building fund. "I think we should establish the goal of having the building in place for the 125th anniversary of the parish in 1992," he said. Walt Decker was the member who seemed most reluctant. Walt, who in his time away from his job at the American Foundation for the Blind kept tabs on the church budget, had revealed that the income from the L. Palmer Brown endowment was not available to help finance a new building. The $18,000 a year St. Mary's was earning on the capital was being used to balance the operating budget. Dwight Douglas had not attended a meeting in two months.

John Donovan and Kathy Munroe arrived at Stelk's office. He'd invited them to review his work on the plans. Stelk looked up and said, "Congratulations, John. It's starting to fill in there."

Donovan stroked his new mustache reflexively. "Well, it's not itching so much, anyway."

Kathy had something on her mind besides the building plans. Kathy was forty-three and worked as a registered nurse with the Putnam County Association of Retarded Citizens. Her husband, George, supervised line repairs for New York Telephone. Kathy, as much as anyone on the planning committee, was sensitive to the shifting winds of the economy. She said she'd been going over some figures in her head.

"Say you have someone who pledges ten dollars a week," she said. "You're going to ask them to add two-and-a-half times that over a three-year period. [That was the percentage Bob Pierpont had suggested as a building pledge.] So you're asking them to give not only five hundred twenty a year, but another thirteen hundred over three. You're asking people who are giving ten to give another eight, whatever it is, a week for the next three years. And you're going to be asking them to increase their base pledge to begin with. Not that we shouldn't ask, and not that they won't do it. It's just that for a parish that has never asked for much money . . . it's going to be tough."

Stelk erased a line and put down his pencil. "Nobody says it's going to be easy," he said. "But if you say we can't do it, we won't do it."

"I agree. But I think it's going to meet resistance. If somebody dropped a million dollars on us to build a building, people would say, 'Great. We love it.' But I think the pocketbook part is going to be hard." Kathy spoke with an exaggerated New York accent and used her hands for emphasis.

"Which is why we need to show where the money will be coming from," Stelk said. "What comes from outside sources. And why we need to cut back on the plans." He pushed the drawings forward.

"The other thought I had . . ." Kathy wondered if the two-story addition should be abandoned for a single large room on one floor.

"You only do that if you have to. Let me show you some of the things I've sketched out here." Stelk used his little finger as a pointer, showing how he'd moved classrooms into the old building to make room for day care in the new and retained most of the essential functions. "You could move my office here . . ."

"You know why the rector's office was moved upstairs in the first place, don't you?" Kathy said. "Because that floor is on a concrete slab and you needed heated hunting boots to sit in there and work all day."

Stelk paused and rubbed his temples.

After a while they drifted outside to walk the grounds to get a feel for the new building and its placement on the property, and I followed them. They decided it would take several parking spaces, but Stelk said they could be replaced behind the building. Fireflies darted and blinked in the gathering twilight under the pine trees in the picnic grounds under Stelk's office window. Sebastian Coti-Curras wandered out of the rectory to see what was going on. He called, "*¡Hola!*" and waved and vanished back inside.

John and Kathy lit cigarettes. John cupped his military-fashion as he smoked. He said he was thinking of trying hypnotism to see if he could quit. Nobody had mentioned the week's major news event earlier, but now the conversation turned to Saddam Hussein's Iraqi army entering Kuwait. John said that when he'd heard the news, he'd gone out and started chopping wood.

✛

That Sunday Stelk preached about the gifts of God, drawing from Matthew's recounting of Christ's feeding a multitude with five loaves and two fish.

"Questions about famines ought not to be directed at God," he said. "They ought to be directed at humankind. It is not God who has impoverished the world. The world is overflowing. It is not God who made famines. There is enough food for everybody in the world. It is humankind that has not made the determination that the hungry shall eat and has instead used food for weapons."

All the news was bad. Stelk offered prayers in the intercessions for Ed Lumley, who had broken his arm exercising, and for Mary Bohun from the vestry, who apparently had contracted Lyme disease.

He continued the intercessions with, "We pray also for the four children killed in New York City . . ."

Here were more of the city's tragedies that faith had trouble justifying. A random gunshot had killed a child sleeping in her family's car after they had returned from a trip to an amusement park; a baby in a walker had been shot through an apartment door; two others had died in equally senseless fashion. Seven children would die in a span of fifteen days, for no sin except proximity to guns and drugs and anger.

"We pray also for the victims of violence in Liberia."

The Anglican bishop of Liberia had requested prayers from the Anglican Communion around the world for victims of competing guerrilla armies in that country's bloody, shapeless civil war.

During the week, U.S. forces were ordered to the Persian Gulf. Saddam's army had quickly overwhelmed Kuwait and was digging in. Saudi Arabia seemed threatened. Oil, not freedom, was of course the issue, but Saddam Hussein was acting with an arrogance that made the threat seem larger. Kuwait and the Saudi kingdom might have been dispensable, but not to a power-mad general with aims of upsetting the established order.

The Prayers of the People followed Form VI the next Sunday. It begins, "In peace, we pray to you, Lord God." There is a place for silence after the lay reader asks prayers "For the special needs and concerns of this congregation." Or, the prayer book notes, "The People may add their own petitions."

At this place, a woman's clear voice rose from somewhere in the pews: "For our soldiers, sailors and airmen, who are in danger."

A second voice, again a woman's, spoke more simply: "For peace."

It was the day of the St. Mary's Festival, a festival St. Mary's had made up for itself by combining the day of St. Mary the Virgin with a celebration of the church's founding. The choir came out of its summer retirement, Carol Obligado and young Billy Bodeker played an organ and trumpet duet—Mouret's "Rondeau," better known as the theme from "Masterpiece Theatre"—and Karin and Richie Efman had a party.

Stelk and Ginny had spent the week on Martha's Vineyard with Sara and all four members of the Coti-Curras family. Stelk worried that Sara had turned the island into her cocoon. She was twenty-four and not interested at all in her job selling ads and taking classifieds at an island newspaper. She saved her real attention for the little theater groups she worked with, and she was growing from a backstage volunteer into a director. But Stelk felt the world of the island wasn't a real world. He fretted that as long as she stayed on the Vineyard she was postponing the pressures and conflicts of real life and would never grow. Still, he had to admit it was a nice place to visit.

Now the whole contingent was sitting around Karin Efman's backyard pool in Mahopac, a few miles from the church. It was a fine, sunny afternoon. Stelk was bedecked in a blue Chicago Cubs baseball cap, a white St. Mary's T-shirt, blue shorts and dark shoes and socks. He positioned himself in a lawn chair at one end of the pool and grumbled about the cost of real estate.

He said he had lost the house in Cortlandt he had hoped to buy to a higher bidder. "Somebody came along who had more money," he said. I remembered his air of expectation when he showed me the house the day we'd visited Harold Van Horne in Peekskill Hospital. Stelk had looked at the cottage with a fixer's eyes. He wasn't handy, Ginny said, but he'd seemed eager to weed and paint and create order, in the same compulsion for the straight row and well-hoed patch he sought in church affairs.

Stelk could not work unless his surroundings and affairs were ordered. "It bothers him not to be on top and have control," said his daughter Marla over lunch one day at Yogi's, the bar and restaurant a stone's throw from the church. She was home between terms at the time.

"Since we've been here he's realized he can't be on top of everything," Ginny had added.

But he tried. Stelk, not Ginny, took care of the family finances, paying the bills and balancing the checkbook. He would actually race around the parish hall after everyone had left on Sundays, straightening chairs, emptying wastebaskets, dusting windowsills, wiping off tables and taking out the garbage. To a few parishioners, this was symptomatic. It meant Stelk was too involved in minutiae to look at the big issues. His devotion to administrative tasks edged out the spiritual. You could control paperwork; Stelk would sooner fill out a piece of paper than contemplate new means of prayer. He was a shepherd, a healer and a unifier, every member of the parish would agree on that, but there still were those who wanted him to be a searcher, too.

"We kept looking," he was saying, talking about real estate. "We've made a bid on a house on Lake Mahopac, here in Putnam County. It's a lot smaller than we wanted, but it's what we can afford." Now they were entangled in the red tape of surveys, engineering reports and mortgage applications.

"My God, this state is ridiculous," Stelk complained. "Going through all this . . . I don't know if it's worth it."

The process was complicated enough that Stelk had had to hire a lawyer. Even so, he said, he wasn't sure they would get a mortgage or, for that matter, that the deal would ever be finalized. The house needed repairs, the seller had agreed to make them but so far had done nothing. "I call the lawyer every day," Stelk said. "Every day he tells me the same thing. 'Nothing new. Call me next week.' "

The rest of the party guests gathered around a picnic table under the shade of a young maple tree, in shaded lawn chairs or in the pool, where Sara and the Coti-Curras daughters sat on the edge and talked quietly and Gerry Cousins played with his two daughters. Ginny and Milagros talked in Spanish. Sebastian sat and smiled. About four o'clock, Kathy Munroe arrived, smiling, from a weekend at Cursillo. Wine was uncorked and, as the sun tipped low, the singing started.

+

The vestry in August created a standing committee on parish expansion and set a goal of 1992 for completing a new building. The vestry didn't vote on the third of David Odell's proposals to Stelk. It would have taken money to create a building fund and there wasn't any money. Nonetheless, John Donovan and the planning committee proposed starting construction by June of 1991.

The house in Somers that John Baynard had left to St. Mary's and Grace Church had been the best hope for the kind of money that could jump start a building fund. But a complication had emerged. Walt Decker had learned when he approached Grace Church about selling the house that it not only had an outstanding mortgage but was in foreclosure. Worse, the life insurance proceeds set aside in Baynard's will to maintain the house were being contested by his business partners. The assumption that St. Mary's would realize $100,000 from its share of the house had to be thrown out the window. Maintaining the house might even cost the church money.

This unexpected blow, combined with the continued bad news about the economy, which by now was almost certainly in a recession, and talk of war in the Persian Gulf, placed a pall over Stelk's expansion plans despite the vestry's resolutions.

"I think it's something that needs to be done, but I'm a little nervous about it," Karin Efman said. She thought St. Mary's could make do for a while longer.

"If we're basing our need to build on the Sunday school, then I'd say we've needed it more in the past and we might need it more in the future than we do right now," she said. "The Sunday school goes up and down. We're in a little bit of a down period right now.

"Of course, we do tend to procrastinate," she added.

Karin felt more strongly than ever the pressures of vestry service that distracted her from worship. She was struggling with whether or not to continue and had almost resolved not to run for another term as senior warden.

Karin also was transparently distraught about Susan's departure for college at Oswego. The time was drawing near when Susan would pack and leave, and Karin's eyes filled every time she talked about it. Laurie, her fifteen-year-old, was stoic. Krissie, the youngest, said impatiently, "Mother! You've got other children."

"I know," Karin told me. "It's not really fair. I think part of it comes from my own childhood. My parents didn't demonstrate affection. I'm sure they loved us, but it just wasn't shown." She said she wanted to show her children the affection she had missed.

✛

Susan stayed out late, saying goodbyes. She wasn't home by two in the morning, when Karin woke up to start packing the cars. She wasn't home when Richie woke up half an hour later. Karin called the New York State Police to ask if any accidents had been reported. None had. She finally tracked down Susan at the home of one of her friends. Susan said, "Oh, God, Mother!" when she came on the phone.

When I arrived around four-thirty the cars were loaded. Karin and Richie had decided to take two cars rather than tow a trailer, which would be empty on the return and hard to control. Sue was taking an unbelievable amount of stuff: a Smith-Corona personal word processor, a desk lamp, a milk crate full of hangers, two large suitcases, a stereo with a turntable, tape deck and speakers, half a dozen cardboard boxes bulging with clothes, linens and blankets, a grocery bag of snacks and chips, two twelve-packs of Coca-Cola and a huge box of laundry soap. Sue would not go thirsty or dirty in Oswego. By five o'clock everything was ready.

Karin reviewed the route for Richie in the floodlight over the garage door.

"I'm going to try to stay behind you," he said. "But make sure you don't lose me, okay?" Richie was a blithe, unaffected man. But now he sounded worried and bounced on his feet nervously.

"He's genetically incapable of driving and reading a map at the same time," Karin said affectionately. She kissed Richie on the cheek. He and Kristen got in an old four-door Mercury Cougar, while Karin and Sue took the newer Chevrolet. I climbed in the backseat with a couple of boxes.

Sue was wearing faded jeans, pink cotton socks and a green sweatshirt. She said she had spent most of last night at Polo's, which was "a happening place in Brewster" that was having its final college night of the summer. Then she put her head against the door and went to sleep.

The two-car caravan wound along a two-lane road through Carmel, past its stately houses, and onto Interstate 84 west. Oswego was on the other side of New York, two hundred and sixty miles away, on Lake Ontario. Light mist mixed with rain. The day bloomed slowly in brightening shades of gray.

The caravan missed a turn, backtracked to the New York State Thruway and exited for gas. Richie hurried up to Karin's window for an updated route briefing.

"Alright, we're going to Exit 34-A," she said.

"Okay."

"Which is 481."

"What's it say, 481?"

"It says Syracuse, 481."

"Alright."

"That's the exit we're going to."

"Okay. We're doing fine. How're you doing?"

"Oh, I'm glad. We're doing fine."

"So now it's straight up to . . ."

"Thirty-four. Unless we have to stop eighteen times."

"Well. A few times," said Richie, smiling sheepishly and bouncing. "When you reach a certain age, you have a bad bladder," he told me, leaning into the window. "You know, falling out hair . . ."

"Now, it's because you're nervous," Karin said.

"I'm nervous, too," Richie agreed.

The caravan resumed. The rain thinned, making the windshield wipers scuttle on the glass. The eastbound traffic seemed to be nothing but military convoys, miles of camouflage-painted trucks with their canvas covers battened down. We decided they were Army Reserve units assembling for departure to the Persian Gulf.

Karin looked over at Sue and brushed a wisp of hair from her face as she slept. "We've had disagreements, and we've had fights," Karin said. "But we've always been able to sit down and talk about it and decide how to go about things. She probably, of the three of them, was the easiest. Laurie went through what I call a gypsy phase. My mother never would have let me out of the house looking like this kid went out to school. It wasn't indecent, but I mean it was bizarre.

"But, really, I've had a good time with the girls."

Karin began a spontaneous monologue on motherhood. I hung over the seat and listened.

"It's hard coming to grips with the fact that she's eighteen. That she's going off. She'll be home again. She'll visit fairly soon. But it's never going to be the same again. She's never going to be the little girl. She's independent. She's registered to vote, for crying out loud. She's going to be responsible for her own actions. Part of me wants to still be there to bail her out and . . . and help her out of the messes that she will get into, but I realize that I can't. I have done—Richie and I have done—all we can do, really. We've given her our values, whether or not she accepts all of them; she has freedom of choice to pick and choose what she wants.

"But, really, it's time for her to fly. To begin to live her life as an adult. And both Richie and I told her, last night, and last week, that we'll always be there for her if she needs us. But you can't . . . you've got to let them go.

"That begins real early. I've done that with all of them, and I continue to do it with Krissie. But I think it wasn't until this year that I realized, well, hey, this is it, now I've really got to let go. And . . . it's hard. And yet part of me . . . When she came home this morning at quarter to three, I said, 'I'm not unpacking the car. You're going.' And, she wants to go. It's just a little cold feet.

"It's the best time of her life. She's got so much going for her. And she's gonna have a good time. It's gonna be great.

"One thing that I'm not going to miss is . . . lying in bed at one o'clock in the morning, wondering . . . where is she? Because I'm not going to know. And that is good.

"I think she's got a lot of common sense . . . most of the time."

The caravan moved west toward Oswego and Lake Ontario, and the land took on a look of Indian country, with swamps and bluffs and rivers. Purple, blue, white and yellow wildflowers bloomed along the roadsides. The clouds broke and sunshine poured through, growing brighter as the sky cleared. Karin drove steadily at fifty miles per hour and kept an eye on Richie in the rearview mirror. We began to see other cars loaded with the paraphernalia of dormitory life.

Sue woke up, stretched and wondered where the doughnuts were.

"They're in the other car," said Karin.

Sue looked back longingly. "What about the potato chips?"

"They're in the trunk. Wait a minute. Cookies. They're in the garbage can."

"Where is it?" Sue asked.

"In the back. No, wait, it's in the other car, too."

"I thought you packed them for the road," Sue said. She sounded pitiful.

"No, I packed them for you. You wanted to save your home-baked cookies."

"Look!" Sue pointed to a pasture along the highway. "Dead cows."

"They're not dead. They're resting," said her mother. A sign at the roadside promoted WASHBURN FOR SHERIFF, in big red letters.

Sue started pushing buttons on the car radio, listened to the Beatles' "Can't Buy Me Love" and part of "Take Good Care of My Baby." Her favorite music was classic rock. She also liked New Kids on the Block, and pushed the seek button until their song "Tonight" came on. She twirled a strand of hair around her finger. Now and then she pulled her hair back into a thick ponytail, then let it go. As the caravan neared Oswego, she grew nervous and twirled her hair more often.

New York 481 followed the Oswego River north toward Lake Ontario. Navigational markers in the river indicated the barge route to Syracuse. The road swooped through fields of ripe corn. Smells of earth and cut grass came in through the open windows. As we entered Oswego County, a sign urged RE-ELECT NELLIS SHERIFF. A Conrail switching yard flashed past. More college-bound cars, loaded to the gunwales, joined the stream.

Downtown Oswego, split by the river, had an idle look. Banners welcomed the returning students. Karin announced there were one hundred and fifty-two bars in the town, some kind of a per capita record. Oswego was a sailor's town. It called itself Port City of Central New York. Between the sailors and the students, there were plenty of customers for the bars.

We passed a side street where Karin slowed to point out an Episcopal church to Sue. "Right over there. That's the last time you're going to see it, right?"

"I'll go to church," Sue said unconvincingly.

"I just wanted you to know where it is," said Karin.

+

The SUNY campus sprawled beside the lake, clusters of buildings among athletic fields. Sue's dormitory was Hart Hall, a high rise near the Student Union at the campus center. The arriving freshmen and their parents were unloading gear into piles on the dormitory lawn for student volunteers with trolleys to transfer inside.

When the unloading was complete, Karin and Richie went to park the cars while Sue and Krissie and I waited. They returned holding hands. The day had become a paragon, clear and bright and crisp.

Sue's roommate was named Jennifer, judging from the photographs collected in a single large frame with her name at the top. The snapshots showed Jennifer as a cheerleader, Jennifer with a boyfriend, Jennifer at the prom. The sixth-floor room was chockablock with boxes. Jennifer was absent. She, too, had brought a jumbo-sized box of laundry detergent.

Karin started helping Sue unpack. Jennifer had brought a gigantic sombrero, Sue her collection of stuffed pigs. "They're for decoration, not security," she said.

Richie asked for her room key. "I want to see if it fits the door."

"Why would they give me a key that doesn't fit the door?" Sue said.

"It doesn't hurt to be sure," her father answered, inserting the key in the lock and wiggling it.

"What side, sweetie?" Karin asked. She was poised with a Laura Ashley-style bedspread, flowers on one side, solid pink on the other. Sue elected flowers. Richie shook pillows into a matching pair of pillowcases. Karin unrolled a beefcake poster, and Sue yelped, "Don't unroll my posters. They'll get messed up. Don't touch my posters.

"We're so much alike," Sue said. "We're both stubborn. I guess that's why we fight."

"Who wins?" I asked.

"She does, now. I don't know. We can still make each other cry."

Karin and Richie left Krissie with Sue and walked together to the lakeshore. Lake Ontario was calm. Gentle waves sparkled in the sunlight and lapped at a shore of stones worn round and smooth by the lake's pummeling in rougher weather. They looked like cobblestones, in all sizes and colors. Karin and Richie sat in the grass on a low bluff above the water. Richie lay back and watched the few clouds drift overhead. Karin smoothed her skirt and stared across the lake. She seemed to be gathering herself.

After a while they returned to the dorm. Karin went to the back of the building to count the floors and windows to Sue's room. "I don't know, in case of fire," she told Richie when he asked.

They said their goodbyes in front of the dormitory. Richie hugged Sue and said, "Don't be a stranger." The tears started into Karin's eyes. Sue hugged Krissie. She saved her last hug for her mother.

"Goodbye, darling," Karin said.

"Goodbye, Mommy." They held each other a long time and then Karin let go and held Sue at arm's length and tried to smile. Her chin puckered as she fought to keep from crying.

Richie put his arm around her shoulders as they walked back to the cars. "She'll be calling. She'll be coming home," he reassured his wife. "She will."

"I did better than I thought I would," said Karin, brushing at an eye.

The caravan began its long return across the state. Karin said, "You can't wait for them to talk. You can't wait for them to walk. Then they're children for such a short time, you don't want to let them go."

9

"There's more to life than shredded wheat." Judy Salerno was standing at her seat, gripping the pew in front of her, asking the congregation for food discount coupons from the Sunday papers. She didn't like speaking before crowds, and she was nervous, drumming her foot as she spoke.

The bulletins were stuffed with her urgently worded inserts. "The Food Pantry needs your help!" they said. "Now that summer's ending, we need your help to restock." Judy had suggested a month's worth of donations: a box of cereal the first Sunday, then a jar of peanut butter, then coffee, tea or juice, then toilet paper or paper towels. Bring in the coupons, Judy said, and she would do the rest.

"Don't clip them. Just bring in the whole ad. It's easier that way. Just bring them in, as many as you don't use yourself," she said. Her foot tapped furiously and she sat down.

Labor Day had passed and St. Mary's had resumed its schedule of two services. The day rang with the crisp clarity of fall. The choir was back, singing in exuberant reunion. Carol Obligado played the organ with a pent-up energy. Eugene Jackson, dressed for fall and smelling of cigarettes, seemed to have begun a beard. John and Vinnie echoed the service from their place in the front row. Kathy and George Munroe and Karin Efman all sat in one row with their children, absent Susan. Sultan and Elaine Jabbour, the couple whose son had been baptized at the Easter Vigil, sat near the back; Nicholas Alexander, for once, was quiet. Exhausted by her withering disease, Caryl Miller never came to church now, but Bill was there with their next-door neighbors, the Tuckers: Mary, Barry, Barry Jr. and Chris, a tall, handsome family. Harold Van Horne had regained his strength. Coleman Hill had been outside before the service, directing cars into the parking lot.

Stelk clearly hoped the vigor in the air would translate into service to the church. Ann Marwick, one of the three vestry members in the last year of their three-year term, had begun the process of soliciting new vestry candidates. "If Ann or a member of the nominating committee knocks on your door, listen closely," Stelk said in his sermon. "You may hear not the voice of the nominating committee, but the voice of God.

"It is God who is calling, God who gives us opportunity, talent, ability. Don't say you don't have those things. None of us do, and then we go from there."

Stelk had baptized three infants last week and had three more scheduled. He told the congregation it was an exciting time to be involved in the life of St. Mary's.

Karin Efman, however, was troubled. She had too much vestry business on her mind. The vestry and Stelk had spent the previous day in retreat at Ann Marwick's house, trying to adapt its structure to the growing congregation. She was talking about it with John Harbeson outside the parish hall after the service when I joined them.

"I didn't see God in a lot of this," she said, raising her hands as if to summon inspiration. "I'm worrying about so much, about the bell tower, about expansion, about reorganizing the vestry, that I'm forgetting to worship," she said.

Karin said her feeling for St. Mary's was undiminished. Her sense of its mission was unchanged. But the spiritual hunger she'd been feeling was beginning to gnaw away, making her uncomfortable. "I still want to get people in all their little cells to support each other, the way I've been supported in this church. But it's got to come from here . . ." She raised her hands and drew them down, as if pulling something from the sky. ". . . This way. It's got to be done with a little more visible prayer. The prayer is there. Maybe it's just thick me, not able to see it."

"No, no," said Harbeson, who was looking at her with concern.

"It's silly, but I feel like I have a ministry here," she said.

"It's a ministry of all believers," said Harbeson.

"If you have a pretty building and people who aren't being fed, you're going to have an empty building," Karin said. Besides, she added, "It makes me crazy when we get bogged down at vestry meetings."

✢

St. Mary's was changing from a "pastoral" church to a "program" church, according to one theory of church management. It had close to one hundred and fifty active members among five hundred or more baptized and needed a better way to run itself. The vestry retreat had been the kind of management exercise that seemed to be in style.

I had arrived at Ann Marwick's pleasant, open house in Yorktown to find the members divided into three groups on its outside decks, introducing themselves to one another in biographical detail. Stelk explained that by reexamining the obvious, they hoped to produce new insights about themselves and the church. His role was to float from group to group, prodding and directing. "What are the things you want retained at St. Mary's, no matter what?" he asked. "What are our weaknesses?"

This was shaping up as altogether drab and earnest when a message from Pluto arrived. David Marwick, the younger of Ann's children, sent it from his upstairs window via paper airplane. Bob Soso, the impeccably dressed vestry member from St. Vincent, picked it up and read, "Hello from Pluto." He, Walt Decker and John Donovan had been in the middle of deciding that St. Mary's lacked a social life. "There's a good feeling on Sundays," Walt said. "But it doesn't extend much beyond that. The card nights, dances, they don't work."

John Harbeson, David Odell and the vestry secretary, Frances Armstrong, sat around a picnic table on the back deck, near a line of drying T-shirts. Harbeson was saying, "Linc is a fine priest, but he has to take on too much. We need to relieve him of some of the organizational stress so he can do more pastoral things. I worry about him. I really do."

Inside, in a family room off the open kitchen, where a framed piece of needlepoint read, A TRUE FRIEND IS GOOD TO FIND, Carol Obligado, Gerry Cousins and Ann decided that St. Mary's strengths started with liturgy and music.

Stelk wrote "Strengths" on a large pad he'd set up on an easel when the groups reconvened as one. Under the heading, he wrote "Liturgy and music." He also wrote, "Family-based," "Diversity of congregation," "History," "Informality," "Ability to self-govern," "Good clergy leadership," "Flexibility," "No factions," "Warm and friendly."

"I hate 'Warm and friendly,' " Carol said. "I picture that as one of those drooling basset hounds."

The weaknesses Stelk wrote down included a low profile in the community, a far-flung membership that hindered church activities, a lack of children's services, the church school structure and administrative work that overtaxed Stelk and diverted him from counseling and other pastoral affairs.

Karin arrived from the dentist's office where she worked. She was wearing a polo shirt decorated not with an alligator or a polo player, but a smiling Mr. Tooth.

The retreat stretched into the afternoon. Stelk admitted to the concern that Dwight Douglas and Harbeson had voiced, that he was doing more administration and less pastoral work than he preferred. "Too much in the financial. And no program planning," he added.

"You're pulled hither and thither by a variety of administrative things," Harbeson said.

"You weren't ordained to do numbers," Carol said.

"So how do we address our weaknesses?" Walt asked.

"Beats me," said Donovan, lighting a cigarette.

The members retreated to their groups. More airplanes swooped from the upstairs window. The notes grew more demanding: "Help, we are being held hostage by Iraqi invaders. Put $1,000 and a handgun in the hanging envelope. Hurry!"

Walt took the envelope dangling by a string from David's window, filled it with pine cones and tugged. Walt's son, Adam, was about David's age. The envelope disappeared into the window. You could hear a fit of giggles.

The vestry arrived at length at a scheme under which members would have "portfolios" of responsibility in such areas as finance, youth and church school, community outreach and membership. Each would chair a committee of church members concerned with that portfolio. They would assign and monitor tasks and report to the full vestry. As it was, the members were simply liaisons to the various church functions.

"Who's the choir liaison?" Odell wanted to know.

"I am," said Harbeson.

"What does that mean?"

"Nothing."

The new scheme meant more delegation, the very thing Stelk had most trouble doing.

"Are you a control person?" Walt asked Stelk bluntly.

Stelk paused. After a minute, he said, "I don't mind letting go if I'm confident. But if I'm not sure, I'm not comfortable. I don't always want to write the newsletter, but I want to know what's in it."

The group talked for a while about hiring an assistant to keep Stelk off the telephone and allow him to do more counseling. "We met for four hours the other day, and he spent half that time on the phone," Carol complained.

"This is a little pie-in-the-sky," David Odell responded. "We're talking about another priest down the road, too. That's two paid positions. Where's the money going to come from? We're talking about expansion. That's going to take all our effort."

Karin had been uncharacteristically quiet all afternoon. She spoke at last in a pained voice. "Are we going to make the vestry a purely administrative thing? What about the heart? Is there going to be any room for spirituality?"

Karin still had been pained the next day at church, still wondered how she would feed her hunger. She told Harbeson as they talked outside the parish hall that she would not seek a new term as senior warden.

✛

My father's name was edging up the prayer list. He had climbed seven rows, to row nineteen, as new names were added to the weekly bulletin and others were removed.

My trips to Florida had continued unabated through the summer. Dad was in the nursing home now, and my routine was much the same as it had been with Mom before her final stroke. I would visit, talk, just be with him for what comfort I could offer. He was there, I told him, to recuperate until he could return to his apartment. This was not entirely disingenuous. He had rejected all surgical options for his prostate cancer. One was castration, to reduce the testosterone thought to "feed" the cancer. I told him this in the best terms I could muster. For a long moment, he thought about his testicles. "Well, I don't suppose they're doing me much good," he finally said. "But I want to keep them anyway." He was taking injections of estrogen instead.

But he failed to improve, and on each successive visit he was more lonely and remote. I would arrive at the nursing home to find him sitting in his wheelchair in the lobby, away from the other patients, looking at nothing, his crossword puzzle forgotten in his lap. He refused to wear the hearing aid I'd made him buy. He said it made his ears ring. "I don't need it anyway," he groused. "I can hear everything I need to hear." Our conversations were equal parts my shouting and his nodding as if he understood. He didn't need to talk to anybody else. He had always been a loner, an artist who spent painstaking hours over work he never really tried to sell. My mother had been his life's companion.

My visits were never long enough for him. They reverberated with his disappointment. He always thought that I was there to rescue him. When he saw me coming, his famous, lovely, grateful smile would break out like a flag unfolding in the wind. "When am I going to go home?" he'd ask. "I'll be alright there. I can hack it." He told friends who came to visit him that I would be moving back to Florida and that he and I would live together while I took care of him.

He liked going out to lunch. We both did. He had decided that he liked nothing quite so much as lobster and that at last he could afford it. He would teeter into a seafood restaurant on my arm, sit down and order the best spread in the house, starting with a Bloody Mary and ending with some chocolate extravagance like Mississippi mud pie. Then he would lean back, nod and say, with the grave satisfaction of a restaurant critic about to give four stars, "That was good."

Soon edema swelled his ankles, and he was unable to get about at all without a wheelchair. One day after lunch I took him back to his apartment. I wanted to reassure him that it was the same, to keep the notion of home alive for him. We rode the pokey elevator to the seventh floor and entered the apartment. The same brilliant light flooded the windows, which gave the same view of the Caloosahatchee River. The same pillow he stuffed behind his lower back while he worked his crossword puzzles was at his same place on the couch. His watercolors and woodcuts were still on the walls, his penknife lying on the dresser, his clothes in the closet and his writing tablet by his place at the table next to the window. Everything was the same as I wheeled him about the small apartment. Except him. My father was not the same. I thought later that it was inadvertently cruel to let him glimpse the life that, in his wheelchair, he would never live again.

The cancer moved quite swiftly. On my next visit, he wanted to go out for lunch as usual, but he couldn't remember what he liked to order. "I'd like one of those . . ." The effort of remembering passed across his face in waves like gusting rain. His eyes darted and his voice groped against the wall of memory. Finally he said, "I'd like one of those . . . fishy things."

We went out and had our final lobster lunch.

I had planned a trip for the following week when the nursing home called to suggest that I come sooner. I arrived late on a Sunday night, a week from the end of September, bringing photos of his childhood home in England that a cousin of his had given me. I knocked until the night nurse let me in a side door.

I was shocked when I saw him, gaunt and rasping. A second nurse raised him in the bed. "John. John, your son is here," she said. He was fogged with Demerol, but the smile broke through.

"Hi, Dad. How are you feeling?" I said, and immediately thought, How stupid. There was nothing to tell him that I hadn't said. It seemed more important that he sleep than talk, and I asked the nurse to let him rest.

"Are you sure?" she asked, and I said I was. By the morning I knew we wouldn't talk again. It was too late to take him home, even on the wings of memory in the pictures I had brought too late for him to see.

I thought all the next day, as I sat by his bedside, how to pray for him. What could possibly matter at this point? What could help? I began to tell him that I loved him. Attendants came in to turn him and to change his bedding. He groaned with pain, and I prayed that he not hurt too badly. His breath labored, and I prayed for ease. Sweat drenched him, and I prayed that he be cooled. He shivered, and I prayed for warmth.

I had rediscovered the attitude for prayer at St. Mary's. The humility to ask for something that I could not provide, and from that the humility to understand that I could provide nothing but the comfort of a touch and a voice, a connection that is finally all we have to give to one another.

It was clear in the late afternoon that he would die soon. His hand was under the covers and I placed my hand over it. His breath came in shudders that grew more and more shallow.

As he gasped and struggled for each breath, I prayed that he would die, that his ordeal would end. But as the pauses between his breaths grew longer and I waited, heart suspended, I prayed in those moments that he would not die, that he go on living just a minute more. Please, God, let him die, let it be over, let this senseless, painful struggle stop. No, don't die. No, no, no.

At last he stopped breathing. He simply did not inhale again. After a long moment, in which neither of us breathed, everything relaxed. The rigid planes of his face and the taut anguish of his mouth, the trembling eyelids, the brittle tension of his chest and the hand he'd curled into a fist, all softened. Everything flowed out. I kissed his forehead and said, "I love you," to his finally peaceful body.

I found the nurse and told her he was gone. I was trembling with relief. She hurried to the room, pressed a stethoscope against his chest and nodded. Two attendants came in, and their expressions were like balm, unguarded, full of sympathy. A woman with skin the color of bruised grapes held out her arms to me, and I sobbed on her shoulder. It was not so hard to lean against a stranger for a moment.

The theology of it seemed quite simple. By giving up, you gained. You dropped your postures and defenses and you could feel, you could be comforted. That was a blessing, and I had found it through the humility of prayer.

And then my father's name was in the intercessions. "I bid your prayers for John P. Taylor, Nick Taylor's father, who has died . . ."

✢

The recession had started in July, said the economists. Only much later was it learned that sales of Kraft macaroni and cheese had risen the same month; trend watchers said that was a sure indicator that people had less money. The Iraqi army continued to hunker in Kuwait, and Mohegan Lake could feel it. Gasoline prices on Route 6 were pushing $1.50 for regular, and people were worried.

Harold Van Horne had surgery to implant a heart pacemaker while I was in Florida. John Donovan, who never got around to trying hypnosis for his smoking habit, had a heart attack that required a triple bypass. His absence from the September vestry meeting helped dampen talk about the parish hall expansion. David Odell, who now chaired the committee on expansion he'd suggested, asked Stelk to name subcommittees responsible for planning the building, developing a fund-raising campaign, exploring grant funding and assessing what he called "the day care option."

That was it for expansion at the meeting, as far as I could tell from looking at the minutes. No one talked about it at church the next Sunday. An abrupt silence fell over St. Mary's. The recession, the price of gasoline and the threat of war as American troops, ships and planes converged on the Persian Gulf, all forced a suspension of debate.

Meanwhile, a new financial problem loomed. Gerry Cousins had received an $8,700 estimate for repairing the bell tower. There was only one bidder. The money designated for the bell tower totaled $2,300, the profits from last year's Harvest Fair. This year's fair was supposed to pay for a new wheeled coffee cart and start a building fund. Now the vestry would have to redirect that money and appeal to the congregation for donations.

Gerry had laid still more repairs before the vestry. The church's exterior stucco needed a sealer coat. That was a $6,000 job that would last three years. Then, Gerry said, new stucco would be needed. Work on the parish hall floor would cost $500. Replacing the rectory's missing roofing tiles would cost $950.

Gerry, according to the September minutes, had hit his stride as junior warden. He'd had the rectory chimney cleaned already. He planned to have the church window frames repainted, the stained glass cleaned and storm windows installed before winter. His list stretched into next spring and beyond. Some of the estimates were staggering.

John Baynard's bequest, the house in Somers, was becoming an albatross. Stelk had been sitting in his office one day when a process server from the county appeared and handed him a summons. He was called to answer the complaint in the foreclosure action. Grace Church in White Plains, the corecipient, had told Stelk it wanted to buy St. Mary's share of the house. But it would be months, pending an appraisal and payment of the mortgage and expenses, before St. Mary's could put any money in the bank.

The final discomfiting note in the minutes was Dwight Douglas's resignation from the vestry. His term ran only through the end of the year, but this was more final. He had written Stelk that he wished "to retire from all church activities for a time." Ann had sent a note saying the same thing.

✛

"We never thought it would come to this point," Dwight said on a Sunday afternoon. He was casually dressed in jeans and a red sweater, Ann in a sweater and slacks. They were alone in the house now; Audrey, their older daughter, had finished college and was on her own, Brian and Jennifer away at college. It was close to Christmas when we talked, and Dwight and Ann were expecting Brian and Jennifer home for the holiday. The tree was trimmed and waiting.

The Douglases said they had decided to join another parish.

"We've been taking the last several months to hash that out," Dwight said. "I think you could look back and say this was likely to happen when Linc came back and did not have a good experience."

He was talking about Stelk's reaction to Cursillo.

Outside the windows, the sky over the Hudson River to the west hung low and dark with a kind of cosmic heaviness. The house, a restored Victorian on a street up a hill, was cozy. It had a bright, spacious kitchen, and a bathroom was decorated with posters from the amateur theater productions Dwight and Ann had written and directed at the Depot Theatre in Garrison—musical reviews with titles like *A Little Lite Music* and *A Four Chorus Dinner.* Ann set out of plate of cookies and offered more spiced tea.

As we talked, the fundamental nature of their rift with Stelk emerged.

The Douglases were people who needed to be challenged in their Christianity, they said. Stelk offered comfort. The Douglases wanted to be part of an invigorated laity. The word they kept using was "empowered." Stelk thought the process of worship was fine the way it was. They seemed to want an aerobic religion, a "no pain, no gain" stretching of their faith. Stelk believed a regular constitutional, the Liturgy, prayer and song and preaching and reading of the Word within the service, was exercise enough.

"I guess I come from a more pedantic, pedestrian tradition," he had told me.

Ann said, "When we went into the call process after Marc [Lee] left, I think what people were looking for was a gentle kind of shepherd, who was not going to break down barriers and wasn't going to be terrifically insistent. So they got what they were looking for. Linc is a very gentle, kind shepherd. He's very accepting. He has a social conscience that he reminds us all to have every now and then. I think that a lot of people feel ministered to, they feel cared for by him, and that's all part of what he's supposed to be doing. But it's hard to be all things to all people."

Versions of that phrase came up several times. The Douglases sounded apologetic when they said Stelk didn't fit their version of a parish leader. At the same time, they damned him with faint praise.

"It's not easy for one person to satisfy everybody," Dwight said. "It isn't so much whether I agree or disagree that there are people who need the comfort that he offers. But sometimes we can set the standard a little low. There's a whole generation of people who've fallen away from religion, so just going to church seems like it's a step up. I think that our purpose on this planet is probably to form a relationship with God and to be stewards of his creation. It's a pretty darn serious business. I don't think everybody should be shook up when they come to church. I think it's good to come into a quiet, pleasant place to celebrate. But one of our functions as Christians is to be empowered and actually go out and do some things that benefit somebody other than ourselves."

"After Communion there's a prayer," said Ann. "It asks the Lord to 'send us out to do the work you have given us to do.' Then there's the dismissal, and we usually use the one that says, 'Go in peace to love and serve the Lord.' Well, I'm not a 'Send me out in peace' person. I'm a 'Send me out to do the work you've given me to do' person. And he's sending us out in peace. Really, he wants to send people out in peace, not charged up to do the work that we've been given to do."

"That's an overstatement," Dwight interjected.

"But that's my fear, that people are leaving in peace, which is okay. But there's that other side, that you are empowered. God said, 'I can't be there, you've got to do it for me.' Somebody's got to do it."

They said the prospects of parish hall expansion had little to do with their decision. Dwight said, "I don't think it would have been a bad idea to build this building." He looked at Ann and said, "You were lucky not to be there." Presumably he meant the vestry meetings. "But there was sort of this lack of the logic of it, which is very upsetting. There were no facts. We never seemed to have any facts to deal with.

"And there was the one underlying premise that we didn't get to: How will we be incorporating into our lives at St. Mary's the tools to help us grow spiritually? I started to push that issue. It seemed like it just got hostility up in the air or something. It wasn't meant as personal criticism. But we have to have a way that we are going to assist our members in growing spiritually and in serving the community around us as we grow. I could never get to that point, that statement of intent."

The Douglases agreed that less challenged Christians could still be happy at St. Mary's. Ann said, "It still has many of the qualities that made it home for years: many warm, intelligent, sensitive people. A strong sense of worship, of putting God first, and not necessarily the church or the parish. If I were a young person coming into the parish I would find St. Mary's a very healthy, attractive place to be."

They said they'd been attending a church that they described as "spirit filled."

+

Stelk hated to see the Douglases withdraw. He said he was frustrated because he had tried, without success, to promote the kind of mission activities they said they needed to challenge them as Christians. A "Midnight Run" expedition to take food and blankets to New York City homeless had drawn one volunteer, John Harbeson's daughter Kristen. No one had volunteered to work with the poor families at the Lakeview Cottages, a colony within half a mile of St. Mary's.

"I end up not being able to do the things that the Douglases and some of the Cursillistas want because that's not what my interests are," he said. "But there are a lot of things not being done that could be."

Stelk agreed that a priest could not be all things to all people. He saw himself as no more holy than anyone else, no closer to God. "Why am I the designated prayer?" he would ask, when the dinner host invariably turned to him for grace. Stelk said he was just a keeper of tradition, passing on the gospel of peace and love. If people needed a personal trainer to exercise their faith, that wasn't Lincoln Stelk.

"It's not what he does well," Ginny said. "He's never felt he had to do a whole lot with those who are well. He really tried to help the Douglases. He recognized that they needed something, but he just couldn't provide it. Years back that could have made him angry or frustrated. But now he realizes he has this shortcoming and deals with it. It's a maturity. You grow into things. I think he has."

So Stelk felt badly, but he didn't dwell on it. Seasonal activities required his attention. The Harvest Fair was just around the corner. The inquirers' classes for Alice Marwick and Cynthia Bondi, his candidates for the Mature Profession of

Faith, would have to begin soon if he was to prepare them for confirmation before the next bishop's visit in the spring. And his daughter Kirsten's wedding was set for the end of November, not that distant now. Ginny already was haunting the bridal shops with Kit, helping to choose bridesmaids' dresses and arrange fittings. Stelk would have to try on his seldom-worn tuxedo for size.

And, of course, there were all the usual things he had to do.

10

Stelk conducted a service once every four weeks at the Field Home.

The Field Home was, as its founder provided in his will, "a home for aged gentlewomen." Cortlandt de Peyster Field had been an active and wealthy member of St. Mary's. It was his $1,000 that had bought from Tiffany the stained glass insert above the altar, which I had learned was not Mary with the infant Jesus, as I had thought, but the virtuous woman from Chapter 31 of Proverbs. The once-elegant frame manse had been his farmhouse. Old photographs depicted Field as a serious, dark-eyed, dark-haired man, with a sweeping mustache and muttonchop whiskers. He drove oxen through winter slush and muck nearly three miles to services at St. Mary's. Later he built a road. Finally he added a wing to his rambling Georgian house, built a chapel that seated more people than St. Mary's and petitioned Bishop Horatio Potter to allow him to hold services as a lay minister. He named the chapel St. Catherine's after his mother. Field died in 1918, leaving the home to the aged gentlewomen, as well as "poor people who owned or who were the descendants of those who owned not less than fifty acres of land in Westchester County."

Services at the Field Home had fallen to successive Episcopal priests, who celebrated in a drawing room since the chapel had fallen out of use. Stelk and the Rev. Robert Taylor, rector of St. Peter's Church in Peekskill, alternated the biweekly services. I went along with Stelk one Thursday in October.

We left St. Mary's a little before ten on an oddly warm, humid morning for the harvest season. The hills were brilliant with fall colors, reds and yellows and purples against the dark and constant pines. Elms shone as bright as gold doubloons. Stelk was in a cheerful mood.

The Field Home was off a country road, not surprisingly called Catherine Street, about three miles south of St. Mary's. It sat atop a hill and gave a marvelous view of the surrounding landscape. Close to the house, the orchards and croplands had given way to scattered woods and ungrazed meadow. A much newer, modern building, the Holy Comforter Nursing Home, where Stelk and Ginny came regularly to visit Ginny's mother, Georgia, shared the property.

Stelk parked and marched up the front walk, carrying his valise with its wafers and jar of wine, bounced up a set of peeling steps onto a wide porch and swung open a screen door. I followed him into a long hallway, where a few gray-haired women sat on chairs. They snapped to attention at the sight of Stelk's clericals.

"Good morning. Good morning," he called out, and hurried off down an intersecting hall past a series of comfortably furnished residential rooms.

At the end of the hall, a woman waited with a worried look. Jean Duff was an eight-o'clocker at St. Mary's and Stelk's regular volunteer at the Field Home services. "They're all waiting," she said, pointedly.

"I got away a little late."

"We have fifteen today," Jean said.

Stelk vested in the hall. He put on a long black cassock and over it, a white surplice. This was an older style of vestments with which the women were familiar. He kissed his stole—the traditional Pentecostal green, not the bright stole Ginny had given him—before he put it on. He produced a Jerusalem cross from his valise, kissed it and hung it around his neck.

When he was vested, he unscrewed the cap of a squat jar

and poured wine into a chalice. The cap had a brand name, "Vita," printed on the top. "Herring, I think," said Stelk. "It's short, so it fits in the briefcase." Then he counted out fifteen communion wafers onto a silver tray and carried the tray and chalice into a large drawing room.

The room was bright, with windows on three sides and light that came through gauzy curtains. Overstuffed chairs and sofas were ranged against the walls. The paintings were from the Hudson River School, landscape and light, except for the portrait of Cortlandt de Peyster Field that gazed down benignly from above the mantel. The founder's view fell upon a white-draped table serving as a temporary altar in the middle of the room. A few straight chairs were set up in front of it. Underfoot, an ugly blue-and-orange rug alluded to being Oriental. I took a seat against the wall.

The women all were wearing sweaters in the warmth. Their hairdos looked like little puffs of cloud. Jean sat down at the grand piano in a corner opposite the television set and struck up the opening hymn, "Take My Life, and Let It Be Consecrated."

Stelk fell into the familiar cadences of the Rite One service: "Lord, have mercy upon us."

"Christ, have mercy upon us," the ladies responded.

"Lord, have mercy upon us."

Stelk used Rite One at the Field Home "for tradition's sake." He said, "The ladies feel more comfortable with it. It's more like the one they're used to." The language, recalling the Order for Holy Communion in the 1928 prayer book, was old but not outdated. God was sterner and human beings more in need of mercy, but the words of worship had a timeless beauty that was evident in the Collect:

"Almighty God, unto whom all hearts are open, all desires known, and from whom no secrets are hid; Cleanse the thoughts of our hearts by the inspiration of thy Holy Spirit, that we may perfectly love thee, and worthily magnify thy holy Name; through Christ our Lord. Amen."

Stelk delivered a brief sermon that focused on St. Francis of

Assisi, whose day it was in the Church. He said it was difficult in modern times to live a vow of poverty and suffering, but one should try for modesty. A woman near the back kept muttering. He and Jean went around the room during the Peace, clasping hands. I rose, too, wanting to connect somehow with these women whose age and dignity reminded me of my mother, and I touched hands that reached out gratefully. The second hymn was "Come, Ye Disconsolate."

A small white cross stood on the table-altar between two white candles. Stelk prepared Communion, and moved among the ladies with the Sacraments. Some closed their eyes and opened their mouths, letting him place the wafers on their tongues. This was the Roman Catholic style; Episcopalians learn to take the bread in their open hands. Catholic services were infrequent at the Field Home, and Stelk said the local priest had given the Catholic women leave to attend the Episcopal services.

Jean played "Blest Be the Tie That Binds" as the closing hymn. Stelk exited, carrying the empty chalice and the silver tray. He returned a moment or two later in his clericals, pulled up a chair and began to chat about the weather. "It feels like you could squeeze the air and wring water out of it," he said, leaning back and stretching out his legs.

One tiny lady didn't want to talk about the weather. "I celebrated my ninetieth birthday last week," she chirped in an accent that was faintly British. "I didn't want to be ninety, but it came inevitably." Jean quickly started a verse of "Happy Birthday" on the piano. Miss Sylvia Clarke said she had come to the United States in 1916, had worked as a nurse at Peekskill Hospital and had run a nursery school in Peekskill for many years.

"I had twenty-two people come from Washington, D.C., for my birthday," she said proudly. "All friends and relatives."

Stelk said he'd been in Washington in September for the consecration of the National Cathedral. "I was ordained a deacon there," he said. "It looked then as if it would never be finished, but it finally was." This led to talk of the Cathedral of

St. John the Divine in New York City, the Gothic and Romanesque Episcopal cathedral in Morningside Heights that was begun in 1892 and was still under construction, employing the archaic skills of stonemasons. Episcopalians called it St. John the Unfinished.

"One of the problems with the cathedral in New York," Stelk said, "is that they've been digging up the street in front of it for so long you can't even see the cathedral."

"I think that's a little bit exaggerated," Miss Clarke corrected him. "You can't hide a cathedral."

A woman named Bess, who wore dark glasses and used a walker, sat next to the talkative Miss Clarke. Bess said she had moved to Peekskill from Canada and had been Peekskill Hospital's director of nursing. Jean remembered her and recalled a time when her, Jean's, mother had undergone surgery in the hospital. "When she woke up from the ether," Jean said, "she looked up and saw this beautiful lady with a white cap and thought she'd died and gone to heaven. That was you, Bess. That was a story in our family for years."

"And look at me now," Bess said.

"Never mind, never mind, you look just as good," said Miss Clarke with assurance.

Stelk listened to all this with a slight smile and arched eyebrows. After half an hour he said his goodbyes and left the group in the drawing room. The women who had been in the entrance hall when we arrived still sat along the wall like sentinels.

A bolted door led from the hall into St. Catherine's Chapel. The chapel formed what was in effect another wing of the house, opposite the residential wing. Stelk asked me if I'd like a look at it, and I said I would. The door had not been used in some time, and it creaked loudly when he finally got it open.

Steep steps led from the door down to ground level and a long, narrow sanctuary with high windows and a raised chancel at the far end where the altar was. "I'd like to have this many seats at St. Mary's," Stelk said. The room was dim and cool. The light through the streaked windows illuminated dust, cobwebs and crumbled plaster on the floor. It was lovely nonetheless, with a nostalgic, sentimental quality. Holding services there would have been impossible, Stelk said. The chapel was too large, too cold, too difficult to heat, even if the women had been able to negotiate the precarious stairs. Stelk slapped dust from his hands. We climbed the steps and closed the door on the monument to Cortlandt de Peyster Field's unusual piety.

✣

We returned to St. Mary's to hear organ music in the church. John Harbeson was practicing for Sunday, when he would play in Carol Obligado's absence. John's long limbs angled over the keyboard and pedals like a stick puppet's. His head was bowed in concentration.

Stelk replenished his home communion kit, and we left for Caryl and Bill Miller's.

The Millers' house was the kind real estate pages call a "splanch"—a split-level ranch—set a short way back from the street on a wooded lot. Stelk kicked up clouds of leaves in the driveway on his way to the door. He climbed the steps to a small porch, rang the bell and waited. A woman with light brown curly hair opened the door, looked at Stelk suspiciously and then invited us into a modest living room.

The room had a brick wall, a wood-burning stove, a sectional sofa and photographic blow-ups, in black and white, of Bill and Caryl in their long-haired hippie days. But it was dominated by a huge orthopedic chair that stood up from its base like an ejection seat. Caryl was standing at a wheeled walker. She was wearing a red dress and red sneakers. "This is Blossom," Caryl introduced the other woman. "My neighbor from across the street." She said Bill was at work and Justin at school.

Caryl shuffled behind the walker as she pushed it toward the chair. Amyotrophic lateral sclerosis is not physically painful to its victims, but it was painful to watch Caryl struggle to move across the room. Stelk followed her progress with concern. When she reached the chair she turned around, leaned back and pushed a button on a control box at the end of a stout cord. A motor hummed, and the chair lowered itself to a sitting position.

Caryl seemed cheerful. She had a new haircut, a short, attractive bob. She indicated the low sofa that occupied two walls. "You couldn't get up from that even if you're well," she said. Her speech had grown mildly slurred from the disease. She said the chair would make her easier to handle for the people helping her. "They won't have to pull me up anymore."

Blossom was just one of many helpers who had materialized since Caryl's illness. St. Mary's Sunday bulletins had advertised her need for help. Frank Doyle's wife, Iris, Eleanor Arnold from the altar guild and Ann Marwick had responded with food, visits and phone calls. Caryl's older sister, Rose, who lived on Long Island, stayed for days at a time. And Blossom, whom the Millers had barely known before Caryl got sick, came almost every day to do housework. (Bill had told me he was amazed by this. He usually sat alone during services and seemed to have few social friends in the church. "You meet nice people in this church," he said. "It's hard to find nice people in the world today.")

This was Stelk's first visit to bring Caryl home Communion. "Will you join us?" he asked Blossom, who had hovered until Caryl was safely in her chair.

"Oh, no. I'm Jewish," Blossom Schecter said. She disappeared into the kitchen.

Stelk conducted a short service, reading from the Order of Worship for Communion under Special Circumstances. When it was over, Caryl looked up and smiled.

"Thank you for coming," she said.

✣

The next Sunday Bill told me Caryl was going to Lourdes. "It can't hurt," he said. "Maybe it will help. I'm willing to try anything if it doesn't hurt."

A Roman Catholic friend of Bill and Caryl's had suggested the pilgrimage to the legendary French shrine in the foothills of the Pyrenees. Steve Ziniti, from Long Island, had a disease called alopecia universalis—head-to-toe baldness. He was going to pray for the restoration of his hair. Bill had decided that Justin should make the trip with them.

"This way he'll be involved with helping her," Bill said. "If I went he'd just be like a tourist on vacation."

A few days later, Caryl talked with me about her expectations for the trip. She appeared at the top of the short staircase that led from the bedrooms to the living room. Rose, a blonder version of Caryl, was helping her today. The six steps between the living room and the bedrooms had been fitted with an elevator chair, but it was broken. Rose positioned herself a step below Caryl and held out her hands to support her as she came down the stairs. Caryl said, "Back up one more."

"Caryl?" Rose sounded worried that Caryl would fall.

"I need room."

Caryl clutched the stair rail with one hand and Rose with the other. She lifted one foot, dangled it briefly, moved it downward until it found the step below. The other followed. It was a slow process. Her feet moved as if they were made of wood. "This'll take nine years," she said.

Reaching the bottom, she gripped her walker and moved slowly to her chair. She looked tired. "It's like a battle every night . . . to get physically comfortable," she said. "I hate the sleeping pills. They make me groggy.

"And I'm not looking forward to the flight. I think it will be hard."

A fourteen-year-old girl had seen religious visions in Lourdes in 1858. Pilgrims flocked there, and miraculous healings were reported in its waters. Caryl said she saw her trip more as a retreat than a pilgrimage.

"Hope," she said. "I want to find some strength within myself. That's why I'm going to Lourdes."

The Lenten healing services at St. Mary's had helped in a similar way. "I felt better when I came home from them," she said. "It had its place. Maybe because they were so small and intimate."

I asked her if she expected to be cured.

"A cure is like a side-effect," she said, toying with the chair's control box. Rose brought a cup of tea and placed it, in a saucer, on a TV table next to Caryl's chair. "That would be lovely. It would be icing on the cake. But inner strength would be the main thing. I'm going mainly to gain some spiritual uplifting. And hopefully it will help Justin come to terms with this." The cup rattled on the saucer as she lifted it. She raised the cup, trembling, to her lips. A black-and-white cat appeared at the top of the stairs, surveyed the room and left.

Bill had told me Justin was ignoring Caryl's illness. "He doesn't want to try to deal with it," he said. "If she's in her wheelchair, he'll act like she doesn't exist." He made no effort to help her. When they were together in public, he stayed a distance from his parents, as if her infirmity embarrassed him.

"He's kind of denying it, in a sense," Caryl said. "He doesn't want to acknowledge it or talk about it."

The greatest burden was hers, of course, and I thought she was bearing it with grace. She was thoughtful and lucid as she talked about groping for faith. She smiled easily. "It's hard when you get something like this," she said. "You're looking for answers. The first thing you think is, 'What did I do wrong? Why did this happen?' Then you blame God: 'Why'd you do that?'

"I've come to a certain peace with that. I don't think he did this to me. I don't think he picked me out. The universe has randomness to it. Like airplane crashes or whatever. Tragedies occur.

"You have a lot of time to think. My faith was never real strong to begin with. Going through this has made it stronger. It's hard to explain. Your faith in God doesn't change, but the circumstances around you change. People come around you, and that changes your faith in humanity, and that reflects on God.

"But I'm still trying to find that inner peace."

She had not turned to Stelk or any other member of the

clergy for answers. "I was trying to find someone to go to, like a psychotherapist," she said. "Because it gets pretty depressing. But I need someplace that's open at night, so Bill can take me, or someone to come here.

"I've tried to work it out for myself. I think I have it pretty good. But I'm not at a place where I'm at peace with it. Every time you get comfortable it poses a new obstacle for you to overcome.

"I cry a lot. Nonstop crying. I'd like to get past that. I'd like to stop crying so easily."

✛

"I worry for Linc, I really do," John Harbeson said.

He'd said the same thing at the vestry retreat weeks earlier. Now we were sitting on a bench in front of the City College administration building. It was another bright fall day, and leaves were swirling around the walkways of the CCNY campus in Harlem. John was between classes.

"He tries to keep on top of everything," he said. "But he has too much to do, and so things don't get done. He's under a lot of stress, and he gets no exercise. I worry about him."

John, along with Kathy Munroe and Walt Decker, had been writing descriptions of the new vestry "portfolios"—the responsibilities of the committees members would chair. The work had been painstaking. Each description required some negotiation. Walt had proposed a top-down scheme of church school management that would have undercut Frank Doyle. Stelk had objected and Harbeson had taken his side.

John nonetheless sensed himself at odds with Stelk on other issues. Stelk and Ginny saw John and Ann Harbeson socially as much as any couple in the parish. But a coolness and a distance had arisen. John traced it to Stelk's eagerness for the parish hall expansion. "He gets impatient with anything that seems to get in the way," he said, "even if I was just trying to see that it was done right."

John seemed to resent, at least mildly, that Gerry Cousins's efforts to spruce up the parish were more appreciated than his efforts to reorganize it.

"Gerry's done wonders," he said. "I've focused on things that are less tangible. And also they've touched more directly on Linc's own roles and functions." A leaf danced along a gust of breeze and landed in his hair. He brushed it free and leaned forward on his hands. "I think there's room for others in the day-to-day running of the parish." John was pushing to give Stelk an administrative assistant, and Stelk was resisting. "The big question is, will Linc let go? I don't know if he will, but he should."

John looked at his watch and consulted an index card he dug from a pocket of his blazer. He stood up and said he had to go to his next class. We walked across the campus toward the North Academic Center. It was a massive building of angles and long rows of windows. As we approached it, John looked up and made a face. "It looks like a beached ocean liner," he said.

His office was up an escalator and down a corridor, in a tiny warren of faculty offices. It was devoid of personality. John's desktop was bare except for a telephone, some odds and ends and a portable computer. He'd tacked a map of Africa to the wall behind his desk and a few posters here and there. He assembled his notes and was about to leave for his class when Jorge entered.

He was a pudgy young man who couldn't keep still. He bobbed and shuffled like a boxer. He wore dirty jeans of bleached blue denim, a jersey-style sweatshirt that was damp with sweat and a plastic batter's helmet covered with advertising stickers. He took the helmet off and held it against his chest. His straight black hair was damp and matted, and he was chewing on a Tootsie Roll Pop. Jorge looked high as a kite.

"I just came from Chicago," he said.

John looked puzzled.

Jorge was there to check his standing in John's class. "Am I okay? Are we okay?" he asked. "I just want to be sure I'm okay with you. I want to give you my house number. Are you married? Or are you a single man? Because I can, you know, the girls, they do favors for me."

He took the Tootsie Roll Pop out of his mouth. A piece of pink gum clung to the ball of candy.

John shifted nervously. He answered in his quick, stuttery voice that abbreviated some words almost out of existence. "What do you think?"

"What do you mean?"

"Married or single. D'you think?"

"I don't guess. You tell me. You tell me."

"I'm married."

"Don't matter. The girls'll be there anyway." Jorge pointed to the island of Madagascar on the map of Africa behind John's desk. "I'm the king here," he said. "I'm known here"—indicating Mozambique—"but I'm the king here." This, he said, was because he was Puerto Rican and Dominican and "I speak black truth." He grabbed a small notepad from John's desk and started printing an amazing résumé, describing it at the same time. "I'm a promoter, choreographer, producer . . . and a rapper. You know rapper? I used to be with Beastie Boys. You know Beastie Boys? But that's over." He added some names and a number and handed the slip to John.

"That's a lot of information," John said.

"And my house number. Call me. Bring your wife, girlfriend. We'll have a barbeque."

John excused himself to go to class. Jorge disappeared as we were walking down the hall. John said something about "serious psychological problems."

+

John's class was an undergraduate introduction to political philosophy. The classroom showed scars of underfunding. Missing ceiling tiles revealed wads of matted insulation overhead. The cinderblock walls were scrawled with graffiti: "God loves you," "Pablo & Pammy," "Individual participation in decision that affects life," "Fuck you," "City College sucks."

John began his lecture about the Reformation, Europe's

religious rebellion against the papacy. Five minutes later, Jorge hurried into the room, still sweating profusely. He sat down, shivered, winced, wriggled into a jacket he'd had tied around his waist, sighed loudly through his mouth, jumped up and left. He returned a minute later, arranged some papers and promptly nodded off. After another few minutes, his head jerked up, he looked around and left the room again. John ignored all this.

John talked about Martin Luther, John Calvin and the movement to separate church from state, gesturing as he did at vestry meetings. He shooed his points into the open, piled them up, patted them into shape and expanded them with widened arms. He looked like the absentminded professor. His striped tie was an afterthought, the shoulders of his blazer were white with chalk dust where he kept leaning back against the blackboard, the soles of his scuffed brown shoes were split, and he walked on the cuffs of his slacks as he paced before the class. "I'm a Protestant, just so you'll know that," he said. "I'm sticking with my own tribe here.

"Who was the enemy here? It starts with a *p*. The pope. You can say it out loud. I'm not going to turn you in."

John talked so enthusiastically that he occasionally would have to stop to catch his breath. He paced constantly, bringing his feet together in a left- or right-face turn as he changed directions.

"These ideas are important to us not as theologians, but as philosophers," he said. "Predestination. What does that mean? Does anybody know?"

A student said, "If you're rich, everybody in your family is supposed to be rich."

Jorge reappeared and flung himself into his chair. He popped a piece of candy into his mouth. Then he thrust a card in my direction. It advertised telephone sex lines.

John described Luther's concept of the priesthood of all believers. Now reverence filled his voice. "Wow! What a mouthful that is," he said. "What do you think the Roman Church thought about that? Each individual could have his own relationship with God. Wow! From that you had community participation. You had congregational hymn singing and things like that."

John was clearly a member of that priesthood. He was an evolved participant: a vestry member, organ player, a singer in the choir. John felt that the church deserved his attention, and he gave it.

He was about to assume yet another role at St. Mary's. Stelk had suggested it during the summer. The Stelks and the Harbesons were on an outing, a sailing cruise up the Hudson, focused on environmental issues. They'd been standing at the rail watching the green magnificence of the New Jersey Palisades slip by, when Stelk had said, "You ever think about becoming a lay reader?"

"I was ready to be asked," John said.

John Harbeson embraced the priesthood of all believers.

✢

By the late October weekend of the Harvest Fair, a construction worthy of Rube Goldberg sat atop St. Mary's. The roof around the bell tower was a phantasm of ascending platforms linked by ropes, as if a group of busy, treehouse-building kids had been at work.

John Sullivan, an affable young contractor, was the thing's architect. He was the sole bidder, whom Gerry Cousins had employed to fix the bell tower. Sullivan had been prowling his platforms five and six days a week, hammering, reinforcing and prying out old wood. The Wednesday morning congregations could hear him scuffling on the roof.

Sullivan had discovered that the bell tower was several inches out of plumb. The timbers supporting the bell's cast-iron frame had rotted nearly through. The tower was sprung at the seams where its old iron nails had lost their holding power.

"Tell you the truth, they called me just in time," he told me.

Roadside signs and balloons advertised the Harvest Fair on

the appointed Saturday. The weather was decent, and when I arrived in late morning the parking lot was modestly full. I ran into Bill Miller, pushing Caryl in her wheelchair. They were just leaving. Bill said he had to take Justin shopping for the trip to Lourdes. A respectable number of customers were browsing among the tables full of schlock and bargains inside the parish hall. St. Mary's had turned out its attics and garages for the Harvest Fair.

Gerry and Diane Cousins stood proudly behind a table stacked high with sports souvenirs. Gerry had been canvassing professional teams for months, begging donations. He'd written the Chicago Cubs and told them St. Mary's rector was a lifelong Cubs fan who prayed for their return to the World Series. The Cubs, who had not been to a series since 1945, had been lavish in return, sending souvenir batting gloves, wristbands and the stocking cap Gerry was wearing as part of the display. The Yankees, the Mets and the New York Giants also had sent donations. Some sharp-eyed kids were pawing through boxes full of baseball cards.

A few tables and chairs were set up like a small café near the entrance to the kitchen. Hand-lettered signs advertised coffee, soft drinks, soup, hot dogs and sandwiches. Ann Marwick and Ginny were waiting tables. John and Vincent from Mohegan Manor occupied a table near the wall, where they would be the first to see any new treat emerging from the kitchen.

Marsha McCoy, a tall, attractive divorcée who was one of the church school teachers, was selling plants at a table next to the choir soprano Melanie Bussel, who was selling samples of home cooking. The samples were fifty cents apiece, but if you liked what you tasted, the recipe was free—a bargain. "You've got to try this. It's mine," Melanie said, offering me a square of her flaky spinach pie with feta cheese. It was delicious. There were tables for games, tables for books, tables for brownies and other cookies, tables for T-shirts and tables for the discards of dozens of households. You could chart the growth of families, from rocking horses and books of nursery rhymes, through toy cars and Barbie dolls, to hockey sticks and roller skates. You could see the sweep of new technology in heavy outsized radios, boxy cameras and vinyl LP records. Electric crock pots and waffle irons testified to the rise of the microwave oven.

Alice Marwick was trying very hard to sell a very ugly ashtray. She said it was a point of pride. "If I can sell this, sales is my future," she announced with a pert smile. Alice had entered the ninth grade at Lakeland High School. She played in the band and had joined the debate team. She said her schedule was "like, really demanding." Cynthia Bondi, her fellow candidate for the Mature Profession of Faith, still worked after school. Alice said it had been "totally impossible" so far for them to meet with Stelk.

John Donovan poked among the tables. He was less than a month from his triple bypass and moved gingerly. "I'm bored with staying home," he said, and felt his shirt pocket for a cigarette before remembering that he didn't smoke anymore.

Lily and Harold Van Horne arrived with their daughter, Joan Ruedi, groped for chairs and sat down to watch the goings-on. Harold said he was just getting out again following his pacemaker implant. He looked a little shaky.

By late afternoon, record albums dropped from twenty-five cents apiece to five for a quarter. Or you could just take them if you wanted to. I took—at full price—an album called *Thrillers and Chillers,* on the Troll label, thinking the narrated stories like "The Tell-Tale Heart" might come in handy over Halloween. Prices were slashed at the book table, too, and I succumbed to a few titles. It was impossible not to buy the Polaroid camera for a dollar, or the Nerf Ping-Pong game that you could set up on the dining room table, for two dollars. Then Frank Doyle rummaged in a straw wastebasket and pulled out the names of lucky raffle winners. The grand prize was a large basketful of wine and liquor.

Stelk canceled church school the next day to leave the tables up. "Fantastic bargains are still available," he announced. "But this is definitely a going-out-of-business sale."

When the proceeds were counted, St. Mary's had another $2,365 toward the bell tower repair and was only $4,000 short.

+

Stelk had barely announced that Harold Van Horne was well enough to be taken off the prayer list and offered thanks for his recovery from his pacemaker implant when Harold nearly collapsed in the middle of the service. Gerry Cousins was the first to notice. It was a folk mass Sunday. Gerry was facing the congregation, playing accompaniments on his guitar, when he stopped abruptly and stood up. He walked to Harold and leaned over him. The congregation held its breath.

"Is everything alright?" Stelk asked.

"He's dizzy," Gerry said.

Harold waved a hand to show he was okay, but he didn't look it. Stelk said, "Would you like to go back and lie down?"

Harold nodded weakly, and Gerry helped him through the door leading to the sacristy. Lily followed. The door closed behind them.

The congregation's concern was palpable. I could see that everyone was keeping an eye on the sacristy door. We seemed to be willing Harold to come through it wearing his familiar smile, or at least hoping that someone would send word. The door stayed closed. Bill Miller and his neighbor Barry Tucker, the day's ushers, took up the collection. They were presenting the plates to Stelk when one of the acolytes entered from the sacristy, leaned close to Stelk and whispered.

Stelk broke into a smile. "You'll be happy to know that Harold is okay," he said. "He's sitting up back there. He just needed to get out of the atmosphere here, the excitement. But he's doing fine. That makes me feel good. I know it makes us all feel good."

He spoke the familiar offertory words, "All things come of thee, O Lord."

The congregation responded with more emotion than usual after the collection. "And of thine own have we given thee."

Stelk served Communion at the altar rail and then disappeared into the sacristy to take the Sacraments to the Van

Hornes. Gerry strummed his guitar and the choir sang the anthem "The Lord Is Present in His Sanctuary."

Harold was a little grumpy afterwards. He was embarrassed about his near-collapse and the solicitousness afterward. "I don't know what happened to me in there," he said. "But something did."

11

Caryl and Justin Miller were booked on an overnight flight to Paris that would begin Caryl's pilgrimage to Lourdes. Bill got them to Newark Airport with an hour to spare on Monday evening. When they got their bags checked in, the Millers headed for the Air France departure gate with Steve Ziniti and his family.

Justin came down the concourse looking determinedly cool, as if he were headed to the shopping mall instead of France. He carried a skateboard under one arm and a backpack on his back. He wore jeans, a purple sweatshirt and a black corduroy baseball cap. He had left behind, as if they were strangers, Caryl in a wheelchair pushed by a skycap, and Bill, walking beside her. I asked Justin if he was going to skate on the Champs Elysées.

"What's that?" he said.

"It's like the Main Street of Paris. Like Fifth Avenue," his father said.

"I'm gonna skate under the Eiffel Tower," Justin said.

Caryl was wearing a sweatsuit. A crocheted blanket lay folded across her lap. Steve, who was tall and cheerful, was also wearing cotton sweats. A floppy cotton hat obscured most of his baldness, but you could see that his eyebrows were hairless arcs of bone. The Millers and Zinitis—Steve and his wife Phyllis had three children—had been friends for a long time; Steve was Justin's godfather.

The families grouped in the departure lounge. Justin stood his skateboard against his mother's knee. Caryl said she was nervous about the flight. She looked drained and spooky, but then she got a sly little smile and beckoned me close. She whispered that she found an old wig, a red one, while she was packing. "I threw it in my suitcase," she confided. "So Steve can come back with hair."

The lounge was crowded. Bill gave Justin elaborate instructions for phoning him. Caryl was called first to board. An attendant wheeled her toward the gate before Bill had a chance to say goodbye. He ran after the wheelchair and hugged and kissed Caryl all at once while the other passengers bunched behind them, waiting. Finally, he gripped her arm and kissed her again, whispered something, and then she, Justin and Steve were gone down the jetway.

Bill waited at the window until the plane had taxied out of sight. Then we found a table in a nearby lounge, ordered a round of beers, and Bill talked about his life with Caryl.

+

They met in 1969, when he was working as a property liquidator at Manufacturers Hanover Trust and she was his secretary. He was ending a bad marriage, and she was engaged. "Caryl was my friend," he said. "I would tell her about the girls I was dating."

Soon they were dating one another. Caryl broke off her engagement. Her strict Catholic parents were furious. She removed her clothing from their house a little at a time. When she had the clothes she wanted, she and Bill quit their jobs and took off across the country. They went to the Woodstock festival that August of 1969. At the end of the summer, when they had to go back to work, they returned to the city and moved in together.

It was a carefree time. They lived in Parkchester, in the Bronx. Caryl liked to fly to Florida for weekends in the sun with a group of girlfriends. Bill was a homebody, happy to stay behind.

"I remembered that when I woke up this morning," he said, sipping his beer. "I leave for work before they wake up, so I leave notes. This morning I wrote her that today was like the old days. 'You're taking off and I'm staying home. Then it didn't faze me. We both were having a good time. This time my prayers and my heart and my love go with you.' "

Bill said he'd try anything to cure Caryl, as long as it wasn't harmful. Lourdes was mainstream medicine compared to some of the so-called cures. He described a friend of Caryl's father praying over her in "a shamanistic ritual" that lasted four or five days. "They'd go into a trance, and they said they contacted and spoke with spirits. They said Caryl had evil spirits.

"They didn't get them out."

The lounge emptied as the last of overnight flights to Europe were called. The barmaid leaned on the counter, watching television, now and then casting a bored glance in our direction. I went to the bar and brought back another round. Bill talked, quietly and unashamedly, of his hopes and fears for his family.

"We need her now," he said. "She's a special person. She's never argued with a person in her life. Except me. It takes a lot for her to argue with me. I told her in the note this morning, everyone needs her."

Bill's face was haggard. It mirrored his fears, and now his brow furrowed in a question. He wondered if by urging her to stay on at her job he had somehow contributed to her illness. "Lou Gehrig was easygoing like that," he said. "When Caryl became a boss, she became a person she wasn't, having to manage people, fire people. She kept saying, 'I want to leave.' I said, 'Stay through Christmas.' She left, but she left a physical wreck."

"It's got to be a worse disease than having pain," he said. "At least you can do something for the pain."

Bill pinched the bridge of his nose for a long moment. "Just a headache," he said. "It'll pass. I don't get headaches."

"What do you pray for when you go to church?" I asked.

"I pray for my friends to remain healthy and well," he said. "With special attention to Caryl and Justin. Once in a while for myself. That I'm able to do all of these things, making sure everything goes all right with Caryl and Justin, that we can get through these hardships."

He looked away for a long moment, appearing to gather himself. A janitor appeared and began running a vacuum cleaner over the carpet outside the lounge.

"I still don't know if I have the resources to deal with this," he said. "I wonder what I'll do afterwards. That bothers me. Sometimes I feel lost. We go to an ALS support group once a month. I wonder what I'll do when she can't talk. When she can't eat. That will happen. They tell me.

"Caryl thinks she'll die. I believe that will happen, too. I haven't given up all hope, but I have in my mind that it could happen. My thoughts are on what will happen then. With Justin. It's hard without a mother."

Of the trip to Lourdes, he said, "I hope to see her come back and have a little more hope for herself. To reach into herself and pull something out. Your brain is the key, and that comes with faith." About Justin, he said, "I hope he has a little more concern. And can understand more about his mother. Not be ashamed. He's ashamed to be near the wheelchair. Hopefully, he'll come back pushing it.

"But, you know, I cope like Justin in a certain way. I don't ignore it, but I try to keep it in a certain section of my mind. Sometimes it comes out and I can't put it back. Sometimes when I'm driving and listening to music, I cry. When I leave here tonight, I might cry."

The departure gates were dark. As we left we heard the barmaid pulling the grate down over the entrance to the lounge. We walked slowly back along the long concourse with its moving sidewalks to the main part of Newark's Terminal B. Bill had left his car at curbside check-in, amid a forest of PASSENGER UNLOADING ONLY signs. It had been two hours, and now he wondered if he might have gotten towed. But the car, unticketed, was right where he had left it.

+

Stelk thought the trip to Lourdes was ridiculous. Medically, it was an act of desperation, like a cancer victim's seeking a miracle cure in some exotic clinic. Spiritually, Stelk begged neutrality. I asked him how a pilgrimage to Lourdes was different from the Lenten healing services. He said, "You don't have to go to Lourdes, for one thing. I don't encourage it for the same reason I don't encourage people to go to Jerusalem. You don't have to go anywhere except wherever church is."

He gave the impression that he placed the trip in a category with Cursillo. As some Cursillistas found expression in what Dwight Douglas had called "the hallelujah stuff," victims found hope at the French shrine. Stelk believed that expression and hope, indeed, everything that religion in all its forms could offer, could be found in the established Liturgy. That was why he looked askance at Caryl's journey.

But, he added, "I hope it works."

Stelk had not mentioned her trip at Sunday's service, and when we talked on Monday night, Bill had wondered why. "I was a little surprised," he said. "It's supposed to help if you arrive accompanied by prayers."

The party was scheduled to reach Lourdes on Wednesday on a charter flight after a night in Paris. That morning at St. Mary's midweek service, when all the names on the prayer list were recited, Stelk said, "I bid your prayers in particular this morning for Caryl Miller, who is in Lourdes this day seeking healing."

And as he prepared the bread and wine for the Communion, he offered the Eucharist for Caryl and her healing.

The pilgrims returned one week after they had left. It was a brilliant fall day. The distant skyline of Manhattan was visible through the big windows of the airport concourse when the Air France 747 taxied into view.

Waiting outside Immigration and Customs, Bill suddenly said, "It would be nice if she just ran right out." He paused for a moment, looking at the doors. "Or even walked out."

Justin emerged first. He was pushing a wheelchair, but it

was empty except for his skateboard, balanced across the arms. Steve came behind, pushing Caryl.

Bill hugged Justin and kissed Caryl as the other passengers parted to pass around them. Caryl looked haggard, pale and oddly dejected. She said she felt sick after the long flight. She whispered that Justin "learned a lot. About faith."

I asked Justin what he thought. He said, "It was the most boring trip I've been on in my life." He didn't like Lourdes, he didn't like the hotel where they stayed, he didn't like the food, he missed his friends, all the television programs were in French, and nobody took the trouble to speak English for him. Poor Justin had had to push his skateboard two miles to another town just to get a candy bar.

When they reached the curb, Justin jumped immediately into the backseat of Bill's Bronco, leaving Bill to maneuver Caryl into the car. Steve had to help to lift her into the front seat. Caryl sagged and put her head back. Steve rifled his luggage for a plastic jug of water from Lourdes and a book, *The Miracle of Lourdes,* which he handed to Bill.

"My face," Caryl said.

"Your face, your face." Steve found Caryl's makeup in the jumble of luggage and handed it into the car. She waved weakly as they drove away.

+

October's vestry meeting lasted just ninety minutes. Gerry Cousins dominated the agenda with his report on all the work he was having done on the parish buildings: the church windows, the rectory roof, the parish hall floor. And, of course, the bell tower. When it was time for John Harbeson's report on the vestry's new portfolio functions, everybody wanted to go home.

"I'd like some time to digest this," Stelk said, glancing at the sheaf of papers John was handing around the table.

"It would just be a quick overview," John said.

"A quick overview?" Stelk seemed to doubt the possibility.

"That's what I offered."

"That's not what I heard. I heard, 'Walk you through it.' That's not a quick overview."

While John fumed, the members tucked his report into their briefcases and folders and Stelk moved to the next agenda item.

John's capacity to take on the details of governance, while insisting they reflect his principles, I sometimes found amazing. Two days after I sat in on his modern political philosophy class at CCNY, I had rejoined him on the campus for a debate in the Faculty Senate. "You're kind to show up for John's crucifixion," Bernie Sohmer, a bearded, barrel-chested man in tweeds said as he welcomed me.

Sohmer was the senate's chairman. The "crucifixion" to which he referred was John's role in an academic brouhaha that dated to the beginning of the year. A CCNY professor, Michael Levin, set off the furor by writing articles contending blacks are intellectually inferior to whites. He'd also railed against feminists and homosexuals. Though Levin had never stated these opinions in his classes, the dean of arts and sciences had warned Levin's undergraduate philosophy students, in a letter, of his "controversial views on such issues as race, feminism and homosexuality." The letter announced the start of another philosophy class, in case students wanted to transfer. The administration said it wanted to head off campus protests over Levin. John chaired the senate's Academic Freedom and Faculty Interest Committee. He was not alone in considering this an assault on Levin's academic freedom.

It was another case of sacred principle. John preferred student protests against Levin to muting the professor's views. " 'Popularity is not required,' " he said, drawing from John Stuart Mill and Justice Oliver Wendell Holmes. " 'Only in the marketplace of ideas can truth emerge.'

"The students are smart enough to make up their own minds. The administration doesn't have to do it for them."

Other senators argued that academic freedom required order on the campus; otherwise, they said, they couldn't teach.

But John, in the end, had won the day. His resolution deploring the administration's interference in students' course selections was adopted with few changes.

It was the kind of debate John relished: finely nuanced, skillfully argued and altogether academic. It shed a light on his vestry performances, showing him impervious to sentiment and committed to ploughing through issues, no matter how exhaustive the discussion.

The vestry meeting adjourned at 9:35 P.M., a record for the year. John would have preferred it go on longer. "We've got half an hour to go over the junior warden's report nail by nail," he complained afterwards, "but we don't have fifteen minutes to go over the most important thing we've done all year."

✛

The unspoken consensus of the vestry was that talking about expansion, for the moment, was a waste of time. Gasoline prices had continued to climb, the winter heating season was beginning, American and other troops of a coalition allied against Iraq were massed around Kuwait, unemployment was up and housing prices were down. The worst news had been the report of the appraisal on the Baynard house, the gift horse that the vestry kept looking in the mouth. The house in Somers was valued at $134,000. With the outstanding mortgage, St. Mary's could expect to net much less than half of that.

"It doesn't add up to much," said Stelk.

We had just returned from Peekskill Hospital, where the vestry secretary, Frances Armstrong, was in bed following a heart attack. It had happened the day after the meeting. Now, just a day removed from the attack, Frances had recovered enough to give Stelk a list of things to do after he said prayers of healing and anointed her with chrism.

"I don't know if we're going to be able to do the expansion or not," he said. The church secretary was off, and Stelk was doing some high-energy bustling around the office. He completed a set of diocesan forms, then dashed into the church office to address an envelope. The typewriter kept beeping at his margin errors. Stelk wouldn't use the word processing program on the church computer. "It's your age, it's not mine," he said. "I'm going to finish my age and die and that'll be that. Don't talk to me about computers."

To Stelk, computers threatened the technological tyranny George Orwell foresaw in *1984*. He worried about things like automated teller cards and Social Security numbers becoming a universal identification code. "I'm old-fashioned," he said. "I'm so afraid of Big Brother."

The appointment book in his shirt pocket was spilling over with notes and business cards. He riffled through them, looking for a misplaced card, and continued to talk about the parish hall expansion. "If we have to put it off, I'll be disappointed because I think it's needed. But it may be one of the realities of life."

He spread the stuffings of the appointment book out on the surface of the conference table and found the card he was looking for. It was a lawyer's, and he picked up the phone and dialed a number. After a pause someone answered, and he said, "Any word from Mr. Lee on the contract? I don't mean to bug you, but I've been out all day . . ."

He listened, frowning. "Well, keep trying," he said, and hung up the phone.

His offer on the Lake Mahopac cottage still was hanging. The owner had accepted the offer but continued to balk at making repairs. He hadn't returned an executed contract. Meanwhile, Stelk had tenants ready to move in, a young family who were members of the parish and needed a reasonably priced rental. The waiting was making Stelk crazy.

"It's this area that's just ridiculous," he said after a long moment of staring at the phone in its cradle. "The prices are so much higher. The problem still is finding a place we can afford."

The Stelks had set $170,000 as the upper limit of their housing budget. That would have bought a handsome house in many areas of the country. "Try to find something for that here," he snorted. "If this deal falls through, Ginny and I may not look in this area anymore. If we can't afford it, we just can't afford it."

Stelk reassembled the jumble of cards and notes, folded them into his appointment book, returned it to his pocket and looked at his watch. He was meeting Ginny for an early supper before the night class she taught on Thursdays. Her students were recent immigrants learning English as a second language.

I had learned that Stelk's clerical forbearance abandoned him whenever he got behind the wheel. His impatience as we zoomed toward Yorktown Heights was emerging as routine. He let his frustrations show like many drivers. Turning into an area of shops and offices, he brusquely waved on a hesitant driver turning from the opposite direction. "Go on! What are you waiting for? Go on!

"People from this area do not know how to drive," he said.

"Only people where you're from know how to drive," I said. "That's an observed truth. Like Murphy's Law."

"People from this area are worse," he said. "I mean it. They just don't pay attention."

He parked in front of Huckleberry's restaurant and we went inside. It was a woody, ferny place with a few customers finishing late lunches and a few more getting started on the cocktail hour. It was a little after five. Busboys were setting up the salad bar, and the waitresses were changing shifts. Stelk ordered rusty nails for himself and Ginny. I ordered wine.

Sipping at his drink, Stelk talked about the seemingly moribund expansion. He blamed a fear of recession. "People are expressing more qualms to me," he said. But he wasn't giving up.

"If we can't expand, we'll have to take a good look at the space we have now and how it's utilized," he said. "Maybe what it means is just scaling back the degree of expansion."

I asked how he felt about the sentiment in the vestry to ease his administrative burdens to free time for pastoral work.

Stelk pushed his drink around in little circles. He said, "There's no way in which the pastor of a parish can avoid administrative duties. You never get out of it. It's just the degree to which you allow it to consume you."

He suggested some pastoral duties could be assumed by lay people. "Other parishes have this," he said. "A lay pastoral calling committee. They could visit nursing homes or call on people who were sick. Lay ministers couldn't celebrate Communion. But they could take the Sacraments from the communion service in the church and administer them to the homebound. It's allowed under what we call the total celebration of the congregation."

Stelk paused and added, with a wry expression, "I say all this knowing full well that people want the pastor and not anybody else."

He didn't want the administrative assistant John Harbeson insisted that he needed. "He hasn't heard yet that I don't want that," Stelk bridled. "I've told him, but he hasn't heard."

Stelk looked at his watch and scanned the entrance. "She's late," he said. He paused and sighed. "I've been at this business for twenty-five years," he said. "It's hard to give up things you're used to doing. You've got to nurse me through some of this stuff. But there's administration and there's administration. I cannot give up oversight. In smaller parishes, I've written the newsletter. And when I've given it up, I've had to get it back. Some of the stuff that went out was heretical." He drew himself up, indignant. "I have the responsibility in terms of communication. Ten percent [of the congregation] never hear what you're saying, but ninety percent need to have the information."

Ginny appeared in the doorway, and he paused. A smile of relief crossed his face, then a frown of concern. Ginny was limping as she came down the entrance steps and across the floor to the booth where we were sitting. Stelk said it was a bone spur on her heel. "I'm worried about her," he said. "This thing better clear up soon."

"If I had a pair of crutches, I'd use them," Ginny said, easing into the booth with a grimace and taking a sip of the rusty nail Stelk had ordered. "I hope it's okay by the wedding." She looked at Stelk fondly. "How are you?"

They talked, as couples do who share each other's triumphs and frustrations, about the day they'd had. There was a fondness in the conversation that made it clear they loved each other. Stelk said he'd made a shopping find that afternoon. He'd been to Thom McAn, the shoe store, anxious to replace the black soft-soled lace-ups he wore with his clericals. The old ones were coming apart. A salesman told him that a sale was about to start. "Two pairs for seventy-nine dollars," Stelk said with animation. "He said it starts tomorrow, but he'd give me the price today. So I bought two pairs. Black and brown."

Ginny hugged him. "Just in time, too. We need to start thinking about a new suit," she said. She took one of his lapels and held his jacket open, fingered the frayed inside pocket.

"This one will hold out a little longer," Stelk said.

Ginny said Kirsten's approaching wedding had produced a series of adventures. Ginny had taken a train to Grand Central the previous Saturday and walked—limped—across town in a driving rain to meet Kirsten at a garment district bridal shop, where they found that the gowns Kirsten had ordered were a disaster. The hems were uneven, and it was clear that Sara's dress had been taken in rather than let out. The dresses were unusable. The recriminations, which included shouting, threats and, eventually, a lawsuit, fell upon the dressmaker. Kirsten and Ginny were left to choose other dresses and send them out to the members of the wedding to arrange for alterations on their own. "I hope they all can get them done in time," she said. The wedding was set for the Saturday after Thanksgiving.

Ginny related all this between bites of her meal. She downed a cup of coffee quickly, then left to teach her night class. Stelk watched, frowning with worry, as she walked with difficulty toward the door.

✣

All Saints' Day featured two baptisms, an appeal by Stelk to vote in Tuesday's elections and an appearance by Dwight and Ann Douglas, who sat in their usual spot near the front on the right. They hadn't made final their decision to switch parishes.

"All of those who are saints, please stand up," Stelk began his sermon.

The congregation laughed nervously. No one stood.

"You are all wrong," said Stelk. "You should all have stood. For we are all saints of God. We are that through our baptism.

"And we this day will baptize two children, who have no way of knowing what is happening to them, but who will be saints of God equally with the rest of us children . . . saints as imperfect as any of us can be, saints nevertheless, saints beloved, sustained and redeemed."

"Voting," he said when he got to the announcements, "is too rich a heritage to allow to go by the boards. Too many people have given their lives for the privilege. If we don't participate in the process, we may not have a process."

Walt Decker, who was trying to project the parish budget for next year, watched the baptisms with interest. Parents and godparents usually were generous on baptism day. The sense of celebration Stelk conveyed not only meant higher plate offerings, but a strong identification with St. Mary's. Walt was the vestry's finance chairman and would be leading the pledge campaign for 1991. He meant to convert those warm feelings into higher pledges.

Stelk already had announced, in the November newsletter, that St. Mary's would be more strenuous in its pledge campaign this year. The low-key canvass of past years would not be repeated. He wrote, "The times, they are a-changing in respect to our needs. We have discovered this year many maintenance problems, which will cost a substantial amount of money to repair, and which must be repaired now before costs go higher and the problems get worse." He added, "A growing congregation means growing expenditures for growing activities."

"Respond with the thanksgiving of God in your hearts and in your checkbooks."

He said nothing about parish hall expansion.

✢

The finance committee met early in November to solidify the pledge campaign. Next year's budget had to cope with rising costs in almost every area. Medical insurance costs were going up. The bell tower repairs had to be paid off. St. Mary's needed new vestments and new hangings. Stelk said new prayer books were needed, too. "The centers of some of them are falling out," he said. Nobody knew what would happen to the cost of heating oil. A postage increase was expected. Stelk would have to have a raise, according to new salary guidelines from the diocese. Even before the cost of the repairs Gerry Cousins had identified, St. Mary's faced a deficit.

Nobody thought the committee should mention parish hall expansion when it wrote the congregation seeking next year's pledges.

"You notice we're not talking about it," said Kathy Munroe, emphatically. "Well, neither is anybody else. All you hear on TV is how all the retailers are saying it's going to be a terrible Christmas season because people are going to hang onto their money and buckle down. People are getting hit really hard. What we need as a parish is to maintain and keep going."

Stelk's shirt pockets sagged with his omnipresent datebook and the case that held his reading glasses. He'd already started filling a new datebook, making appointments into 1991. He put his glasses on and took them off again. "Well, right now we have a number of immediate problems. As usual."

"Like the stucco?" asked Kathy.

Stelk paused with his glasses in his hand, halfway to his face. "How do you know about the stucco?"

"From Gerry."

Gerry had reported in September that sealing the stucco exterior of the main church building to keep the moisture out would cost $6,000. The sealer would last three years at best. What was really needed, professional engineer Joe Bierwirth had told Gerry, back in the summer as he went around tapping at the church walls with a nail set and nodding his head when he heard a hollow spot where the stucco had separated from the masonry beneath, was a more permanent repair. He suggested stripping and patching all the hollow places, adding an inch of insulation that the church had never had and adding new stucco over it. That, according to the people at Garden State Brickface & Stucco, whom Gerry had invited to provide an estimate, would cost $60,000.

"We're talking about megabucks here," said Stelk.

"We can't raise that kind of money," Kathy said. "We'll have to either mortgage it or finance it."

Walt laughed and said that the budget would be ten thousand dollars short without funding any building repairs. "With them it's sixteen or seventeen thousand. I don't see where we can get it other than pledges. We have to do more on stewardship this year and tie it to some of these needs and do a hard sell. We have to be more aggressive.

"We're projecting pretty well on plate offerings," he mused. "If we could project the baptisms . . ."

"If it's a cold winter, we should have some baptisms next October," Karin Efman said.

Stelk launched a dreamy digression. He sounded like a solicitor on a public television pledge break. He seemed to be struggling with how to ask the congregation to price the sustenance of souls, to place a value on the comfort of prayer, the relief of surrender, the uplifting of communal worship. "Think about the functions the church fulfills," he said. "We're a point at which people can come and cry together over the crises of their lives. That's part of what we do in the worship. It's part of what we do as a parish family. That's an important thing. You can't price it. We do have something to offer. We're an ongoing place in which some of the basic questions of life . . . life and death . . . the meaning of that . . ."

Kathy said, "You go to the pizza place once a week and spend twenty-five dollars. Look how much more you're getting from the church."

Stelk picked up the thought. "We could suggest spending as much on church as they spend on scotch for the week."

Kathy said, "You might want to say beer to this congregation."

Recent events, which some people chose to call trends, Stelk said he found encouraging. "There is a return to institutional religion," he said. "There's less of the 'everything goes' and the 'me greed' approach that we've seen in the recent past. The other thing, I read that people are beginning to give more to individual charities that they identify with."

+

The bell tower was starting to look new. Amid the tiers of scaffolding levitated onto the church roof, it glinted with new siding. Bright copper flashing shone around its base. John Sullivan, the contractor, was almost finished with his work.

Early on a Wednesday morning, the first ice was on the roads, but a blistering cold wind had dropped, permitting Sullivan back on the roof for the first time in three days. He was squatting like a monkey on a piece of scaffolding as a few worshipers gathered for the midweek service. I waved, and he yelled down a greeting.

You could hear Sullivan's thump-clump on the roof during the informal service. Stelk talked about the first Episcopal bishop in the United States. Ann Marwick, the morning's lay reader, read through the prayer list. Richie Efman, wearing an Oswego sweatshirt, threw his arms open to embrace everybody when the Peace was said and added a cheerful, "Praise the Lord!" Eugene slept heavily, breathing in whispery snores, until Stelk delivered Communion to the people.

Sullivan had fashioned a mountain goat's route to the roof. He parked his pickup truck close to the church on the rectory side. Then he lengthened an extension ladder and braced it in the truck bed. The ladder lay flat against the steep church roof, leading to a set of wooden chocks Sullivan had nailed against the roof tiles. A yellow rope dangled from the bell tower to the lowest of the chocks.

"Climb on up," he called. "Hang onto the rope when you get past the ladder."

Sullivan hadn't wasted any lumber on the chocks, I noticed, as I stretched a long, high step from one to the next. The nylon rope was comforting to hold. The uppermost platform, a slab of plywood, lay across the roof peak thirty feet above the ground. There was a nice view from the rooftop. The surrounding hillsides had faded from the reds and golds of fall into winter buff. Sullivan's cheeks were flushed with cold. A St. Christopher medal dangled outside his army green jacket, and a pouch on his carpenter's belt sagged with galvanized roofing nails. He started speaking proudly of the bell, as if it were his own.

"It's a heavy thing, bronze. I was told it weighs four or five hundred pounds. That's what Gerry Cousins said. It's twenty-four inches in diameter and an inch-and-a-half thick on the bottom. No telling what would have happened if they'd kept ringing it. The whole thing could have come down. Can you imagine if that thing fell into the church? But it wouldn't. It would have gotten stuck," he said.

"Look, it was cast with the name: 'St. Mary's Church, Lake Mohegan.' Over here it has a date." He pointed to a foundry casing: "The. Jones & Co., Troy Bell Foundry, Troy, N.Y., 1874."

"Now I've heard the tower wasn't here when the church was built," Sullivan said. "That's what I heard."

St. Mary's history was unclear. The church was completed in 1872. If the date on the bell was any indication, the tower was added two years later. It appears in a photograph taken around 1885, the same picture that shows the church walls covered with Sir Walter Scott's ivy. No earlier photographs exist. The tower's proportions certainly were part of the church whole.

Sullivan showed me the cast-iron wheel that swung the bell when the rope was pulled, setting the clapper ringing against the bronze bell wall. He'd attached a new synthetic bell rope, which he'd led through existing holes into the back of the nave. He'd made a copper rain shield, slotted where the rope led downward from the wheel, but he said he still was worried about rainwater descending the rope. "I'm going to try some surgical tubing," he said. "Somebody told me that if you tie surgical tubing around the rope, tight, the water will follow the tubing and just drip off of it and the water won't get below the tubing. I don't know. I guess it could work."

The new braces for the bell frame were four-by-fours of treated fir, doubled one on top of another and bolted together to bear the bell's weight. It was this frame that had nearly rotted through. Sullivan said he'd also shored up the whole tower from its slump in the direction of the altar.

"I could only move it two inches," he said. "It was leaning three-and-a-half, but that was all she'd go. Then I went around and shimmed it here and there. They used iron nails on this thing when it was built. They lost their holding power over the years. I had to go through and renail the whole tower with galvanized nails."

The vinyl siding seemed to fit on the tower—both its outside and open inner walls—like a loose glove. It was made to resemble clapboard siding, and there was some flex at the corners. The faux clapboards and the brilliant white of the new vinyl didn't quite fit with the stucco of the church, but the visual separation of the roof softened the contrast, and time would dull the vinyl's shine. The copper gleamed. "It'll last, too," Sullivan said.

All Sullivan had left to do, he said, was repair the housing of the wheel shaft. The shaft had worn a rut in the housing over nearly one hundred and twenty years of bell ringing. He planned to insert a sleeve of polyvinyl chloride pipe. The plastic would last longer than the iron original. It probably would last longer than the church.

When I was ready to climb down, the descent from the roof looked like a straight drop. I asked Sullivan the angle. "It's twelve and twelve," he said. "Twelve inches up and twelve inches across, give or take. Almost a perfect forty-five degrees."

"Any tips for getting down?"

He grinned. "Hang onto the rope."

A day later the rope and the scaffolding were gone. Sullivan, his work finished, had dismantled it and carried it away, leaving the refurbished bell tower alone and spanking proud astride the roof. The vestry was left to figure out how to pay the remainder of Sullivan's bill.

12

Justin Miller let himself be coaxed to church after he returned from Lourdes. For two Sundays in a row, the thirteen-year-old went to church school and hung out with the other young teenagers like David Marwick and Adam Decker, Walt's son. They would come into the church after the offering and sit in back, whispering behind their hands and giggling.

Bill, meanwhile, felt increasing stress from Caryl's illness.

He rubbed an eye and then his temples. "These headaches," he said. "I never had headaches before."

It was an early November afternoon. I had arrived to find the Millers' house still decorated for Halloween. A cardboard Dracula pinned to the front door wore a button that said, "Give blood." Bill had answered the door with a bottle of pills in one hand. He said he'd gone to the office infirmary at American Express one day with an unusually sharp headache. The nurse took his blood pressure. It was 180 over 100. He was suffering panic and anxiety attacks. American Express put Bill on indefinite medical leave at three-quarters pay.

We sat down on the sofa. The living room TV was playing in the background. There was a lot of gunfire. Rod Steiger was playing Al Capone. As the tommy guns rattled, Bill said Justin was still complaining that Lourdes had been boring. But at Lourdes, he had gone into the healing baths. He had told his godfather Steve Ziniti that he wanted to return as a *brancardier,* a volunteer, to help crippled pilgrims get in and out of the baths.

"If I had gone, Justin would have got nothing out of it," Bill said. He studied the label on the pill bottle, shook one out and took it.

He said he thought Justin was beginning to acknowledge his mother's illness. The boy had come into his parents' bedroom one night, as Caryl was trying to get comfortable in bed, and said, "You moved more quickly, Mom. Maybe you're getting better."

"He usually doesn't talk about it at all," Bill said. "Sometimes he talks to me when we're alone. Usually to say she's going to get better. He won't admit or recognize she might die. Once he said we'd name the cabin up in the woods after her."

The cabin was a dream of Bill's. He brought out a map to show me the five-acre shard of property he'd bought in the Adirondacks, near Glens Falls. He'd outlined it on the map in red. Next he showed me a flyer for a log house kit. It looked nice: three bedrooms, a porch on two sides, a large room for living and dining under a cathedral ceiling. Bill said he'd staked a driveway.

He rummaged some more and found some photographs. They were snapshots Bill, Caryl and Justin had taken of each other at the cabin site last winter. The scenes were clean and white, fresh, new, the smiles cheerful and full of expectation.

Caryl appeared at the head of the stairs. She had a new hairdo, tight curls that looked good on her. Rose, who had been helping her dress, turned her around and steered her onto the elevator chair. Caryl came down in a whine of machinery, clutched her walker and came across the living room.

"I'm a little slower every day," she said.

She reached her chair and turned slowly to lean against it. More machinery noise, and the chair brought her to a sitting position. Her forehead shone from exertion; her face was puffy, and she looked exhausted. Her voice was harder to understand than it had been before she left.

"I haven't been the same since I've been back," she said.

"It took a lot out of me physically. I was fine while I was there."

Bill went into the kitchen and came back with a mug of tea. He set it on the table next to Caryl's chair and asked, "How do you feel today?"

Caryl shook her head. "No energy."

I asked if she had found what she was looking for at Lourdes. Her face grew thoughtful. "I think so. A nice spiritual uplifting. It was sad to see all those people suffering. It makes your own problems seem smaller."

And the inner peace she had hoped to find?

Caryl made a face. "I still haven't gotten it where I want it. I'm looking for something that will make me feel more at ease with the situation. Not so depressed."

I asked her what the baths were like, and she described them as almost a revolving door. "Six ladies carried me into the pool, dunked me, said prayers, took me right out," she said. "They don't dry you off. They say you're not supposed to dry the waters off. Oddly enough, when you come out you feel warm. Maybe because the water is so cold. When they dunked me, I lost my breath."

She went into the baths four times. "You go in and you pray," she said. "But I gave it up twice." She meant that she had prayed for others, not herself. She prayed, she said, "for all the other people who were suffering." And she prayed for Bill, "that he would have the strength to deal with all this."

She chose to be cheered by Justin's behavior on the trip. "I don't think he'll ever forget it," she said. "It wasn't his normal vacation time. It was more like a retreat. He couldn't watch TV, so we had to rely on talking. Talking to each other, being with each other . . ." She looked wistful. "Being there among all those people showed him that there are a lot of other people around like me. I know a lot of times he's embarrassed by the wheelchair. He's told Bill that. But there he said he wasn't.

"I guess encountering the people from all different countries . . . All the selflessness, all the volunteers who come to help people. They do the most menial jobs, cleaning streets, helping people in and out of the baths. Justin said he wanted to do that, help people go into the baths, people in wheelchairs, people on stretchers."

Bill had waited for the tea to cool. Now he picked up the mug and held it to Caryl's mouth for her to drink. "It wasn't easy to get him there," Bill said. "He said, 'I don't believe anything that goes on there. I'll never go.' " Caryl added, "But while he was over there he was saying rosary prayers. He got into the spirit of what went on." She paused and smiled sadly. "I guess it didn't last long.

"Now that he's back home, he's back to normal."

That worried Caryl. She was worried more for Justin than herself, she said. She didn't feel he was coping with her illness well, was bottling up the turmoil it was causing him. "He hasn't really said how he feels inside," she said. "It's more about how he feels outside."

Caryl was finishing her account of the trip when the phone rang. The cordless phone lay on her lap. She groped at it, but she couldn't grasp it. Bill moved to her chair, picked up the phone and held it to her ear.

✣

Terry Donaghy, the church secretary, told me Stelk was at the post office, so I sat down to wait. Stelk enjoyed his daily errands. He liked being visible in the community, going about in his clericals, waving, stopping to talk when he had time, as familiar as a small-town mayor. Mohegan Lake wasn't a walking town. There really wasn't any town in the sense of a main street with sidewalks, a bank and a five-and-ten-cent store. The daily morning mail call at the post office was as close to a town square gathering as Mohegan Lake could offer.

I heard the door swing open and then Stelk hurrying up the stairs. He dropped the mail on his desk and said, "Come on." He collected the black case containing the Sacraments from the sacristy and rushed out again. We were headed for the Field Home.

Stelk drove with his usual impatience. The sun shone

through trees where a few tenacious leaves still clung. Suddenly some random snowflakes fell from a single heavy-bellied cloud, and Stelk switched the wipers on to brush them from the windshield. He still had the parish hall expansion on his mind. He said he'd met in Manhattan with officials of the Episcopal Church in the United States to inquire about low-interest loans. What he'd learned had not encouraged him.

"The Episcopal Church Building Fund will loan up to $100,000 for ten and three-quarters percent," he said sourly. "They've got plenty of information and support to offer, but they really are more into theoretical architecture than loaning money at this point."

The wisps of snow stopped falling as quickly as they had begun, and Stelk switched the wipers off. He said he thought the parish could afford to build a bigger parish hall, but was gripped by a climate of fear. "Expansion has as much to do with attitude as economics," he said.

Fourteen women waited in the Field Home's big salon. Feisty Sylvia Clarke, the chatty little Englishwoman, was absent. She'd been feeling poorly and was preparing to enter Peekskill Hospital for tests. The room missed her vitality. The other women sat there waiting, as quietly as bedding plants, for the service to begin.

Stelk prepared the Sacraments at his usual station in the hall, counting out wafers onto the silver tray and pouring wine from the Vita herring jar into the chalice. A gray-and-white cat surveyed him haughtily. Stelk got into his vestments, hung a wooden missionary cross around his neck and entered to begin the service.

His assistant and piano player, Jean Duff, was on vacation. "We'll sing a capella," he announced. "Hymns we all know." He opened a hymnal and began singing the first verse of "The Church's One Foundation."

Midweek services were devoted to obscure saints who were rarely mentioned otherwise. Stelk, who sometimes thought he would like to retire to England to study medieval English history, knew them all. Today's was St. Willibrord. "Willibrord was an apostle to the Low Countries," Stelk began his homily. "He did not get much success himself. He is not one of the great missionary figures. He laid the groundwork for somebody else. It's not unlike what goes on in most of our own lives." He spoke of the value of small contributions. The women did not seem to care about St. Willibrord.

One of the congregation, sitting in a wing chair, nodded off. She looked up and blinked when Stelk woke her to offer his hand in the Peace. "God's peace be with you always," he said. Stelk celebrated Communion, going around the room, first with the wafers and then the wine, and had to wake her again to offer the Sacraments.

Stelk had just led "Now Thank We All Our God" and made his formal exit when a large woman wearing a green suit with a bubble skirt swept into the room. She was carrying a table lamp. She stopped by the altar, peered into a corner of the room and narrowed her eyes. "What the hell do they do this for?" she exclaimed, and marched toward the offending corner.

Stelk returned in his clericals as the woman was turning a lamp shade's seam from view. He was followed by a workman wearing a white T-shirt and painter's pants and carrying a stepladder.

"Would you like us to move?" Stelk inquired politely.

"No, there's no need," the woman said brusquely. She barked some orders at the worker. He opened his ladder, set it up next to the altar in the middle of the room, climbed toward a chandelier and began replacing standard light bulbs with flame-shaped ornamental ones.

"Well, I think we'd better . . ." Stelk said.

"No, no, no. Not necessary," the woman in the suit interrupted. She took the white altar cloth from the table and began to fold it.

Stelk got up. His face was red. "We'll let the work proceed," he said. "I hope we'll have more time together next time." The woman glanced at him and kept folding the altar cloth. Stelk walked out, leaving the residents in their chairs quietly watching the new attraction.

Stelk stopped to visit Sylvia Clarke in her room. When he came outside he was in a funk. "That was really uncalled for," he complained. He stopped at Peekskill Hospital to look in on Frances Armstrong, the vestry secretary, still recovering from her heart attack. We entered her room to find Frances in a state of high dudgeon. Her untouched lunch tray was pushed off to one side. "Roast beef!" she said. "I'm on a low-cholesterol diet. I don't know what they're thinking." Frances, who was seventy-one, had started paying attention to her hair again.

Stelk held her hand and prayed for her recovery. Leaving the hospital, he said, "She seems to be coming along fine."

He slipped back into his funk as we drove toward St. Mary's. He said his house hunting had taken a bad turn.

"We've withdrawn our offer on the Lake Mahopac house," he said. "The owner was just . . . It was outrageous what he wanted. He wanted us to pay him to keep the house off the market while he took his sweet time with repairs. We just said, 'Enough.' "

The deal's collapse not only left the Stelks without the retirement house they wanted, it left the parish family they had planned to rent to without a place to live.

"We're rethinking whether to buy something here at all," Stelk said gloomily. "Ginny and I are going to take a while to decide whether we even ought to continue to look. We'll probably return to central Ohio if we move out of this area."

They had come to Mohegan Lake partly for its proximity to New York City, but Ohio's charms were growing in retrospect. "Columbus has a big airport," he said. "We could still travel if we lived there. We always did before. But when we came here it was also . . . There was something about being near the sea.

"One of the most exciting things when we moved here was the sea gulls. The sight, even the sound of sea gulls."

Wherever they retired, Stelk wanted to be near water. He spoke of the seacoast, rivers, streams, the sound of water flowing by. Now a babbling brook might have to do.

"I guess that would be okay," he said. "But it wouldn't really be the same."

✢

Karin Efman was free. Her decision not to return as senior warden had liberated her. Her term would not officially be over until new vestry members were installed next January, but even now there was a new lightness about Karin. She went about her parish chores unburdened.

She told me she was looking forward to her next Cursillo weekend. The retreat was planned for January. Ann Douglas was going to be her team leader and had asked her to give a talk about piety. Karin was enjoying the assignment. She'd sketched some ideas and was playing with a metaphor she'd drawn from the shadows thrown by the cross against the wall behind the altar at St. Mary's. She saw in the three images the tripartite nature of God and liked the way the metaphor was working out. As for her successor as senior warden, she felt no reason for concern.

"God will provide a good one," she said one day in the church office as she folded newsletters for mailing, just so, according to Frances Armstrong's instructions from the hospital.

Karin had gotten over the first shock of her daughter Susan's absence. Sue wrote frequent, chatty letters that often dwelled on food: "They had stir-fired tofu again the other night, Mom. Isn't that scary? You can feel free to send Pop-Tarts (chocolate). HINT HINT! Wheat Thins are always good, and of course, chocolate candy." The Efmans had driven cross-state for Parents' Weekend at Oswego. Oswego decals plastered the family cars. Now that the weather was turning cooler, all the Efmans were wearing Oswego State T-shirts and sweatshirts in a variety of styles.

Laurie Efman was the eight o'clock acolyte the next Sunday. The sky was pink and it was blustery, the first real cold of the season. Laurie was wearing an Oswego State T-shirt. You could read it clearly under her white acolyte's robe. It read: "Oswego Coed Naked Hockey—Twice as Nice on the Ice."

Stelk had been working on a cycle of sermons about love: love of God, love of self and love of neighbor. Today he had reached the love of neighbor. He found a theme in the New Testament's emphasis on mercy, contrasting it with the attention given justice in the Old Testament. "If all we have to face is justice, that's the day of the Lord," he said. "To do mercy, to be merciful . . . A life of mercy is what we are called to live . . ."

A gust of wind ripped across the church roof and made the timbers creak.

"Our neighbor is the one to whom we show mercy," Stelk said. "We learn that it is by showing mercy that we love our neighbor."

We prayed for Sylvia Clarke that morning. Stelk read her name among the intercessions. She was facing surgery on Monday. Whatever it was that had been bothering her last week, that sent her to the hospital the day I had been with Stelk at the Field Home, had been serious. "I don't know what it is," Stelk said later. "But surgery, at ninety . . ." He shook his head ominously.

Coleman Hill was in his accustomed place at the early service, sitting with his mother. He ducked down into the collar of his insulated jacket to light a cigarette as soon as he got into the parking lot, and I caught up with him and asked how things were going.

"Uh, okay," he said.

He looked glum, like things really weren't that great. He said he had a job servicing oil heaters "three, three-and-a-half days a week." I wondered if he was doing any driving.

"Nah," he said, and paused. I waited. After a moment he continued. "Well, what happened, I was going to drive two days and do service three days. But Palisades Fuel, they made me take a physical. I found out I got an umbilical hernia, and the doctor said I couldn't pull the hose." He squinted his blind eye and took a drag off his cigarette. "Thing is, it would have been a full-time job, with benefits. As it is, it's just part time."

He said he didn't expect to find much painting or construction work during the winter. "We'll get by," he said. "We always do."

Coleman's mother said she had been packing for her annual winter in Nokomis, Florida. She was on her way out of town later in the week when she dropped by the rectory and told Stelk that Coleman and his family would appreciate a turkey for Thanksgiving.

"How do we know our neighbor?" Stelk had asked. "Our neighbor is the one that we pass God's mercy on to. No demographic description. Our neighbor is an action. Our neighbor is the one whose wounds we bind, whose needs we look after."

✛

I was about to get a lesson in shopping.

Judy Salerno had been writing more urgency into the food pantry notices in Sunday's bulletins. Donations had grown steadily. Bags of groceries and wads of discount coupons filled the big wicker basket in the narthex. But supplies were running thin.

"The good news of the approaching holiday season is also accompanied by some bad news," Judy wrote at the beginning of November. "The number of families served by the Food Pantry has grown by one third in the past two months. If this trend continues, we'll be depending on your support, weekly donations and extra help more than ever."

"It could be the economy," she told me. "You have the feeling that it's getting worse. But St. Mary's is the only food pantry that serves anybody and doesn't ask too many questions. Word could be getting around."

It also could have been the sea change in the food pantry's operations. To Judy, a meal was more than the four basic food groups. It was an element of celebration, something to be savored. She was a fine cook herself and wanted to liven the meals people were getting from the pantry. Her goal was to give every client family a real Thanksgiving meal. She was asking for yams, cranberries, nuts and candy in addition to the routine cereal, peanut butter, juice and paper goods. She'd appealed for volunteers to bake desserts, and now a sheet on the parish hall bulletin board was filled with promises of pies, cookies, cakes and bread.

What's more, Judy believed a real Thanksgiving meal was a turkey dinner. So every food pantry family would have a turkey for Thanksgiving. She rose in church on Sunday mornings, drumming her foot nervously, and pressed the congregation to donate turkeys. She asked for cash register receipts she could exchange for free turkeys in supermarket promotions. The twenty-eight turkeys she'd amassed so far were stashed in freezers around the parish, pointing up the pantry's lack of storage. Judy planned to give them out the day before Thanksgiving. She had called the Butterball Turkey Hotline for instructions on thawing turkeys safely, and the woman there was very nice when Judy told her the turkeys were for a food pantry but, to be honest, no, they weren't Butterballs. Now, a week before the holiday, it was time to shop.

Judy picked me up at St. Mary's on a drab, gray afternoon. She was wearing a variation of her standard outfit: a black-and-raspberry-pink oversized sweater, gray acid-washed jeans, a pink band holding her ponytail. Her Chevy hatchback was littered with grocery coupons.

Judy drove east, through Shrub Oak, Somers and Croton Falls, to pick up the interstate to Danbury, Connecticut. She said she shopped in Danbury because the stores there gave double coupon discounts. She had learned about coupon shopping years before from a secretary at an advertising agency where she'd worked. Not long afterward, she quit work and started clipping discount and refund coupons.

"It's very addictive, and I have a compulsive personality," she said. "I love the idea of beating the system. It's too good a deal."

The Super Stop & Shop in Danbury was a big modern supermarket, its parking lot half-filled with cars in early afternoon. "It's better than Shop Rite because they don't have any limit on double coupons," Judy said as she pulled into the lot.

"At Shop Rite they have a limit of four of the same item, so you have to split your orders." She explained that meant it took two people, or two trips through the checkout line, to buy eight items at the double discount, an inconvenience when you were shopping for dozens. Judy and her helpers sometimes had to visit several supermarkets to use the coupons effectively.

Judy got out of the car, carrying a small yellow gym bag that was bulging at the seams with discount coupons. She showed me how she'd separated the coupons into Ziploc bags. "I arrange them alphabetically by product name," she said. "I know people who do it by product category, but I can never remember if crackers are under snacks or crackers or where."

We entered the huge market, and Judy plopped her gym bag into a shopping cart. She instructed me to get a cart as well. I followed her to a service counter, where she picked up a store flyer. "They usually have two flyers," she said. "One that they hand out to anybody and one behind the counter with a pink stripe that says these coupons can be tripled." She stretched and peered over the counter. "I guess not. No triple coupons today." She sounded disappointed.

Judy steered her cart into one long aisle and paused, a jouster entering the lists. She began to move, peering at prices as she went. She rounded the corner and came down the next aisle under bright fluorescent lights. At the end, she paused and reconnoitered. "So far there's nothing on sale that we have coupons for," she said. "This is very underwhelming."

In the next aisle, she spied a display of crackers and her eyes lit up. NEW! NABISCO CHEDDAR WEDGES, read the sign. She picked up a box and found a price. "Now here's where we're going to make a killing," she said with satisfaction. Ten-and-a-half-ounce boxes were on sale, two for three dollars. "We have seventy-five-cent coupons, which are gonna get doubled to a dollar and a half, which is how much they cost."

She stripped the display of Cheddar Wedges, twenty-seven boxes, and had five coupons left. "Maybe they'll have an end display," she said. "Well, that was exciting. That paid for the gas already."

Next, piling Cream of Wheat into her cart at $1.49 a box, Judy said she was annoyed. She'd expected to find it at $1.39. She fished in her coupon bags, discarded some outdated coupons and found some current ones worth 65 cents that would double to $1.30. "So that's nineteen cents a box. But free would have been better. I'll just get ten boxes. It'll be cheaper at Shop Rite."

She stopped at the canned fruit, looking tempted. "Fruit is one of the hardest things to keep stocked," she said. "People never give us fruit, and it's always so expensive." She studied the prices and shook her head. "No, not today."

I asked her why New York supermarkets didn't double coupons.

"Some people think it's because of me," she said.

She piled several boxes of Aunt Jemima pancake mix into her cart and plucked a variety of coupons from the gym bag. In the next aisle, she loaded twenty-four cans of College Inn low-salt chicken broth, two for 89 cents, into the cart. She held up a fistful of 35-cent coupons.

"Here we make a quarter on each can," she said. "Depending on what else we buy, that will offset that. We're not here to make money from them, just to make our groceries cost as little as possible."

An aisle later, she decided to apply the chicken broth profits against the cost of spaghetti sauce at an after-coupon cost of 59 cents a can. Judy shrugged. "It's the best I can do."

She was disappointed not to find Star Kist chunk white tuna to go with some "very good coupons." She said, "That was going to be our coup de grace today. Free tuna." Margarine at $1.19, after employing a 40-cent coupon, "wasn't good enough." We headed for the checkout counters.

"Most of the checkers are amazed when we come through," Judy said. "Sometimes they give you a look. Mostly it's the crotchety old ladies who do that. Only in a pinch will I go to anyone over twenty. They'll take every coupon as if it were coming out of their own pocket. I look for boys first. They don't shop or have any concept of shopping; you give them the coupons, they take them off. Then young girls. Kids are in awe. They think it's a great kick, beating the system. When they hear it's for a food pantry everyone except the store managers are very nice to you."

The checkout girl was young, blond and visibly bored. She cracked her gum and dragged the groceries item by item across the light beam that read their universal product codes. No addition was needed. It seemed excruciating work. The bill totaled $103.43.

Judy held out her wad of coupons and the checker's jaw set. She gave an exasperated little huff, cracked her gum again and then started entering the coupons, using the register keys this time. People behind us moved to other lines. The cash register receipt peeled out endlessly, curling on the floor. It was five feet long before all the discounts had been taken. They brought the bill to $13.11.

Judy counted out the money, and we took six bags of groceries to her car. Then we headed for the Shop Rite.

The Shop Rite deli counter was offering samples of Nabisco Cheddar Wedges. Judy hunted for the crackers only to find they were sold out. She packed the five remaining coupons back into her bag.

"Damn!" she said when we reached the hot cereal shelf, pushing carts in tandem. She was looking at Cream of Wheat for $1.59. "Damn! I thought I was going to get them for $1.39 here," she said. "Damn! Now I'm pissed."

Apple-flavored Cheerios restored her humor. With her coupons, small boxes would cost 49 cents each. Judy piled eight into her cart and eight into mine. We would each make two trips through the checkout line.

She stripped the shelves of store-brand chunk light tuna, on sale for 49 cents. "You can't get it any cheaper than that," she said. "Excuse me. I'm going to see the free-turkey lady."

Judy headed toward a matronly woman seated at a table. The woman looked like the original Betty Crocker, before makeovers. She was surrounded by signs advertising free turkeys to customers with $200 in register receipts. Judy returned in a minute. "That's what I was afraid of," she said. "The free turkey is after coupons, not before. Which is pretty hard to do. For me to spend two hundred dollars is not an easy thing."

We moved swiftly down the aisles now, loading our carts without regard to coupons: thirty-six boxes of macaroni and cheese at four for 99 cents; thirty cans of pork and beans at three for $1; three packages of chocolate mints at an after-coupon net of 49 cents; Hershey's four-ounce chocolate bars with almonds, net 9 cents; Dole raisins, net 39 cents; Dole pear halves, net 14 cents; Green Giant frozen white corn in butter sauce, net zero.

Necessities in hand, Judy slowed and ambled through the aisles, searching for odd bargains. She hummed along with the Traveling Wilburys' "It's All Right," playing over the store loudspeakers. She studied the shelves like a browser in a gallery, a hand on one splayed hip, looking for something meaningful in the displays before her. Raspberry preserves were two for $1, marked down from $2.19 each; she took eight. Some pantry clients would spread their toast with raspberry jam. She tore off a handful of coupons good for refunds on frozen chickens and stuck them in her bag.

A store employee walked past as Judy was buying some smoked turkey for her own pantry. The woman said, "Oh, that's a good deal with the coupons. I used mine already."

"Yeah," Judy agreed. "Do you want some?" She handed over several coupons.

The woman's eyes widened at the sight of Judy's gym bag. "How did you get so many?"

"It's a long story," Judy said.

We headed west at sunset with twelve bags of groceries in the car, net cost some $60, and two five-foot-long cash register receipts.

✢

Sylvia Clarke, the ninety-year-old Field Home resident, died in surgery. Stelk read her name in the intercessions on the Sunday before Thanksgiving. The Field Home would be a duller place without Miss Clarke and her bright whimsy. Stelk had been right to worry about her undergoing surgery.

St. Mary's was ripe with harvest bounty. The altar was moved forward, and behind it, a cornucopia spilled out onto white linen ruddy heaps of leaves, pale gourds and glistening dark eggplants, Indian corn, red cabbages, yellow grapefruit, pumpkins, oranges, grapes, lemons, onions and potatoes. Brick-red asters decorated the corners of the reredos. The altar guild had outdone itself.

Stelk preached about stewardship. His sermon was part of the annual appeal for pledges.

"Show me a Christian's checkbook and I'll tell you his priorities," he said. "That's not a joke. Money is an incarnate, in-this-world enfleshment of who we are and how we have our priorities. The way we use it indicates who we serve."

He argued that just putting money into the collection plate each week was not enough. Without pledge commitments, the parish was unable to plan. "Imagine how it would be if you tried to make payments on a car or house without knowing what your salary would be," he said.

Judy Salerno was balancing two bundles of food and struggling with the door to the food pantry when Fred Bodeker, who had done the pantry's shopping before she took it over, approached her after the service. He opened the door and stood aside while she put the bundles down. Then he told her she was being too extravagant.

"They don't need brand-name cereal," he said. "It's too expensive. There's too much sugar in it. What they need are just the basic food groups."

"Brands are less than generic when you use the coupons," Judy countered.

"Well . . ." Fred said he worried that if word spread that St. Mary's was filling grocery bags with the kind of brand-name products people saw on television, the food pantry would be overrun by scam artists. He remembered that the pantry had experienced fraud in the beginning when, flush with generosity, it was giving groceries to anyone who came on distribution day.

Then a check of addresses revealed half the recipients were clients of other food programs as well.

The notion of cheating put Judy on the horns of a dilemma. Generosity, not suspicion, was her nature. She wanted to serve her clients well. "What am I supposed to do?" she said. "Fight fraud by making people not want to come here because they get lousy food?" She didn't want to treat clients like potential criminals, either. She believed people lining up for handouts had enough trouble hanging onto their dignity without income checks and identification cards. Judy was making a point of learning the names of all the pantry's regulars. She wanted to see them not as clients but as human beings.

But she was seeing new faces all the time, and now, as the food pantry had been forced to do at its beginning, she had started asking people where they lived. If they were from Peekskill, which had food programs of its own, Judy would give them a bag of food anyway and tell them to go to one of the Peekskill programs the next time.

Fred was repeating what he'd said about the four basic food groups.

"They're getting the four basic food groups," Judy said. "I'm just trying not to bore them to death."

13

I shared the road with hunters as I drove to St. Mary's on the day before Thanksgiving. Deer season in southern New York had opened, and cars and trucks whizzed by on the Taconic State Parkway, laden with early season kills.

At nine-thirty, half an hour before the food pantry normally opened, St. Mary's parking lot was filling with a variety of aged and battered cars. It was a cold morning, and the pantry's recipients were pressing into the hallway adjacent to the sacristy that the acolytes used as a robing room. The men and women queued at the door leading to the parish hall, where Judy had set up her distribution point. They all were talking and exchanging greetings. The noise spilled into the sanctuary, where Stelk was conducting the midweek service.

Susan Hafford, a young wife and mother who had become Judy's main food pantry assistant, asked for quiet. "There's still a service in the church," she said.

Mary T. was first in line, as usual. She was a leathery-faced woman with a loud, abrasive voice. She shouted back to those behind her, "Hey, shut up, everybody, there's turkeys in the church."

Judy Salerno and Susan were filling the last few bags with canned yams, boxes of stuffing and gravy mix, and bags of nuts and candy when Carol Obligado arrived to deliver the sixteen turkeys she'd been storing in her freezer. Judy had collected forty-four turkeys altogether. I helped Carol unload hers and bring them inside; it took two trips with a grocery cart.

"What was the count on the desserts?" Judy asked. She was wearing her standard shades of black and purple.

Susan worked with her three-month-old, Jennifer, in a carrier strapped against her chest. I found Susan matter-of-fact and refreshingly sardonic. She was a cradle Episcopalian who attended church because she always had, and she and Judy spent long hours in theological debate. Susan glanced at two long tables that held foil-wrapped plates of home-baked cookies, pies and cupcakes. She shifted the baby and said, "I stopped counting after a trillion."

More people joined the line that now stretched outside the door. To look at them was to put a face on hard times too easily viewed as an abstraction. There were men and women, all ages, in hard-worn clothes, and their faces showed embarrassment, defiance, pain and resignation.

Judy told them to help themselves to the food in a couple of boxes she'd set out beside the line. The boxes held a variety of orphaned canned goods that were either exotic, like sardines in tomato sauce, or unpopular, like beets and kidney beans. Susan had drawn turkey feathers with crayons and stuck them on the boxes.

Judy's invitation set off a scramble, while she found her clipboard with its dog-eared list of names and sat down at the table. She was poised to hand out groceries when Mary T. announced, "I'm gonna have to get through there."

Judy raised her eyebrows.

"I need some help carrying. I've got a fractured leg."

Judy stood up and moved the table, and Mary stepped into the parish hall with a limp and an air of triumph, as if by passing the barrier she had separated herself from the rest of the recipients. I carried her groceries to her car and was placing them in the backseat when she confided, "I saw some of these people collecting bags yesterday at St. John's. I thought you should know." She looked at the people standing in the line and shook her head disdainfully.

Judy was repeating thawing instructions for the turkeys. "It's frozen. Keep it in the wrapping. Put it in cold water for six hours. Breast side down. Change the water when it gets too cold. This is a recording. We don't want you getting sick."

A man with deep crow's feet and a Southern accent reached the head of the line. "Ah, Mr. C.," said Judy, smiling. "We've got your turkey in the kitchen." She, Susan and Diane Cousins each had cooked and sliced turkeys at home for pantry clients who, like Mr. C, were single and had no use for a whole turkey. Others had broken ovens, no ovens or simply couldn't cook. Susan brought a foil-wrapped platter from the kitchen, placed it in a bag of groceries and added a dessert.

A thickset woman with a cane shuffled to the front. "I canceled my physiotherapy today," she announced. She, too, wanted to go through the parish hall and out by the wheelchair ramp. When Judy got up and moved the table for her, the woman gave her a big hug. "Happy Thanksgiving, honey," she said.

"Why, thank you," Judy said.

Twenty minutes after the pantry opened, the grocery bags were running low and still the line stretched into the parking lot. Judy said, "There are too many people here. People I haven't seen before."

A woman with wings of dark hair fanning from the corners of her narrow face asked Judy if she could pick up a friend's groceries in addition to her own. She said, "Her baby's got pneumonia."

"No pickups today," Judy said. "I'm only doing bodies who are here unless they arranged it in advance. I told everybody that. I did."

Judy normally allowed the food pantry's regular clients to pick up groceries for their relatives or neighbors. But she had been telling the pantry recipients since she started taking turkey orders at the beginning of November that for Thanksgiving they would have to come in person.

The woman's face clouded. "Her baby's got pneumonia," she repeated.

"She could bring it and leave it in the car," said Judy. "It wouldn't be that long."

"With pneumonia?" said the woman angrily. She tucked up her groceries and left, pushing through the people standing in the line behind her.

"Where's your little one?" the next client asked Susan.

"Sleeping." Kristen, Susan's three-year-old, was napping upstairs in the church office. She still was wearing Jennifer, the baby, on her chest.

"Sleeping, with all this noise?" The young woman took her bag of groceries and her turkey and handed the bag to the young man at her side. He wore a grease-stained down vest over a flannel shirt, and his bashful smile showed missing teeth. "Have a good holiday," the woman called as they turned to go.

By ten-thirty, all but a few of the Thanksgiving bags and turkeys had been given away. Now a woman in a long black coat and round, very dark sunglasses stood before Judy. With her was a woman wearing a stained parka over a Harley-Davidson T-shirt. Judy traced a pencil along her list, looking for a name. "I don't have you down," she said.

"I was here," the woman in the sunglasses said. She was very certain.

"I have her down," Judy said, indicating the woman in the parka. "But I've never seen you before at all."

"I was here." The woman was adamant. "I talked to the lady upstairs. She took my name specifically."

"Well, I have a problem with names that aren't on the list. You weren't here last week to sign up, so you'll have to go to the end of the line. I have to take care of the people whose names are on the list." Judy took a quick count of the line and called back to Susan and Trish Symonds, a dark-haired young mother who had just arrived to help, "I need five more as-close-to-Thanksgiving bags as you can make."

She turned back to face a woman in a handsome wool coat. Judy traced down her list and found her name, Cecilia F. Judy was topping off her bag with a plate of cookies when Cecilia stopped her, speaking with a West Indian accent. "Can I have a pumpkin pie?" she simpered. Judy took out the cookies and put in the last of the pumpkin pies.

"I want to also pick up for Mrs. C.," Cecilia said.

"I never found Mrs. C.," Judy said.

"What do you mean? I gave you her number and told you I was deliverin' to her." Cecilia quickly grew indignant.

"You gave me her number," Judy said. "I called and they said there was no such person at that number."

"You must have dialed the wrong number."

"I can't give a bag for somebody I can't confirm exists," Judy insisted. She hated saying no, but she also hated to be taken advantage of. Cecilia was a challenge to her charitable instincts. "You'll have to give me the right number, or have her call me, or something."

Cecilia wouldn't budge. "The lady's dependin' on a turkey," she said. "She's waitin'."

"You knew the rules," Judy said. She looked at her watch. "Go have her call me, or get the right number."

Cecilia flounced out. Susan and Trish brought more bags of groceries to the front. "These are as close to Thanksgiving as we can get now," Susan said. "They've got cranberries and yams."

Five more people stood in line for five bags of groceries and three turkeys. The turkeys were gone when the woman in the sunglasses and her friend in the parka reached the head of the line.

"Wait, wait," Judy said. "We have two hams." She hurried to the kitchen and returned with two small canned hams from the refrigerator. She radiated pleasure, announcing, "I'll put one in each bag."

At ten forty-five, the hall was empty. Judy flopped in a chair with a weary smile of satisfaction and said, "That was only slightly painful."

"Did everybody on the list get a turkey?" Susan wondered. Kristen was up from her nap and munching Cheerios from a plastic bag. Trish's daughter, twenty-nine months and also named Kristen, wanted Cheerios, too. She began to wail.

"And five who weren't on the list," said Judy. "They'd been here before but didn't come to sign up. And two who did sign up didn't come, so there were two extras. Everybody got a turkey except for those two hams." She went upstairs to take a phone call in the church office. She returned and was locking the outside door when a knock sounded. A young couple were standing on the steps. "We heard there were turkeys here," the man said.

"There were," Judy said. "They're all gone now." She told the couple about the regular Friday food pantry. She closed the door as they left, turned the latch and said, "The cupboard is bare . . . and the door is locked."

She took stock with Susan and Trish. The pantry had given forty-four turkeys to forty-six families. Coleman Hill had called Stelk to say he didn't need the turkey his mother had requested. The two hams brought the total of families served to forty-eight. Each family had received cranberries, yams, gravy and stuffing while it lasted, juice, nuts or candy, some kind of special vegetable like fancy peas or onion rings and home-baked cake, pie or cookies. The turkey-decorated boxes of odds and ends still contained a few cans of garbanzo beans. The beets were gone. Susan looked through what was left. "I never thought anybody would take that can of smoked octopus," she said.

As recently as September, the pantry had served an average of twenty-two families each week.

Cecilia returned at that moment. She came in through the parish hall door and strode to the pantry in her wool coat. "She called," she said. "May I have her basket now?"

"She called," Judy agreed. It was the phone call Judy had been called upstairs to take. "She sounded very old or very drunk," she said in an aside. "So we did confirm that she exists. But I've got to get a valid phone number for her." She produced a bag of groceries and a plate of cookies that was the last of the desserts. She went to the refrigerator in the kitchen and brought back the last of the main courses—a duck.

As Judy handed her the bag, Cecilia asked, "Do you have a little piece of ham for me?"

Judy was nonplussed. "No, there's a duck in there," she said. "She wanted a turkey. We only had two little canned hams, and they're gone."

"No," Cecilia said. "Do you have a little piece of ham for me?" She spoke in a wheedling child's voice, and it dawned on Judy that she was asking for herself.

"No," she said, exasperated. "You got a bag with a turkey and this bag for her. Go on, get out of here. Come back next Friday."

She hugged Cecilia by the shoulders and steered her toward the door.

✣

By Thanksgiving night the rectory was filled. The wedding guests were gathering.

Stelk had tried to put to rest his doubts about Kirsten's marriage to Joe Byrne. When the priest had finally met the gray-haired carpenter, the two had been wary of each other. Stelk and Ginny and Joe and Kirsten had spent stiff Sunday dinners feeling their way around the differences in age and class and education. Stelk had marched against the war in Vietnam, where Joe had served two tours as a demolitions expert charged with defusing mine fields. Joe had done his share of drinking, a habit he insisted he now was able to control. Among his four children was a son with Down syndrome who was in an upstate institution. All those pitfalls loomed in Stelk's and Ginny's minds.

"You just never think anybody's good enough for your first child," Ginny said.

Gradually the wariness between Stelk and Joe had relaxed and was showing signs of ripening into camaraderie. Any doubts that lingered now took a back seat to logistics. Marla had missed her plane from Colorado, but Stelk was saved (by the grace of God, as he saw it) from making two trips into the city, because she finally reached LaGuardia just as Suzanne Hartley, a friend from Stelk's first parish, was arriving from Ohio. They all stayed up late, drinking sherry and reminiscing.

By Friday night there was no room in the house. Kirsten had come up from the city to prepare, and Sara arrived from Martha's Vineyard. Stelk and Ginny turned the house over to Suzanne and their daughters. They moved to the Peekskill Motor Inn, where the groom and his best man were staying. Then everybody assembled over drinks because it was Kirsten's birthday.

"I turned twenty-six and then got married," she would say.

There were still the bundles of birdseed—rice was passé, since it harmed the birds that ate it—to be tied into lace bundles to be showered at the bride and groom, and more reminiscing and more sherry.

The wedding day dawned, and Stelk was coordinating train schedules from the city. Gwynyd the sheepdog was exhausted from barking. Ginny touched the pouches underneath her eyes. "We've been stupid staying up so late," she said. "We really haven't been very smart."

Only Suzanne's formidable energy was undiminished. The wedding program listed her officially as "Assistant to the Bride." She took the job seriously and as her due, having baby-sat with Kirsten as a student at Ohio Wesleyan. "Oh, I've been hustling her bustle," she said, describing how she'd made Kirsten try on her elaborate gown and train.

The ushers were using Stelk's office as a changing room. I was standing in the parish hall when Stelk came pounding down the stairs and into the main room, practically sliding across the floor as he tried to change directions. The coattails of his black tuxedo flapped behind him as he hurried across the room and burst out the door leading to the rectory. "No, I'm not having fun yet," he called back. "All these details."

Stelk returned through the same door a moment later. He looked about and disappeared in the direction of the church. He was looking for somebody he wasn't sure he'd recognize, a friend of Kirsten's who was to give a reading.

"Aha!" He spied the woman near the sacristy door. "I've been looking for you. It is you, isn't it? Yes. Well, here's the reading."

He dashed off to confer with lay reader Ed Lumley, who was assisting in the service, then hurried back to the rectory, where photographs were being taken in his dining room.

"Oh, he's much calmer now than he was two hours ago," Ginny told me. She was wearing a lovely dress of rich brown satin. Sara and Marla and Byrne's two eldest daughters, Deirdre and Catherine, wore bridesmaids' dresses that were just darker than the green of Ireland. Two photographers were arranging the families at one end of the room, triggering their flashes as they shot from one angle and another.

Ginny's mother sat at the center of the portraits. At eighty-four, she was lovely in her frailty. Ginny had inherited her face, her hair, the shape of her eyes. The stroke had left Georgia Horn with little speech or movement. Her frustration must have been enormous, for you could see the comprehension in her eyes struggling to express itself. She looked as if she wanted to say something, like an English teacher impatient to correct a point of grammar, but all she could do was bark out the words, "All right, all right." Her legs were twisted awkwardly and caught on each other at the ankles. Ginny wanted to rearrange them, but the photographers were in a hurry. No, that's all right, they said, and the flashes blinked.

"These down, that up, then that one up, then one more, then down and another down." Stelk nodded to himself as he counted the steps between the rectory and the church, gauging the effort it would take to get his mother-in-law in to the service. He leaned and spoke close to her ear. "I'm going to escort you on over. Can I do that?"

"All right, all right," she said.

✣

The soft notes of the organ prelude died, and the guests in the church turned and watched the door. Carol Obligado launched into the fanfare of Handel's "Sound the Trumpets."

Susan Byrne, the youngest of Joe's daughters, led the bridal party up the aisle. She was fifteen, chewing gum and struggling with a nervous titter as she tossed flowers from a small bouquet.

Catherine and Deirdre were more contained. Sara, officially the maid of honor, looked serene, Marla radiant.

And then came Kirsten and her father. Stelk's face shone with relief and pride. In his tuxedo he looked like the diplomat he might have been. Kirsten's white dress trailed ten feet of train. She wore hardly any makeup, and she looked virginal, innocent. Joe waited at the altar in his gray tuxedo. His face was beet red. His burly best man, David Wright, seemed too large for the small church.

Father Paul Nicely—a priest's name if ever there was one—was a longtime friend of the Stelks who had come from Ohio to conduct the wedding. He asked the traditional question: "Who gives this woman to be married to this man?" Stelk lifted his daughter's hand from his arm, gave it to Joe Byrne and stepped aside.

Nicely's homily spoke indirectly to the differences that had so worried Stelk and Ginny from the beginning of Kirsten's relationship with Joe. "You obviously have courage," he said. "It takes immense courage for any man and woman to approach marriage. There are certain odds, I suppose society would say, that are against you, that you are defying, with courage."

Kirsten and Joe stood before him, holding hands. The priest swayed like a metronome, appearing between them briefly and then disappearing behind one or the other as he talked. He said that Joe had known pain and loss, that Kirsten had a gift for lifting people up.

Standing in the choir stalls, Byrne's daughters nudged each other and giggled, furiously chewing gum. Sara and Marla wore quiet smiles.

"Human resources alone are never enough," Nicely warned. "So the good news is, God's grace is sufficient. Your resources, human, limited, powerful as they are but limited, God takes, magnifies and makes them adequate."

Kirsten and Joe spoke their vows in unabashed voices, looking into each other's eyes and holding hands.

A Eucharist followed. During the Peace, when Joe and Kirsten greeted Linc and Ginny, hugged them, and greeted

Ginny's mother, Georgia yelped out, "All right, all right." Gerry Cousins pulled the bell rope, and the church bell pealed in celebration as the guests exited into a fine rain and circled to the parish hall.

A bagpiper was playing at the entrance to the parish hall. Syd Henry, with his height and bulk and pinkish Irish tan, looked the part of a cop in a Jimmy Cagney movie, twirling a nightstick by the fruit stand. It turned out he was a cop, a retired sergeant from the Mount Pleasant Police Department. Syd was a pipe major "For All Occasions," according to the card he handed me. He wore the blue-and-gold kilt of the Westchester Police Emerald Society, and the Irish police shield on his chest read *Garda Siojcana,* which Syd said was Gaelic for "Guardians of the Peace."

Syd was skirling "Amazing Grace" when, after an hour, the wedding party dashed through raining birdseed and the drizzle toward two waiting limousines. Kirsten paused to press a tip into his hand. "Thanks," she told him. "It's Joe's favorite."

✣

"Throw your coat in the corner. Take off your tie."

Joe Byrne was greeting wedding guests inside Charlie's Inn, a neighborhood pub in Throgs Neck where the Bronx narrows into a snout that pokes into Long Island Sound and launches the Throgs Neck Bridge toward Queens. The neighborhood is Irish working class, with low buildings on wide streets with trees and yards and lots of sky. Joe was more relaxed now that the wedding was over and he was close to home. He grinned. "The fight starts at seven. Divorce in the mornin'."

The wedding party occupied a long table across the back of a crowded room. There was a contingent from St. Mary's, a few of Stelk and Ginny's longtime friends and a group of Kirsten's friends from LAN Systems, the software consulting firm for which she worked in marketing. But the bulk of the crowd seemed to be Joe's relatives and friends: union men who tugged at their collars with callused hands, flint-eyed old men in dark suits, watchful women in dresses, scampering children, teenagers, swaggering boys and flirting girls, couples who held hands and whispered.

The sound of champagne corks popping came from a bar in the corner.

Sara sat at the head table. She was the quietest of the Stelk sisters, and on the few occasions when I'd seen her, she often seemed wistful or distracted, lost in thought. Her interests lay in the theater and in literature. Deirdre, Catherine and Susan Byrne, by contrast, were young women of the moment. They were noisily fond of everything new: clothes, music, television. This clash of styles had caused an early rift between Sara and Joe Byrne's daughters. Sara felt that they had blocked her out. But the wall had slowly fallen.

Still, Sara seemed the least likely of the party to be the first to rise and silence the large crowd. She stood at her place and tapped on a glass until the room fell silent. Then she raised a glass:

"To my sister, to my new brother and to my new family."

Cheers and applause followed. Stelk and Ginny looked at each other, surprised and proud. A wave of the tinkling of glasses swept the room, the crowd's way of calling for a kiss between the bride and groom; they complied.

A band started playing between courses of the meal. Susan Byrne danced to a song popular before she was born, "Kansas City," holding her white shoes in her hand. The sedate white dress she'd worn as a flower girl now was off the shoulder. She'd wanted to wear it that way at the wedding. Kirsten had said no, setting off spasms of disappointment. But Kirsten told her the reception was a different thing, and Susan had accepted that. Kirsten said the Byrne daughters had adjusted surprisingly well to the idea of having a new stepmother not much older than they were, once they got used to the idea that they no longer had the run of the house.

The salad course arrived at the same time an accordion joined the band. Soon a bouncy jig was drawing dancers into the center of the room. Stelk pulled Ginny onto the dance floor. Afterwards, more swells of tinkling glass, more kisses. More food and wine. Then Joe walked to the front of the room and spoke to the kid leading the band. "The groom's goin' to sing for us now," the leader announced. "Joe's goin' to do a song that was popular back in the old country: 'The Wedding.' "

Joe brushed his hands on his pants and stepped to the microphone. He began to sing in a rough baritone. Kirsten came to the front of the gathering audience and watched, linking arms with Catherine Byrne, her new stepdaughter, who was just nine years younger. Deirdre, who was wearing rapaciously long fake fingernails, and Susan joined them. Joe sang, "I close my eyes, and I can seeee us . . ."

Kirsten rewarded him with a big hug when he was finished.

Joe's father then took the microphone. Hugh Michael Byrne was eighty-three years old and nearly dead of cancer. He was a volatile old man with a fierce eye and a quivering jaw. He had brought his wife and five youngest children from Rutland Street in the slums of Dublin to New York in 1964. Joe was nineteen then, already a carpenter for four years since his father caught him sleeping when he should have been in school and took him off to work. He'd seen Joe go to Vietnam and return, seen him suffering from a damaged child, a broken marriage, the death of his children's mother. He was a father who, like Stelk, wanted to see a smooth path before his child. Now he had seen this thing with this younger woman, this priest's daughter, blossom into love and marriage.

There was a legend in the Byrne family, Kirsten told me, that several generations ago, a Hugh Michael Byrne had married the daughter of an Anglican priest. The Irish Byrnes were so outraged they disowned him.

But this Hugh Byrne felt differently, and he had willed himself to stay alive to see this wedding. And if the priest could dance, Hugh could sing. His bones were too brittle for the jigs, but his lungs were good enough, the voice could still be raised.

He grasped the microphone and his choice, too, was a song about a wedding. "It's a wonderful day, for a wedding in May," he sang. ". . . the birds are singing, for me and my gal. The bells are ringing, for me and my gal."

He finished the song and stood with his head bowed to the applause.

Kirsten and Joe cut the cake together, fed each other slices thick with icing. Susan Byrne caught the bouquet. Stelk danced with Kirsten and Joe with his mother, and the dance floor filled.

Stelk danced that night. He danced the jigs of the Irish and the slow, sweet waltzes of his Midwestern youth. He danced in his embassy tuxedo in the ballroom of his soul. He danced with Ginny and with Suzanne Hartley, who closed her eyes and laid her head on his shoulder, as if in unrequited love. He danced in a circle with Kirsten and Sara and Marla and Ginny, kicking his legs and reversing directions and making them laugh. He laughed, too, and his face was red from the laughter and the wine.

✢

"A forty-five-year-old son-in-law. That I haven't been able to get used to," Stelk said.

"That's a challenge," agreed David Odell, twirling his glasses.

"And a grandfather. An instant grandfather. With four grandchildren." Stelk was trying his best to sound indignant.

The vestry members were arriving one by one for their November meeting. David confessed, in sympathy with Stelk's new status as a grandfather, that he had attended his thirty-fifth high school reunion earlier in the fall.

"You're old," said Marilyn Trudeau.

"In 1955 you could still walk the streets of Peekskill without being mugged," David pronounced.

"I was eleven years old in 1955," said Karin Efman.

"I was born in 1955." Mary Bohun brought that line of conversation to an end, and Bob Soso opened the meeting, reading An Order for Compline.

The vestry's agenda was dominated by familiar issues of finance and organization. The first was how to pay the balance remaining on the bell tower repair. "You can't just walk out to people and say you need forty or fifty dollars per family as people are trying to pay their Christmas bills," David argued. "Christmas is on everybody's mind. The decorations are out there."

Gerry Cousins said he needed money, too, to protect the stained glass windows. He handed out an ominous report. "The Plexiglas we now have is broken, cracked and heavily scratched," it began. He recommended replacing it with glass over the fixed part of the windows and Lexan (". . . believed to outlast Plexiglas by apx. 4 times") over the parts that opened, at a cost of $1,140.

"I think our timing is terrible," David moaned. "The bell tower. Windows. We are entering a stewardship campaign."

He wondered if the church could borrow from itself, dipping into one of the endowment accounts for a short-term loan. "For a couple of months," he said. "So that we can get through stewardship. Get through Christmas. Give people a chance to rebound, get to February or March and have a campaign to raise funds for the bell tower and maybe the windows at the same time. We need a breathing space."

"If we want to borrow, I think we should borrow from a bank," Walt Decker said.

"But why pay interest?" Mary asked.

Walt shook his head. "I have hang-ups about borrowing from an endowment fund," he said. "It just seems wrong to me."

"On the other hand," said Ann Marwick, "if we borrow from a bank we're costing the church money."

"It's a hairy kind of thing," David agreed. "Still, we need the money."

The question was passed back to the finance committee with an order to explore the options.

Unpleasant financial news continued to rain down. Walt and Bob Lockhart, the church treasurer, reported that the diocese was recommending that each parish contract for an audit of its books. Groans went up around the table. Walt reported that the 1991 budget was likely to show a deficit. And Grace Church in White Plains had offered St. Mary's just $21,345 for its share in the house John Baynard had left to the two churches.

Grace Church's letter revealed a certain unfamiliarity with its co-owners. The Grace Church delegates had addressed their offer to Reverend Lincoln Stelk and Vestry, St. Mary's, Scarborough, a church some ways distant, south of Ossining. The letter had arrived only by virtue of a facsimile transmission. It suggested reasons for the low appraisal on the house: a deck that wasn't built to code and a nearby electrical tower. The Con Edison tower, said the letter, "sits directly behind (actually quite close) to the house. There has recently been much negative media regarding the possible dangers of long-term exposure to the electromagnetic fields transmitted from these towers."

The letter went on, "However, we are empowered to make the following offer . . ." Deducting the mortgage due from the $134,000 appraisal, dividing the balance and deducting the appraisal fee, legal and closing costs, emergency roof repairs and other costs, Grace Church came up with an offer of $21,345.

"Wait a minute," said Walt. "We're paying all the expenses?"

Walt and Bob Soso were delegated to make a counteroffer, in which the expenses of the sale would be shared by the two churches.

That left the vestry reorganization, which was how St. Mary's hoped to manage itself better as it grew. The new system of portfolios called for committees on liturgy and worship, finance, Christian education, membership, property management, communications, outreach, youth and building expansion. Each would have a vestry chairman, some designated members and a varying number of at-large members appointed by the vestry.

Stelk groused that the vestry was taking his appointment powers. He pointed out that he was the equivalent of the parish CEO and said that he and the wardens should make the nominations and send them to the vestry for approval. "This could all be kept informal," he said. "As long as there's not some kind of subversive activity."

Stelk also balked at John Harbeson's continued efforts to push an administrative assistant on him.

"I don't think the vestry ought to be in a position where they can tell me I'm going to be working with an administrative assistant," he said. "I'm sorry, it doesn't flow that way. You should consider it after the rector, as the chief administrator, has laid it on you that this is something that is needed."

The members agreed, and Stelk sat back, his leadership intact along with the administrative burdens he cherished and could not bring himself to share.

14

Stelk appeared wearing, at long last, a purple stole. The long season of Pentecost had ended, and Advent, the beginning of the church year and the season leading up to Christmas, was upon the parish. St. Mary's echoed with the sounds of children rehearsing for the Christmas pageant. Frank Doyle, the church school supervisor, was collecting Toys for Tots. Judy Salerno launched a new food pantry campaign. She wanted to add hats, scarves and gloves to the pantry's Christmas distribution.

"In the joyous season of Christmas, we can share our joy by making Christmas special for our Food Pantry families," Judy wrote in her bulletin insert. "Please note the extra items we've added to our weekly listings and give generously, with love, to all those God has placed in our path."

She was proud of that last line. It came from the Linda Hunt character in *The Year of Living Dangerously.* Judy was like Billy Kwan in many ways, an outsider, noticed for her size, and also disturbed by injustice, sensitive to suffering and, finally, unable to stand aside without getting involved.

Judy put stocking stuffers high on the list of food pantry donations she was requesting. Mittens and knit caps and scarves began to pile up on the pantry shelves, along with toiletries, pens, candles, crayons, decks of cards and games. Her Christmas entree was to be canned hams.

And then someone broke into the food pantry.

Judy had never before missed more than a can of tuna fish, and she had a hard time begrudging that. This time she had gone into the pantry to find bags torn open and the stocking stuffers stolen. The hats and scarves and mittens that Judy had been begging from the congregation all were gone.

It wasn't difficult. There was no lock on the door. There never had been. Time was long past when church doors could go unlocked, but the food pantry was inside the parish hall, and there was almost always someone there when the hall was open.

"I feel abused," Judy said, looking distressed as she fumbled with an unfamiliar key one Sunday after the ten-thirty service. I had gotten into the habit of helping her carry the food back from the basket in the narthex. "I feel guilty that I wasn't smart enough to hide them, and bad for everyone in the church who brought stuff. I don't know who did it. I'm not Sherlock Holmes. So now we have a lock on the door, which is very depressing." She turned the key and opened the pantry and took the bags I handed her.

Stelk broke off from a coffee hour conversation and looked into the pantry. He wore a look that suggested a weariness with human nature. He tested the new lock and said, "I'm disappointed that somebody had to come in here and mess things up like that. I'm sorry they felt they had to do that. If somebody needed something, we would have tried to give it to them."

His impulse, though, was no less generous. With his talent for drawing inspiration from unlikely sources, Stelk introduced his sermon on the second Sunday of Advent with a cartoon from that morning's paper. It showed a family at a bountiful table as one of the children said, "There are some people in the world who never see this much food in their whole lives."

"God is a giving being," he preached. "We, when we are at our most human, are giving beings, because that's when we most thoroughly reflect the nature of God. When we let go and give."

The theft failed to dampen St. Mary's Christmas preparations. The church was filled with song. The Liturgy was elevated to reflect the joy of Christmas; the lay readers chanted rather than read the Prayers of the People, and the choir and the congregation responded by singing the Greek for Lord, Lord have mercy: "Kyrie, Kyrie eleison."

The chanted prayers were a tradition borrowed from the Taizé community of Protestant monastics in France. They were a challenge for the lay readers. Stelk routinely sang the Sursum Corda, the Great Thanksgiving and the Sanctus in the Eucharist. He had his tenor under reasonable control even in the difficult construction from the Great Thanksgiving: "It is right, and a good and joyful thing, always and everywhere to give thanks to you, Father Almighty, Creator of heaven and earth." But singing the prayers wasn't as easy as Stelk, with his practice, made it sound. The form used was Form V. It took up over two full pages in the prayer book. The rhythms of the prayers and the local inserts did not always lend themselves to chanting. Ginny lost her rhythm in the prayer for "those who suffer from AIDS, and who are imprisoned by addictions." Ed Lumley stumbled during the one for "Edmond, our Presiding Bishop, for Richard, Walter, Harold and Paul, our own bishops, and all bishops and other ministers. . . ." But the lay readers were supported by Carol Obligado on the organ, who held a long note, then dropped to a lower note at the end, and the choir swept in to lead the response. Combined with the language of the prayers, the effect could be majestic:

"For a blessing upon all human labor, and for the right use of the riches of creation, that the world may be freed from poverty, famine, and disaster, we pray to you, O Lord:

"Kyrie, Kyrie eleison."

The music and voices that rose within St. Mary's made beauty of the worship.

✛

"We're looking for a gig," said Carol Obligado. The choir had performed at the annual Christmas pageant of the Yorktown Historical Society in recent years. Bob Lockhart, the church treasurer, had arranged it. But now Bob's term as the historical society's president was over, and so was the gig. Carol lined up a date at the Field Home.

An audience of thirteen awaited the performance in the salon where Stelk held services. The room was decorated for the season with gaudy foil snowflakes hanging from the chandeliers. Red roses stood in vases on the tables. The women sat around the walls in the overstuffed sofas and chairs. "We have new chairs," one lady told me. "But we don't have permission to have them out. They're heavy, too. They have to be wheeled in on a carrier." She sat back as if the thought of it exhausted her.

Ed Lumley, turned out in a blue blazer and a red striped tie, conducted Evening Prayer from the 1928 Book of Common Prayer. The choir sang easily remembered standards like "O Come, All Ye Faithful" and "Silent Night." Ed insisted on reading the closing prayer as the choir softly sang "O Holy Night," an act Carol dismissed as corny. The choir closed with "Joy to the World" and then rushed to Carol and Fred's for a tree-trimming party.

A week later the choir sang for Caryl Miller.

Bill had worked hard to make Caryl's life as normal as it could be. He tried to surround her with familiar routines and take her to familiar places, to keep her engaged and interested in life. They camped at Woodstock every year on the anniversary of the festival, and Bill had insisted on taking her again this year. He gave parties and invited friends, and he resented the "former friends," as he called them, who withdrew after Caryl became ill. Since he could not get her up and dressed in time to take her with him to church, he decided to bring the church to her. He asked Carol if the choir could carol at his house. He didn't mention it would be a little like singing in Times Square.

Bill decorated for Christmas. He decorated big. He decorated inside and out, and he and his neighbor Barry Tucker competed to see whose house would be the brightest. The two houses attracted drive-by spectators from miles around.

This year Bill had plunged into his decorations as if they were the cure for his anxiety attacks. Early in the fall, he showed me an old horse-drawn sleigh he'd found upstate and dragged home to add to a collection that included Santas, elves, reindeer, a manger scene, toy soldiers that glowed, lit from within like paper lanterns, and enough lights of all colors to guide sailors lost at sea. He started stringing lights and setting up his figures in November. When he turned the lights on early in December, the house and yard glowed like an aurora. Inside, Bill arrayed tiny Santas and elves and Christmas trees and candles. He arranged scenes from a Lionel train set to which he'd once devoted an entire room: miniature streetlamps and stores and houses and trees, covered with a sprinkling of aerosol snow. He set out family photographs from Christmases past, of Justin growing up and one of Caryl with the Santa at Macy's, looking like Natalie Wood in *Miracle on 34th Street.*

Justin told me he thought the whole thing was "totally embarrassing."

It was bitter cold the night the choir came to sing. I had spent the afternoon at Dwight and Ann Douglas's, talking about their decision to leave St. Mary's. When I arrived at the Millers', a steady stream of cars was cruising by the light display. Caryl was watching the choir set up from across the street at Blossom Schecter's, where she and Bill had eaten dinner earlier. She said the view was better.

The choir assembled in the Millers' yard, wearing gloves and stocking caps and hooded parkas. Justin was inside watching "Starman" on TV. He promptly disappeared.

Carol conducted from atop a bright red railroad engine, which she shared with a waving Santa figure. Lights blinked in the trees overhead. Bill balanced a video camera on one shoulder and carried a 35-mm camera around his neck. Stelk wore a long red stocking cap. Caryl watched, framed in the Schecters' doorway. The choir sang half a dozen Christmas hymns as the gawkers slowed their cars to listen.

The choir continued its caroling next door at the Tuckers', whose house sported an identical Santa-in-his-sleigh-with-reindeer on the roof, as profuse a collection of figures and lights in every tree and bush.

"I can't believe this neighborhood," said a woman who parked her car and came into the yard. She was carrying a baby. "I always come here. It's even more exciting this year."

From where Caryl sat, the scene looked like Currier and Ives on a carnival midway. The bundled choir played flashlights on its lyric sheets. Stelk tucked his flashlight under his chin and kept his hands stuffed deep into his pockets. Fred Obligado shivered and resisted looking at his watch. Chris, the younger of the Tuckers' two sons, mimicked Carol as she waved her arms, conducting. Barry Tucker recorded the scene with his video camera. He said, "If you're not in the spirit, you will be after tonight." Overhead and all around, the lights blinked and shimmered.

A couple with a small daughter got out of their car and walked into the Tuckers' driveway to listen to the singing. "We just happened by," the woman said. "It's so wonderful."

The singers reached into their pockets for bells to jingle as they sang "Jingle Bells." When the jangling stopped, they crowded inside the Tuckers' for punch, cookies and a fire in the fireplace.

Caryl Miller still watched from the Schecters' as the yard emptied. In all the riot of color and light on the street that attracted the curious from miles around, in all the extravagance of Christmas, the Schecters' house was almost dark. There were only the lights that silhouetted Caryl in the doorway, and in a window to one side of her, the glow of candles on a simple red menorah lighted five days earlier for Hanukkah.

✢

Walt Decker's pledge solicitations became a regular part of the ten-thirty service during December. "Income that keeps up with inflation isn't enough," he would say, mentioning all the necessary repairs Gerry Cousins had identified. "We have no secret benefactor. We have no big endowment fund (that isn't already being used to balance the budget). We have only the parish family here to support us in what we do."

He asked the congregation's families to increase their

pledges. If tithing—the traditional ten percent benchmark for giving—was too much, Walt said, "Think of what you spend on entertainment every week. A movie can be family bonding, and this is family bonding of a different sort."

By December's vestry meeting, he was ready to put a budget into place. It was one of several year-end matters that had to be resolved.

First, Stelk handed around copies of a December 17 *Newsweek* cover story. The story, headlined "Young Americans Return to God," told of middle-aged baby boomers who were returning to organized religion after having been church dropouts, and younger parents attending to convey basic values to their children. "This is the kind of thing we're seeing here," Stelk said enthusiastically.

John Donovan was attending his first vestry meeting since his bypass operation. He wasn't enjoying not smoking, and he was in a sour mood. He managed to provoke Stelk by complaining, in an exasperated voice, about the National Council of Churches' position against celebrating the five-hundredth anniversary of Columbus's first voyage to America. He said he thought that was preposterous.

"But John," Stelk said, "when Columbus 'discovered' America there were already people here. Columbus destroyed a whole tribe of Indians in the Caribbean. There were people in this hemisphere who had advanced civilizations. The National Council was just trying to set the record straight."

John rubbed the back of his neck and said, "I'm just too damned old to be politically correct."

Gerry Cousins was decked out in a bright sweatshirt stenciled with holly leaves and berries and "Fa la la la la la la la la" across the front and down one sleeve. He was a one-man Christmas pageant, but when Stelk asked for his junior warden's report, Gerry said, "I don't want to be a Scrooge here tonight, but I have bad news."

The roofer who'd installed the church roof seven years ago apparently had done it on the cheap. Asphalt shingles designed to last twenty years were starting to blow off because they'd been put down with two nails instead of four. The roof needed replacing. "Ideally by removing the two old roofs and starting over," Gerry said. "It would cost more, but that would be the right way to do it. We're legally in the right. The question is, what will the contractor do about it?"

"It will be a fight," Donovan said, predicting that the contractor would not willingly replace the roof.

"I think we should try harassment," said Ann Marwick.

"Isn't that Wife Training 101?" said Walt Decker, rumbling with a laugh.

"Moving right along," Stelk said in a hurry, before Ann could take the bait.

Walt reported that borrowing from the L. Palmer Brown endowment to pay off the bell tower repairs was "cautionary" but, in his view, not legally restricted. The vestry voted to take $3,000 from the endowment fund and repay the money before the end of 1991.

So St. Mary's 1991 budget already was $3,000 out of balance when it was approved. It was a conservative budget of $104,810, a $5,110 increase. Walt said the stewardship campaign had produced a potential for $70,000 in pledge income in 1991. He'd budgeted only $65,610. Stelk got a raise to $25,750. Combined with his car and furniture allowance, St. Mary's would pay him $30,750, a four percent increase from $29,500 for the parish CEO. The budget included no money for major property improvements, although Gerry had asked for $50,000.

The details were revealing in their modesty. The budget included an annuity for Stelk to which he and the parish would contribute $400 each. The vestry designated a portion of his income as utility and housing expense so he could pay less in taxes. Carol Obligado got a $500 raise, to $4,500, "a gesture of respect," said Walt. There were no stock options, bonus provisions or golden parachutes.

David Odell had no report on the parish hall expansion; the question was virtually dead. As liaison to the acolytes, however, he provided a footnote to 1990s lifestyles. "There are fewer smokers," he said. "The acolytes are having trouble before the services finding people with matches to light the candles." Stelk laughed and promised to keep a supply of matches in the sacristy.

Karin Efman said the greening of the church for Christmas would be held the next Sunday, after the ten-thirty service, followed by the children's Christmas pageant. "We're going to pretend we're Baptists and be in church from morning to night," she said.

✢

Christmas brought children home from college. Ted Obligado was home from Bucknell, and Tom, his younger brother, home from the University of Hartford in Connecticut. Eric Harbeson, a tall, loping, redheaded young man, was home from the College of Wooster in Ohio. Susan Efman returned from Oswego.

Karin told me she felt the way she did before Sue went off to college. She wanted to reassert her motherhood. Sue and Karin's other daughters wanted her to let go of it.

"There was so much I wanted to tell her that day," Karin said one Sunday after church, reminiscing about the drive across New York that had delivered Sue to Oswego. She was standing in the parish hall with her arm around Sue's shoulder. "And she slept. This is part of severing anyway. But I wondered, have I told her about this boogeyman, or that one?"

"But I slept," Sue said. She sounded relieved that she had.

Laurie had assumed some of her older sister's roles; now it was Laurie who would shuck her acolyte's robe when the service was over and head for the car and sit listening to the radio until Karin was ready to leave the coffee hour. Now it was Laurie who grew impatient and reacted to treatment she thought was unfair.

Just then Laurie entered from the parking lot and stood on the fringes of Karin's conversation. "The car is leaving," she said pointedly.

Krissie followed her. "Laurie's breaking the radio," she said. "She's leaving the radio on."

Laurie rolled her eyes. "She hates me anyway," she said.

Susan, meanwhile, was asserting her new freedom, and Karin had been unnerved by it. Sue was inclined to keep late nights. Karin wanted her in early, but she couldn't argue with Sue's contention that she'd been on her own for months now, and she wasn't going to put up with a curfew.

The night came that Karin waited up for her until three-thirty. She decided that night that if she couldn't put a curfew on her newly independent daughter, she could put one on the car. Karin put her foot down. The car had to be in by two.

✢

On the night the choir sang for Caryl Miller, Judy Salerno led a bake-in. She and seven friends baked bread at a house in Stormville from three-thirty that afternoon until nine at night. The owners of the house were teachers who catered on the side, and their kitchen had two commercial ovens.

"It was nobody from the church," Judy told me. "These were people who think the church part is crazy, but they're active in all kinds of other things and wanted to do something. They're do-gooders from the sixties, tie-dyed kids. So I said, 'Get some people together and we'll bake.' "

Judy and her tie-dyed friends baked pumpkin bread and apple bread and threw raisins into everything. "We should have had a calculator," Judy said. "We had to keep asking, 'What's twelve times one and seventh-eighths?' It was messy, flour everywhere. But the loaves all rose and did what they were supposed to do. It came out pretty nicely."

Judy came away with fifty loaves to add to the Christmas food pantry.

She and Susan Hafford started putting the Christmas bags together after their aerobics class on the Wednesday before Christmas. Judy had wheedled some grocery bags with Santa Clauses on them and bought some red paper stockings for fifty cents apiece. The two women worked to the sound of Christmas carols, the choir singing at its regular Wednesday night practice in the Pine Room.

Patrick Hafford didn't like it, this business of coming home from his job at Met Life and having to take care of Kristen and Jennifer while their mother put ribbons on Christmas stockings for other people's children. Both girls were still up and cranky when Susan had called to check in at ten-thirty, and Patrick had pleaded, "Come home now." They had it out when she got home.

"Husbands!" Judy said.

Judy's husband, Dan, like her friends, thought she was crazy for having anything to do with church. Dan's routine, like Patrick Hafford's, had been turned upside down by the food pantry. "I don't think he resents it," Judy said. "It's just that he's not used to it. Everybody's discombobulated. Patrick expected Susan to come here for an hour. That's what he told her. Except that he always tells her she should get out. Dan always says the same thing to me: 'You're always home. Go out.'

"She likes coming here and doing this. I like coming here and doing this. We're not here every night."

Judy and Susan were unlikely friends. Judy was tall and dark, Susan short and blond. Judy was fifteen years older. They had different attitudes about children. Judy didn't like children at all. Quite surprisingly, they found themselves simpatico.

Judy said, "Everything we discuss we actually agree on, like clothes should be cotton and wool, not polyester or fiberglass. It's weird. You hardly ever meet people like that, especially people who you would never in a million years suspect. I mean, she lives in a high ranch, real suburban, the most Levittown type of house you can imagine. But we go to aerobics together, we shop together, we do stuff together. We get along really well. When we come here we laugh and joke about other church people, about life in general, about our husbands . . . We just get along."

Judy, unlike Susan, thought about religion quite a bit, about these Episcopalians who went "all tappy-lappy to the altar for Communion," and who sometimes didn't sing the hymns or follow the prayers in the prayer book. She was mystified by that, she said. The biggest mystery was the new attraction of attending church. It gave her a high that she had trouble sustaining if she didn't attend the midweek service.

"I'm still trying to figure out what's happening to me," Judy said. "My friends give me strange looks. They say, 'We're going to watch you very carefully, and if you show further signs of deterioration, we're going to take you away.' " So far, all she'd figured out was that it was fun. Church was fun, the food pantry was fun. "What can I say?" she shrugged.

Susan took it for granted that being an Episcopalian involved things like working for the food pantry. She did it unquestioningly, just as she attended church on Sunday. She had been surprised to learn there were services on Wednesday, too. "Are we supposed to go?" she asked Judy.

"Huh," Judy said. "Try to get Father Stelk to tell us anything we're supposed to do." She was used to priests who gave people more direction.

After Susan went home on Wednesday night, Judy had stopped work, too. She came back the next morning and resumed work on the packages. She assembled fifty-four Christmas bundles of food and gifts. Then she'd gotten nervous and put two more together, just in case. The food pantry lines still were getting longer every week. She had ended up without enough canned hams, so she'd rummaged for coupons and gone out and bought ham steaks at a discount of fifty cents a pound.

"It's going to get back to normal," she said. "These last two months have been abnormal. I mean, these are holidays. You're not just sitting here handing out the same bag of food you hand out the rest of the year."

+

The food pantry on the Friday before Christmas was festive with the Christmas stockings tied with ribbon, Christmas cards, the fruit bread wrapped in cellophane and shiny oranges heaped into the bags. Judy had bought ten hat-and-mitten sets to replace the ones that were stolen. The stockings, depending on the family, contained scarves, teddy bears, toy cars, candy canes, little perfumed soaps, bottles of lotion.

The bags were lined up alphabetically over three long tables. One had food and gifts for nine children. Judy, who was always making notes, knew by now which of her regulars were on diets, which had children and how many.

Trish Symonds set the last of the bags in place and then stepped back to look at the bright packages. Susan was with Patrick at his office party in the city. Trish shook her head. She said, "When I did this last January, they'd get two cans of beans, two cans of soup and cereal. The food pantry has totally changed since Judy took it over. Totally."

Judy sat down at her table in the doorway. She was wearing faded jeans, a loose cotton sweater and soft ankle boots that laced up the front. For a large woman, her feet were surprisingly small. She scanned her clipboard, looked up at the line and said, "Okay, who's ready?" Trish and I stood by to carry groceries to the front.

The crowd had swollen since Thanksgiving. The line at the door was longer and more cheerful, but no less demanding. Mrs. H. squared her shoulders and told Judy she wanted to pick up for Sandra O. "She broke two ribs," said Mrs. H. The woman had a weathered face and was wearing a hunting vest and an old red-and-black checked flannel shirt. "She was up putting the star on top of the tree, and she fell and landed on the chair arm." She planted her hands on her hips and dared Judy to deny her.

"She called. Don't worry," Judy said as Mrs. H. gathered in the bags Trish handed her. "Have a good holiday."

Mrs. C. peered closely at the Christmas stocking in her package. It was labeled: "Boy, 8 yrs." She smiled shyly and said, as if surprised, "That's right."

They were talking to her now. Judy's effort to know the food pantry's clients was drawing them out in conversations. "I got married," Diane M. announced with a smile. She was a friendly looking woman, neatly dressed.

"Well, congratulations, I guess," Judy said. She still was incensed about husbands.

"I changed my name," Diane continued.

"No. Don't do that. Leave it," Judy said. "It's better for you."

"Well . . ." The woman looked down. "I already did."

"It's your funeral. No, tell me. I'm just kidding." Judy wrote the new name on her pad and looked up. "Lee C." She remembered the man's name without looking at her list.

"Very good," the man said, pleased. He gave Judy a firm handshake when he took his bag.

"Barbara." A large woman in a threadbare wool coat stood at the head of the line. Judy beamed. She beckoned Barbara to lean down and said conspiratorially, "Somebody gave us a jar of caviar. Diabetics can have caviar, can't they? Oh, good. 'Cause it's in your bag."

Barbara gave Judy a big kiss. "Thank you, honey," she said. "You're so nice. I hope you have a Merry Christmas."

Not all the people could look at her as they accepted the bags of groceries. A young man wearing a denim jacket and jeans and a baseball cap stitched with the name of an excavating company took his bag and turned away without a word.

All the regulars had come and gone, and only the generic bags remained when, just before eleven, a short, plump woman in a black T-shirt opened the door and peeked tentatively in. "Is this St. Mary's Church?" she asked. "They told me in Peekskill I could get food here."

"Where do you live?" Judy asked.

"Lake Mohegan."

"Who told you to come?"

"The Peekskill Community Health Center."

Judy took her name and gave her a bag of groceries. "We're open every Friday at ten o'clock," she said. "Happy holidays."

One grocery bag and one ham steak remained at the end. "Oh, good," she said. "I can give Mr. B. something when he comes next week. Because he'll ask for it. I know he will."

Mr. B. was another of Judy's regulars, an irascible old man whose bad moods challenged Judy. She plotted ways to make him smile, and having a ham steak the next time he came was calculated to break through his gloom.

I asked Judy what she thought it would be like to be one of the people she served. "To me, this would be very hard to do," she said after thinking for a moment. "I would rather be working in McDonald's. I think. I've never been poor. I don't know at what point you get beaten down for the last time. Here today Diane M. tells me that she's gotten married. I would think that if you were single and struggling, and you got married, you could hope for a change of status. Upward, preferably." Judy laughed. "Otherwise, why would you bother? She has a very nice raincoat. She always looks real well. She's very friendly. She's very nice. She's still coming. Why? How desperate do people need to be?"

She sat back and surveyed the tables, empty but for the solitary bag of groceries. Trish took her daughter and went home. Judy said, "That's fifty-five bags we gave away. Two and a half times what it used to be. We're still seeing new people every week.

"But I have no idea if the people who came today for the first time will come back. Some of them, I think, are going to disappear back into the woodwork. The way it was going, even though I had fifty people on the books, only thirty-five of them would show on any given Friday. Except for the past month. They got good stuff on Thanksgiving and wanted to stay in good standing for Christmas. You come when you get something special, but what are you doing the rest of the time? It's free food, so if you need it . . ."

Free food for hungry people. It would not have taken a great leap to get from Judy Salerno, pleading for donations and double discount coupon shopping, to the miracle of loaves and fishes.

+

Old Hugh Byrne, Joe's father, died early on the Sunday before Christmas, a day on which war in the Persian Gulf loomed ever closer. He'd sung for his son, who had married a priest's daughter, and that had been enough for him. He'd lasted only four weeks longer.

Marla and Sara, both home for the holiday, sat with each other at the ten-thirty service at St. Mary's and now and then talked quietly and laughed. It had been a long time since Marla, as a baby, had crawled under the pews of Stelk's first parish church in Delaware, Ohio, to visit her father as he prepared Communion. The rising swell of laughter from the congregation had puzzled Stelk until she crawled into the open, chortling, and Ginny had hurried toward the altar and swept her up in her arms. Marla and Sara's presence made Kirsten's absence more acute. It dramatized her role within another family and the shift within the Stelks'.

The season's growing joy was tempered by a sense of apprehension. It seemed as inevitable as Christmas, as the deadline imposed by President Bush for Iraq's withdrawal from Kuwait grew closer, that the American-led coalition of forces called Desert Shield would attack the Iraqis in Kuwait. Churches stepped up their calls for prayer.

St. Mary's had included a prayer for peace in the Mideast in the Prayers of the People since the Desert Shield force was assembled. Now, Stelk announced a bishops' request "to engage in a very heavy concentration of prayers for peace within the next few weeks." He said the Peekskill Area Pastors' Association was organizing prayer vigils at a series of area churches at noon daily up to the January 15 deadline.

"Prayer is a powerful thing and we need it," Stelk said.

Oddly, there had been little talk among the congregation of St. Mary's about the possibility of war, whether it would be a good thing or bad, right or wrong, necessary or just a way of distracting attention from a declining economy at home. Nobody was debating if the economic sanctions imposed on Iraq should be continued. At vestry meetings and over coffee after services, St. Mary's was largely silent. But Stelk was responding to an internal force. He had been a warrior. His sensitivity grew from his career in the Strategic Air Command and the cargo of nuclear bombs he would have flown into war. He would have done it then, but now he was unshakeably convinced that all war was immoral. It was one of the issues on which he and his new son-in-law still differed. Joe Byrne, after defusing mine fields in Vietnam, thought wars should be fought to be won. Stelk no longer thought that they should be fought at all.

Stelk said he had compiled from the Book of Common Prayer a pamphlet of "prayers for peace, for those in the armed forces of our country, for our enemies, for our nation, for the president and all in civil authority." They were stacked at the back of the church. "You might take this and pray by yourself if you're not able to be at the services," he said. "We can take seriously the power of prayer and we may have some effect."

+

Whatever was going to happen in Kuwait was still three weeks away. Christmas was immediate. After the service, I joined a spirited crew of two dozen for the greening of the church. We transformed the church inside of an hour into a pine-scented, garlanded, festive place. Lowell Warnecke, the husband of lay reader Chris Warnecke, and George Munroe, Kathy's husband, along with a parishioner I didn't know well named John Banu, climbed onto aluminum extension ladders and started hanging a garland of pine boughs. They started at a peak above the altar, swooped down past the worn marble tablet in memory of Catharine M. van Cortlandt Field, to the side wall. The garland passed from hand to hand, peaked above the window arches, dipped gracefully, peaked again, until 225 feet of it—according to the altar guild's Eleanor Arnold—was swagged around the sanctuary. Eleanor, who arbited these things, pursed her lips. "It's not as full this year," she said. Lowell distracted her with questions. "How's that droop look up there?" he asked, pointing to the arch above the altar. "Nice, huh?"

Marsha McCoy, the attractive church school teacher, fixed bundles of pine boughs tied with red ribbon at the end of each pew, using rubber bands. Marsha had a son, Morgan, a big, quiet kid who had just turned thirteen and didn't know what to do with himself. "Morgan's father was an acolyte in this church," she said. "His grandfather made the cross. I still have the plywood pattern." She indicated the cross over the altar, with the Greek letters alpha Α and omega Ω, the beginning and the end, at the tips of the crosspiece and the entwined chi and rho ☧, the first letters of "Christ," at the ends of the upright piece.

Billy Bodeker, the young trumpet player, was up on a stepladder his father Fred was holding. They were under the arch in front of the altar, where Billy stretched to hang a lighted star.

Joyce Donovan, John's wife, and Karen Banu joined Marsha as she placed pine boughs around electric candles on the windowsills. Gerry Cousins hung pine wreaths bright with red ribbon in the top of each of the church windows. I climbed a ladder to place pine boughs and sprigs of holly into the Advent wreath on the iron trendle suspended above the choir, where a new candle had been lit each week since the beginning of Advent. The crèche—the manger scene—was placed before the altar, and Eleanor Arnold began to carry in dozens of poinsettias.

And then Chris Warnecke was vacuuming pine needles from the carpet and Diane Cousins was asking, "How many Episcopalians does it take to green a church?" Ginny Stelk served barley soup with bread and butter in the parish hall. Angels started to gather for the Christmas pageant, accompanied by their anxious parents.

Redheaded Amanda Korr wore a sparkling foil tiara but had left her wings at home. Today was her fourth birthday, and everybody in the family was excited. Her mother, Linda, said, "I forgot the cookies. I had to go back to the house. Then halfway here I realized I forgot the wings, and she had to have those. I sent my husband, Tommy, back for them."

Walt Decker arrived with his wife, Mary Jane, their daughter Cheryl and son Adam, who wore the robe and turban of a king of the Orient. Jimmy Bodeker, another king, came up tugging at his turban and complaining, "I can't even see with this." Walt shouldered his new video camera.

At ten to four, Carol Obligado on piano, Gerry Cousins on guitar and Billy Bodeker on trumpet were tuning up. Walt had taken a seat in the front row with a clear view. A tall, gaunt man from Mohegan Manor chewed pensively on the stump of his left index finger, as if worrying a fingernail. Suddenly an angel burst into the church, crying, "Mommy! Mommy!" Pat Bujarski, the architect's wife, adjusted her daughter Katie's wings and straightened her halo. Katie stayed with her mother and settled back to watch the show.

The three kings, some shepherds and a gaggle of angels entered from the sacristy. Amanda Korr now had her wings. Kristen Efman, the narrator, wore the same angel's outfit that Susan and then Laurie had worn before her. She marched to the pulpit and started reading the first lesson, the annunciation to Mary by the angel Gabriel, from Luke. She read in double time, as if she were trying to get it over with. When the angels moved to the front of the altar, Katie Bujarski jumped up and ran to join them. They started singing. Katie hesitated, turned back toward her mother, then rejoined the angels.

Mary and Joseph entered. This year Mary was a blond—Tricia Cousins—and Joseph, Christopher Banu, wore sneakers. Between the hymns and anthems, Kristen breathlessly speed-read the story of Mary and Joseph's trip to Bethlehem, the birth of Jesus and the arrival of the shepherds and wise men.

Adam Decker's Gaspar, carrying his gift of gold, self-consciously sang the second verse of "We Three Kings," while Walt videotaped him. Snapshot cameras flashed. Parents in the pews craned their necks to see their sons and daughters.

Kristen Efman's final breathless lesson was from Isaiah: "Sing for joy, O heavens, and exult, O earth; break forth, O mountains, into singing! For the Lord has comforted his people . . ."

"She's a funny kid," her sister Laurie said when the pageant was over and all the children and parents were back in the parish hall eating cookies.

Susan said, "I can't believe I wore that same costume."

Laurie said, "I can't believe we both did."

Then Christmas came with services that jammed the little pine-garlanded church for the hymns and the story of the birth of Jesus, who would be called the Prince of Peace, and the year ended and war loomed closer.

15

Two sons of the congregation were assigned to Operation Desert Shield. Army Private Charlie Laughlin's family wasn't among the Sunday morning regulars. But Eric Taylor's mother, Beverley, attended the ten-thirty service every Sunday. She had learned three days after Christmas that Eric, a twenty-three-year-old Navy ensign aboard the supply ship U.S.S. *San Diego,* was in the Persian Gulf.

Mohegan Lake bloomed with yellow ribbons. They signaled from front doors, mailboxes and trees that the folks at home supported the troops of Operation Desert Shield. An intensifying patriotic fervor seemed, as much as anything, to want to heal the wounds of Vietnam. Television stories from the Gulf featured troops saying they were getting bored with training exercises. Let's go ahead and get it over with, they said. There was a swelling eagerness to deal with the recalcitrant Saddam Hussein. But for Beverley Taylor and everybody else with someone in the Gulf, what mattered most was getting that someone back home safely.

Beverley was a beautiful woman. She was black, light skinned, with a serenity and bearing that enhanced her striking features. She was regal without being haughty, well dressed but not flashy, serious but not severe. Eric was one of three children, all as attractive as their mother. Shaw, named for his father, was the oldest. Eric was in the middle. Kimberly was about to turn sixteen. She was tall and willowy, and in her regular turns as an acolyte, exhibited her mother's grace.

The family joined St. Mary's in 1972, the year Shaw Taylor, Sr., an engineer for the pharmaceutical manufacturer Eli Lilly, moved his wife and two sons from Queens to Yorktown Heights. There was no religion in his background. Beverley, however, had been raised an Episcopalian and saw to it that he got some. Shaw and Shaw Jr. were baptized together at St. Stephen's Episcopal Church in South Ozone Park, Queens. When they moved to Westchester, Beverley went looking for a church. She missed a turn in Granite Springs and couldn't find the Church of the Good Shepherd.

"St. Mary's was just sitting there waiting for me," she told me. She said she came to think of it as "the small church with warm people."

Kimberly was baptized at St. Mary's in 1975.

Beverley said she had always believed that priests had a special capacity to comfort people with the lessons of faith. She grew disillusioned, however, after her husband was operated on for pancreatic cancer. Marc Lee was St. Mary's rector then. She had asked him to visit Shaw, hoping that would give him faith and comfort. But when Lee left, she heard her husband laughing bitterly. He said, "You asked him to come here to comfort me. He asked if I was afraid of dying."

Beverley said she was stunned at the question. It seemed to me to be a reasonable way of approaching a discussion of faith. Perhaps it was too direct. In any case, it made her believe that priests were not extraordinary people after all.

The Rev. Deborah Dresser, the interim priest who served between Lee's departure and Stelk's call, conducted Shaw's funeral.

"We laughed," Beverley said. "Mother Dresser presided, Joanna White assisted, a female police officer directed traffic. My husband was a chauvinist. He would have liked that." Beverley said Mother Dresser restored her equanimity and her faith in priests.

Beverley was forty-four when she was widowed.

"For the last, almost seven years now since he got sick, I pretty much have provided my own strength," she told me one evening in her neat suburban home. "When I need extra help I go to the people who can provide. Just letting Father Stelk know that Eric is part of the Middle East crisis is my way of seeking the bonding. I wouldn't be sitting down and trying to have quiet time with him." "Quiet time" was a phrase from Beverley's job; she taught a transition class of children between kindergarten and first grade. "Just being in the church, being part of that fellowship, is comforting to me," she concluded.

✢

Stelk spoke of war for the first time in his sermon of January 13, the first Sunday following Epiphany. The morning's headline in the *New York Times* was CONGRESS ACTS TO AUTHORIZE WAR IN GULF. Beverley sat in her usual place on the aisle in the second pew on the right, with Shaw Jr., home from Oakland, California. Kim, her hair pulled straight back from her high, clear forehead, was the acolyte who led the procession to the altar, carrying the cross between and slightly ahead of two acolytes bearing candles.

The Sunday following Epiphany is the day that celebrates the baptism of Jesus, and Stelk began by talking about water, flowing like the spirit. But soon he came to the war for which the world seemed to be holding its breath.

"Our focus is once again upon the desert, the desert where there needs to be the water of life," he said. "We're at a very serious time in the life of this world. We may see World War III begin this week. It is possible. But thank God it is not necessary. And it is not inevitable. And we are not yet committed to it. The world still has a chance.

"I have been urging you to pray for weeks, and I am urging you now to let that spirit of God flow through you in prayer this week like it has never flowed before."

There were many opportunities for prayer, Stelk said. Almost every major religious leader in the country had asked that people pray for a peaceful resolution to the conflict. He rattled off a list of prayer services in northern Westchester and said Episcopal, Catholic, Lutheran and Jewish congregations in the New York area would hold services on Monday night from five to six P.M., "for prayers for justice and peace in the Middle East."

Stelk said prayer offered "a chance yet to affect the future of our world."

He repeated a line from the recent Sunday comics to relieve the tension and get a laugh from the congregation: "This Christmas there's something our troops in the Middle East could really use. Something that hasn't been seen in those parts for quite some time. Wise men.

"And so we pray for wisdom. And for courage. And for peace. And for justice. Now I bid your prayers by using a prayer, composed and used widely throughout this country by Christians, by Jews and by Muslims. A prayer for both Saddam Hussein and George Bush, and we will later in this service include in our prayers Eric and Charlie and all the rest of our people. But I ask you to join with me in this prayer.

"Oh, God, you fill the universe with light and love. In you we live and move and have our being. We pray for Saddam Hussein and George Bush. Enlighten their minds and fill their hearts with the power of your creative love. Guide their actions, so that all civilians and all military personnel in the Gulf area are protected from the sufferings of war. Inspire their decisions so that the crisis in the Middle East is resolved peacefully, and all peoples of the world learn to walk in ways of justice, love and peace. Amen."

The congregation responded with a subdued "Amen."

The Peace was more somber than usual. The word, for a change, was not an abstract, personal greeting that accompanied the handclasps between members of the congregation. It was an expressed desire, a wish for an absence of war. You could feel, as it was said, the air of uncomfortable waiting that overhung the country. We said "Peace" to each other with sadness and feelings of inevitability. The word was offered like a prayer that was not likely to be answered.

People surrounded Beverley and her children after the service, offering their wishes and prayers. I felt as if I wanted to embrace her, but I hesitated. "That's okay. You can hug me," she said. "I'll take all the hugs I can get."

She said Eric's assignment aboard the supply ship rather than a fighting ship "is the only thing keeping me sane."

✣

Four people, including Stelk, attended the Monday evening prayer service. The January 15 deadline passed on Tuesday, and on Wednesday, planes swept into Iraq and Kuwait and began pounding Iraqi positions. Operation Desert Shield became Operation Desert Storm.

When Kim Taylor came home from school that afternoon, her mother met her and opened her arms, and Kim fell into them and fell apart. That Friday was Kim's sixteenth birthday. Beverley gave her the grandiose gift of a limousine to pick her up and take her to school.

"I'll always remember my sixteenth birthday," Kim told her mother. "I got picked up in a limo and we were at war and my brother was there."

Stelk, too, was absorbed by the war. He scrapped his plans to write about baptism and confirmation in the newsletter and renewed his call "to lift this situation to God in prayer. Apparently," he wrote, "God is the only one who can affect it. The unanimous appeals of the religious leaders of this land have failed."

The Anglican Communion since the 1930s had been officially opposed to war in settling international disputes, and presumably to civil wars as well. Defense was not at issue; what was was the willful killing. The Church's position had never stopped wars.

"But when nations go the way of war anyway," Stelk wrote, "the Church stands ready to support those who will suffer as a result of the actions of the State." He announced that St. Mary's would start a prayer scroll containing the names of men and women in Operation Desert Storm who were connected to the parish, beginning with Eric Taylor and Charlie Laughlin. The scroll would be placed on the altar with a single lighted candle as a sign of constant prayer.

As Sunday approached, Stelk brooded over how to treat the subject. Judy Salerno had pressed her view on him in a passage she'd found in an old library copy of Thomas Merton's *Seeds of Contemplation.* It was a dark passage in which Merton said mankind only wanted peace in order to exploit, rob and consume without sharing. It ended, "So instead of loving what you think is peace, love other men and love God above all. And instead of hating the people you think are warmakers, hate the appetites and the disorder in your own soul, which are the causes of war." By Sunday morning Stelk was in a curt mood, impatient with distractions.

The choir was practicing before the service. The church school classes were gathering in their circles of chairs in the parish hall while Frank Doyle and Marsha McCoy went over the morning's lesson. Little Jenna Soso, starched and crisp, sat on a table and swung her legs. Acolytes were robing outside the sacristy.

Stelk was still in his clericals at ten twenty-five, bouncing around in the sacristy and fussing over details. The morning's lay readers, Ann Marwick and Bob Lockhart, had their robes on. I wandered into the sacristy as Bob, unswervingly conservative, was complaining to Ed Lumley about the Diocesan Council's approval of a New York City Board of Education plan to distribute condoms in the schools.

"It sends the wrong message," Bob was saying.

The sacristy was too small for the three of us to be standing there arguing, and Stelk interrupted brusquely to remind me I was underfoot. "You'll excuse me," he said. "I've got a few other things to worry about at the moment. We're supposed to be out there."

He poked his head out the door. "Acolytes! Get the choir in here."

The church bell rang. Stelk vested quickly and urged the

procession out the door and to the back of the church to begin the service.

"Come and reason together," Stelk began his sermon. "The words of the prophet Isaiah. 'Come now, and let us reason together. . . .' These are the words of God to the people of Israel.

"Did God create Iraqis as well as Americans?" he asked rhetorically. He reached for an answer into the Midrash, expositional footnotes to the Torah, to relate God's reaction to the rejoicing of the Israelites after the Egyptians who pursued them out of Egypt were destroyed in the Red Sea: " 'Stop, Moses, you don't understand. Those are my children. All made in the image of God.' "

Stelk paused for a moment. His brow wrinkled, and he seemed lost in thought. "It is so easy for us to admire the ability and technology of our bombing attacks. And as a former Air Force pilot, I do admire them. It's amazing, the things that we can do these days.

"I also wonder what happened to that peace dividend we heard so much about a few months ago. The peace dividend which was to clothe the naked and feed the hungry and house the homeless and do all the humane things which we had not been able to do because of the immense amounts of money that we had poured into these sophisticated weapons. And now all I hear on TV is how wonderful the weapons are and we need more.

"There is an awkwardness that I find as a Christian in my admiration for our technology. It's also something that as a former pilot I know: it is so easy to wage war from the air. You never see who you kill."

It was quiet in the church then. Only the children made noise. Nicholas Jabbour, the baby baptized at Easter, happily oblivious, was chortling in his parents' arms. He would be a year old on Tuesday. He was playing with his father's hair, and reaching for his mother. He was bouncy, always moving; the sounds he made were happy ones. The adults were intent on

Stelk's words. Beverley Taylor sat in her self-contained dignity in her usual seat in the second row. People watched her. Kim, once again, was serving as an acolyte.

"The ground war is coming. You and I will see who dies because it will be poured out of our TV sets into our living rooms and our kitchens and our bedrooms. We will not be able to escape it. And we will be part of it, for we will be living it as if we were there.

"God created *all* humankind . . . It hurts. It is difficult. We need to recognize that from the standpoint of God all war is evil, even that in self-defense, because it takes human life. It may at some times be necessary, and that is not what I am arguing nor am I saying Saddam is a neat guy, we need to pat him on the head. He's a rat.

"What I am saying is that we must not take lightly what we do."

He quoted William Tecumseh Sherman: "I am tired and sick of war. Its glory is all moonshine . . ." He quoted Thomas Merton, from the reading Judy had provided: "Love others, and love God above all." He quoted a byword of the civil rights movement: "If you want peace, work for justice."

Finally, "If indeed the lion can lie down with the lamb, as Isaiah predicts, perhaps even Iraq can lie down with the United States, the Israelis with the Palestinians, and all the rest who seem to have to be at each other's throats.

"Peace. The peace of God that passes all understanding is the peace that we are talking about. A peace that is more than tranquility and quiet and the absence of conflict. A peace that is a positive relationship with human beings, of respect, and love, and understanding. 'Come now, let us reason together,' says the Lord."

The war already had touched more of the congregation of St. Mary's. Stelk added the name of Michael Tortarelli, a parishioner's nephew, to Eric Taylor's and Charlie Laughlin's on the Desert Storm prayer scroll. Melanie Bussel said she had been unable to reach her husband's family in Israel since the Scud missiles from Iraq began falling on Tel Aviv and Haifa. But it was Beverley Taylor, whose mailbox was tied with a yellow ribbon, who focused the thoughts and attention of the congregation with her presence.

+

Stelk signaled the official end of the parish hall expansion at January's vestry meeting. "This is not Scarsdale," he told the members as they listened sympathetically. "We are not a rich parish. We do darn well with what we have. But the fact is, the type of million-dollar expansion we're talking about, it would have been a huge bite anyway, and with the downturn in the economy, it just doesn't look like it would fly."

No one at the sparsely attended meeting was surprised. Stelk for months had been the only one pursuing expansion possibilities. Dwight Douglas had not been a factor since last summer. The other vestry and planning and development committee members simply had felt the weight of the recession on the parish.

"And maybe it's a good thing we didn't get into it anyway," Stelk was saying.

He reported what he called a "providential" development: the house next door to the rectory was for sale. It was a two-story Victorian cottage in the same style as the rectory. The Realtor owner was merging with a firm in Croton. She wanted $300,000 for the house.

Since the FOR SALE sign had gone up, Stelk had been thinking of St. Mary's space needs in "a slightly different, but viable perspective." He described his ideas to the vestry. "There's an outside entrance [connecting] with office space in the top which could be used by AIM [the Agency for Improvement in Mohegan, which rented office space in the parish hall]. The ground floor could be used by AA, and on Sunday it could be used for church school classes. The parish offices in here could be moved to the first floor, and these rooms up here"—he swept his arm around to indicate the parish hall's top floor—"could be used for church school, too, and we could get a decent library up here.

"There are some options here which would enable us to get more space at one third of the cost we were talking about."

Stelk confessed that there were drawbacks. The house had no large meeting room and would preclude day care. On the other hand, it would give the church a few more parking spaces. He urged the vestry to consider it. "It's adjacent property," he said. "If you paint it white and blue like the rectory it would fit right in with everything else."

Stelk, the wardens and the finance and parish expansion chairs were delegated to look over the house and assess it as an annex, assuming that the doctor who currently rented a ground floor office didn't exercise his option to buy it first.

Stelk believed St. Mary's could afford the house even if it could not afford a million-dollar parish hall. Results of the pledge campaign had been encouraging. Walt Decker had smoothly covered last year's $9,000 deficit in repair costs with the money from two Harvest Fairs, the loan from the endowment fund and a small surplus from 1989. Now he reported that new and increased pledges pointed to a 1991 pledge total of $73,433, well above the $65,610 he'd penciled into the preliminary budget. "And we're still growing," Stelk added with enthusiasm. He said three families with children had appeared at recent services and appeared likely to join the parish.

The vestry, using Walt's new figures conservatively, finalized the budget at $109,200. It still included no money for major property improvements, but added repair funds and a small reserve for capital improvements.

Gerry Cousins shook his head, puffed out his round cheeks and passed out lists of the parish's maintenance needs. The $30,000 stucco job headed the list, then $10,000 for stucco repair and paint inside the church, $13,000 for paint and stucco on the rectory, $8,000 for painting the rectory interior and a couple of other things. He didn't put a price on surfacing the parking lot, which he said was also needed.

The shoddy church roofing job remained a problem. The roofer who'd put two nails in the roofing tiles instead of four still wasn't returning Gerry's calls.

The mission committee list of recommendations included spending $375 for a freezer for the food pantry, so Judy Salerno could repeat her Thanksgiving turkey giveaway. Judy also needed storage space for frozen bagels; since she'd struck a deal with a local bakery, the food pantry recipients, still averaging about fifty a week, had started to find bagels in their grocery bags.

+

Stelk continued to brood about the war in the Persian Gulf. It presented a dilemma. Turning the other cheek was not really possible among nations, and Stelk knew it.

The morning of January 27, the third Sunday after Epiphany, was cold but not bitter. I passed pockets of snow in the roadside hollows and among the tussocks of winter grass as I drove to Mohegan Lake. Bare trees cut the low sun into serrations of shadow and light.

It was a Normal People Sunday at St. Mary's, the day once a month when the church school and the choir were suspended to give the teachers and the singers a day off. Stelk wore the bright green Guatemalan stole Ginny had given him as a birthday present the year before. Judy Salerno had printed her Thomas Merton quote on the bulletin's food pantry insert, under the heading "Food for Thought." The congregation was singing, "Glory to God in the highest . . ." when John and Vinnie ricocheted into the church. They reached their spot at the left front and looked frantic when they found it taken. John Harbeson moved to give them a place.

Walt and Mary Jane Decker straggled in late, and then John and Joyce Donovan. It was as if there were some distraction in the community this morning. In the last week the Desert Storm coalition had continued bombing Iraqi troops and installations, while Iraq launched more Scud missiles at Israel and Saudi Arabia. Late in the week came news of refinery fires that were spreading black smoke and a fear of global cooling. Then the news, more sickening still, that Iraq had opened the valves at a Kuwaiti terminal, spilling millions of barrels of oil into the

Persian Gulf. Television showed cormorants dying in the goo. Everyone was struggling to make sense of the demons that had been unleashed. But so far, no troops had engaged. There was only the terrible, incessant pounding of the bombs.

Stelk's sermon was dense, fraught with the anxiety of war and the struggle to keep one's soul in the midst of it.

For the record, he was talking about evangelism, in line with the Anglican Communion's declaration of the nineties as a "decade of evangelism." Stelk began with Jesus' words from the Gospel according to Matthew: "Follow me, and I will make you fishers of men."

But he quickly posed the complicating question: What does evangelism mean? Does it mean drawing people "out of the world, a place of conflict and of evil"? Or does it mean to live and serve "within the brokenness of this world, to take social action and social concern seriously because it is a ministry, a way to proclaim the good news of God in Christ, that God loves and so we love, and we act in love.

"The argument continues within the Church . . . also in the area of war and peace."

This was where he was headed.

"It is quite clear that Jesus taught, Turn the other cheek. Walk the extra mile. Those who have over the years tried to deal with an imperfect world and can't accept the absolute pacifist position have evolved what is called the just war theory. It is taught in seminaries. There are eight points to it: One, war must be proclaimed by lawful authority; two, the cause must be just; three, the belligerents should have a rightful intention, that is, to advance good or to avoid evil; four, the war must be fought by proper means; five, action should be taken against the guilty; six, the innocent should not suffer, which is meant to mean should not suffer loss of life; seven, war must be undertaken only as a last resort; and eight, there must be a reasonable chance of success.

"You can see how easily anyone can justify any action they want to take."

Stelk confessed his own ambivalence as a former pilot.

"I can speak to this from personal experience. I believe it is a sin to take a human life. But I served as a bomber pilot in the Strategic Air Command in the fifties. I did so knowingly, and willingly. I served on occasion on the Number Two target in our strategic war plans, downtown Moscow. It was very odd, later on, walking around downtown Moscow when I was there, wondering who had those plans at that point.

"I knew that if I went to war, and flew, I would kill thousands and thousands of people with the one weapon that I had . . . and I was thoroughly convinced that I would lose my own soul in the process. But I opted to do it anyway, and to accept the consequences, because I felt that at that time, in that place in history, this was an effective deterrent to a holocaust of unimagined proportions. The only effective deterrent was a group of people who were committed to do the insanity that we were committed to do.

"It is not an easy decision either way."

This was stretching into one of Stelk's longer sermons. The church was crowded, not only with the new families that recently had come to St. Mary's, but with the church school children and the choir. Justin Miller, Adam Decker and David Marwick were clowning in the back row of folding chairs. Adam was wearing a Bart Simpson T-shirt. Babies were crying, and Stelk spoke over them, telling of being an Air Force veteran at seminary.

"There was a group called the Episcopal Pacifist Fellowship. A Navy veteran and I were the lions in a den of Daniels. It was an argument between pacifism and peacemaking, about the relationship between those of us who might well take a human life to defend ourselves or our loved ones . . . or who might take a life in a war that we considered a justifiable one . . . and were yet committed to peace and the peaceful solution of conflict. The group evolved to be the Episcopal Peace Fellowship, not an absolute pacifist organization. I have been a member for many years."

Stelk was saying that warriors as well as pacifists could work for peace. "Ultimately," he said, "in refusing conflicts or working in the midst of them, we must remember that our duty is the same . . . to do whatever is necessary that the world might be transformed into the divine intent . . ."

"What was that all about, anyway?" Judy Salerno said afterward when we were taking the day's food donations to the pantry. It sounded to her as if Stelk was letting the end justify the means. She thought the bombing had been started too soon, partly to distract from the deteriorating economy she was seeing signs of every week. The food pantry still was serving fifty families every Friday. The numbers hadn't dropped the way she thought they would. Judy thought all the yellow ribbons around Mohegan Lake were less a signal of support for the troops than a sign that people had let themselves be fooled.

Stelk, of course, had a constituency that almost forced him to equivocate. The conflict lay within his family as well as within his church and, perhaps, within his heart. Kirsten had been wearing a copper MIA bracelet, the kind you hardly saw anymore, since she started going with Joe Byrne. Joe felt the Vietnam veteran's lingering bitterness over the restraints imposed on the fighting there. Kirsten had said, "He's not a warmonger, but if you're going to fight he believes you might as well do it." Joe wanted to kick ass and take names, and Kirsten, with her MIA bracelet, exhibited her sympathy. Marla was a pacifist, and an antinuclear demonstrator. The irony was that she attended Colorado College, in Colorado Springs, the city that was the home of the U.S. Air Force Academy. The town was full of young men who could, for all anyone knew, turn out like her father. And she wanted nothing to do with any of them.

Stelk said he could respect both sides. Each could be right, each justified, he said, "as long as it's something you've worked through and fought through." Stelk would honor your position on the war if you got there by wrestling with your conscience.

✣

Judy by now was attending services every Wednesday and Sunday. The food pantry absorbed her not only on Fridays for the distribution but throughout the week. Her friends and Dan, her husband, continued to tell her she was crazy.

"But Dan got his last Friday," she said, chortling.

Dan, a special-education teacher who was tall and rugged looking, with a rebel's requisite long hair, had determined to goad Stelk when he finally met him, Judy said. He wanted to engage Stelk about the underpinnings of the Church, which he considered faulty. He had seized on the legend of St. George slaying the dragon. A Church that venerated a saint who may never have existed, who slew a nonexistent beast, even if that saint was the patron saint of England and a martyr, was in Dan's view on pretty shaky ground.

His opportunity had come as he and Judy were at the parish hall unloading cases of canned goods she'd found on sale at Shop Rite. They were schlepping the cases when Stelk came in the parish hall to see if he could help.

Dan greeted the priest cordially enough. There was no meanness in his point of view. Judy said she had the feeling that for all his fulminating, Dan was going to back off. "I wasn't about to let him do that and keep going on at home about St. George and the dragon and how ridiculous that is, which he's been doing for eight months now, since I started coming here," she said. Acting the provocateur, she said, "Linc, Dan has a question for you. But watch out, it's a trick question."

Judy said Dan tap-danced for a while, then said, "Isn't this Church part of the Anglican Church, and what about St. George?"

Stelk pointed out that St. George was a hero of the English Church, and wasn't on the American Episcopal Church calendar.

"Well, I just wasn't sure," said Dan. He thought Stelk was begging the question.

Stelk's eyes twinkled. "We really don't believe in St. George," he said. "However, we do believe in the dragon. The name we have for him is Clyde."

The parish of St. Mary's met for the one hundred and twenty-fourth time on the last Sunday of January. The annual parish meeting conjured, for me, visions of a New England–style town meeting. However, it started very slowly.

Fifty chairs fanned out from a podium at the juncture of the Green Room and the Pine Room. The podium gave a view in both directions. Stelk could see Judy Salerno huddled with John Weber, soliciting more mission committee support for the food pantry. Ann Marwick was darting in and out of the kitchen, where she had two soup pots simmering. Lily and Harold Van Horne sat in front, watching alertly, and Mary Jane Decker, behind them, was doing needlepoint on a round form. Marilyn Trudeau, the mathematics teacher on the vestry, and Karin Efman both were wearing yellow ribbons pinned to their sweaters and gold crosses on chains dangling outside their turtlenecks. Super Bowl Sunday, with the New York Giants playing Buffalo, had limited attendance to the most committed members of the congregation.

Stelk convened the meeting and started the voting for new vestry members. Ann Marwick, John Donovan and Dwight Douglas, who already had retired, were the members whose terms were expiring. Ann had done some arm-twisting to come up with a slate of five nominees. Gerry Cousins was unopposed for junior warden, and Joyce Donovan—a handsome, bluff, good-natured woman who had an aplomb John, her husband, lacked—had agreed to run for senior warden to succeed Karin Efman. The voting took about five minutes. A New York State law, the Religious Corporations Act, said the polls had to stay open for an hour, so everybody stood around talking and eating Ann Marwick's tasty chicken noodle and vegetable noodle soups.

When Stelk reconvened the meeting, he thanked a long list of parish groups for their work during the past year. He recited the year's highlights, ranging from the Eagle Scout landscaping project dedicated on Rogation Sunday, to the bell tower repair, the Easter Vigil and the new organ pipes.

"The food pantry has really blossomed. That's something to

celebrate," he said. "It's also something to lament. It's a shame that we have to be feeding fifty families in this county." He seemed suddenly overcome by emotion, and his voice broke. "It is an utter shame. It's a blasphemy. But the fact is that we have to, and we're able to do it, and that is a blessing and a real blessing. Judy Salerno and Susan Hafford have done just yeoman work on building this thing up . . ." The group interrupted with applause. Judy looked embarrassed.

He was talking about the lectors, the members of the congregation who read the Lesson and Epistle at ten-thirty services, when Harold Van Horne spoke up.

"A lay reader's not a lay reader? How come?" He focused on Stelk with his bright bird's eyes.

"What do you mean?" Stelk looked perplexed.

"The lay readers don't read. They don't read the Bible."

Stelk explained the terminology that designated the readers as lectors and the lay assistants in the service as lay readers, but Harold had a look of triumph as if he'd gotten onto something. Stelk admitted the jargon was confusing.

Stelk glossed over the frustrations of his year. He had never met with Cynthia Bondi and Alice Marwick, his candidates for the Mature Profession of Faith for whom he'd held such hope a year ago when they'd knelt before the bishop. School and work schedules had continually gotten in the way. The frustration was greater, Stelk had told me, because Bishop Grein had commended St. Mary's program to other parishes. Stelk's enthusiasm remained unchecked, however. "This is not a puberty rite, this is not a bar mitzvah, it is something different, a way of helping people make a mature decision," he said. He confessed, "I must admit I have not done a good job of building on the beginnings."

David Odell, chair of the dormant parish expansion committee, shook his head sadly when Stelk asked if he had a report.

"The economics have stalled somewhat," Stelk said ruefully. But he brightened with the news of more baptisms to come, and marriages, "a whole bunch of marriages." That means, he said, "We are still growing."

Stelk described the new vestry structure that grew out of the retreat at Ann Marwick's. He said the vestry members would take over their "portfolios" when the new members were sworn in and officially adopted the new scheme.

The year's big news, which Stelk saved for last, was that he and Ginny had managed to grow tomatoes outside the rectory. "We had tried for years," he said.

Beverley Taylor, prim in a yellow sweater and blue slacks, said, "Father Stelk, it's because you've been planted in the proper location."

Stelk was taken aback by the applause that followed. He tried to avoid looking flattered.

Ginny, Fred Obligado and Ed Lumley returned at that point to announce the winners. There was some hooting from the audience, most of whom had done their time on the vestry. "Winners?" somebody called.

"Victims," another voice responded.

Joyce Donovan, the new senior warden, chose a phrase from the baptismal vows as she undertook the senior warden's job. "I will with God's help," she said. And, she added, "at Ann Marwick's urging." The new vestry members were Rosemary LaPointe, who was received into the Episcopal Church in 1988 and attended her first Cursillo the next year; Gerald Morrison, a longtime parishioner and former member of the vestry; and Beverly Harris, an IBM employee. She and her husband and two acolyte sons had been members of St. Mary's for sixteen years.

16

The Desert Storm prayer scroll grew quickly. By the end of January, when eleven Marines were killed in the battle around an insignificant Saudi town called Khafji, it contained seventeen names. Stelk added the name of a cousin's son. Four names turned up in the collection plate one Sunday. Pat Bujarski rewrote the names in calligraphy, and the scroll rested on the altar under the constantly burning candle.

A handful of worshipers clustered in the choir stalls for the Wednesday service on January 30. It was a colorless day, neither bright nor dark, just cold enough to set the radiators rattling. Richie Efman, wearing his latest Oswego State sweatshirt, read the lesson. Stelk, stuck by the calendar with Brigid, the abbess of Kildare, explained her Druid background and conversion to Christianity. Eugene Jackson fell into a gentle sleep with his hands folded in his prayer book.

Eugene awoke for Communion. When the service was over he followed Judy Salerno to the food pantry. He approached her awkwardly and thrust a small, wrinkled envelope at her. She took it from him, and Eugene backed away in a series of oddly formal bows. He looked embarrassed and grave at the same time.

Judy opened the envelope to find a dollar bill wrapped in a piece of notebook paper, on which Eugene had printed, "Food Pantry." By this time Eugene was out the door. She ran after him and called, "Thank you. Thank you." Eugene bowed again, gave a half wave and kept walking.

"Wow," Judy said. "Wow." I thought I saw a tear in her eye.

The new atmosphere surrounding the food pantry was inspiring such notes of grace. Its renewed sense of mission was pulling parishioners and recipients alike into its orbit. Mr. W., a tall older man who during the winter wore a blue parka bearing an ABC Sports logo, had taken Judy aside one morning after he'd received his groceries and said, "Would it help if I came early and helped carry the bags?"

She said it would.

Mr. W. had been coming early ever since, helping to make up the bags and carry them to the front where they were handed out.

New volunteers were appearing from within the congregation, responding both to Judy's transformation of the food pantry and to the sharply higher numbers of recipients. One was Joan Ruedi, Lily and Harold Van Horne's daughter, who had Lily's eyes that drooped at the corners and Harold's high cheekbones. Joan offered to sort coupons. Judy had her own way of organizing the coupons, but finally she accepted because they were piling up on her kitchen table.

"You just cut them out and put them into these envelopes with these categories, and I'll do the rest," Judy was saying. She and Joan had taken a table in a corner of the parish hall, where Judy was explaining the contents of a large cardboard tray full of coupons and a wad of envelopes labeled from "Baby" to "Yogurt." The coupons were ones with no expiration date, and some were yellow with age. I sat down to listen.

Joan sifted through the mound of coupons, which was close to spilling over. "This would be potatoes, right? And this would be plastic bags? Okay, I'm getting this. Fruit Wrinkles. That would be snacks. Dog food? You have coupons for dog food?" She looked questioningly at Judy.

Judy shrugged. "Because people give us coupons for dog

food," she said. "And because someday there may be a refund offer that says, 'Buy a box of dog food and we'll give you a dollar back,' and the same week there'll be a seventy-five cent coupon in the paper, which I'll take to Danbury and double it, so I would buy the dog food and give the church the dollar and give dogs the dog food. So you might say, 'I'm never going to spend food pantry money on dog food or cat litter, but someday, if Shop Rite's having a half-price sale, it might be cheaper just to buy it, especially if there's a refund on it. I'm also thinking that down the road I might say, 'If you have a dog, do you need coupons?' I mean, people are still going to the store."

Judy's success in shopping lay in that kind of doggedness and inexhaustibility. She would leave no stone unturned, including dog food coupons, if it meant a bargain for the food pantry. Her energy had a momentum that carried others in its wake.

"Drinks. That would go in drinks." Judy looked at the coupons Joan was holding. "And that, that would be under a category called 'Mexican,' because you have an abundance of Mexican kinds of things."

"Did you cut all these out?" The sheer number of the coupons was impressing Joan.

"Who knows? Some of these I've had for ten years. But as long as there's no expiration date, they're good."

✛

The Cursillo scheduled for that weekend was an important one. The Cursillistas saw it as potentially revitalizing. Cursillo at St. Mary's had been at what Karin Efman called "a low ebb" last fall. But Karin and Rosemary LaPointe were involved in this one, as part of the leadership team of which Ann Douglas was the lay rector and Dwight a participant. George Munroe, Kathy's husband, was "making" his first Cursillo.

"That might fire us up a little bit," said Karin.

Stelk had even bought into this Cursillo, or at least was

giving it lip service. He had written, in the January newsletter, "Cursillo is a major renewal movement in our church, and we are blessed to have a sizable number of persons who have taken this particular walk with Christ."

Karin had been looking forward for weeks to the retreat at Mariandale, a Catholic monastery in Ossining. She was working on a string of successes. Susan had made the fall dean's list at Oswego (and assured Karin she wouldn't make it in the spring because of sorority rush). Laurie was named editor of her high school yearbook for her upcoming senior year. Now her expectations and excitement focused on the Cursillo weekend and the talk she was to give on piety. Karin had worked on it long and hard, using the computer in the office at St. Mary's to write what eventually became an eleven-page text. It began by defining piety, but in the end Karin told the story of her own spiritual journey.

She described being baptized and confirmed, defecting from the Episcopal Church because the Methodists had a better youth group and then, after high school, falling away from church. "I graduated from nursing school in New York City and went to work. There was no time for God in my life. But our God is a patient God," she wrote.

Soon she was living a version of the American dream. "I had a husband who loved me and whom I loved, the house in the suburbs, the station wagon in the driveway, two kids, the dog, the whole nine yards. The material things were all there. But something was terribly wrong."

Karin realized she was looking for God in her life when she made baptismal promises for Susan and Laurie. She wrote, "God was calling me back, and I finally heard him."

Her text was larded with loving references to St. Mary's as "a community of people trying to live as Jesus taught so long ago." She recalled that they had welcomed Richie before his conversion. "Surely these are not members of God's 'frozen chosen,' " she wrote, using the term for aloof, high church Episcopalians.

She wrote, "Being able to worship is very important to me, and when I'm absent I feel something is missing. Through praise and prayer, word and sacrament, I seek and find renewal."

But Karin had found the essence of her spiritual journey in the journey she'd made to Oswego at the end of last summer, when she'd dreaded delivering her first baby into a new life.

"I had so many things to say to her, and she was sleeping," Karin wrote. "There is a saying that your children aren't yours to keep, but God loans them to you for a while. It was time for me to step to the sidelines.

"God has blessed Richie and me with three daughters. Driving north that morning, I thought about the past eighteen years and how different my life has become. Would I be the same person I am if not for this sleeping young woman next to me? Again, I realized God had put Susan and her sisters into my life for a reason. In making sure they had a religious education, my own knowledge and love of God has been deepened immeasurably. The void I felt so long ago has been filled."

Karin gave the talk and cried when she sat down. She told me later she thought that would end her crying over Susan's leaving home. She had said the things it had been impossible to tell Susan that morning on the highway, and she felt at peace at last.

"Of course, Laurie will be going away at the end of next year," she said. "I don't know how well I'll cope with that."

+

Richie Efman was as enthusiastic about Cursillo as his wife. "Have you heard what it is like living with a convert?" Karin had asked her Cursillo audience. "It is true. Richie really wanted to be a cradle Episcopalian. He jumped in head first."

She described Richie's altar guild service and his embracing of Christianity. "He has shed a new light on what it means to be a Christian," she said. "He sees things I never saw or had lost over the years in the familiarity of growing up a Christian. I have sometimes envied his joy and excitement."

Richie truly was an enthusiastic Christian. It had to do with his natural effusiveness as well as his embracing of the faith, which he would happily describe to anybody who would listen. Judy Salerno asked him one Wednesday morning after the service what he thought was so great about Cursillo.

"It's a great experience, is all I can tell you," Richie responded eagerly. "It's intense. You're doing some singing, you're doing some acting out, all for the glory of Christ. That's all. It's unique. It's a lot of laughing." Richie was earnestly breathless.

"But why?" Judy wanted to know.

"Why what?"

"Why Cursillo? Why do you do it? Why is it necessary? What's wrong with church?"

"Oh. A lot of this is not given at the parish level," Richie said. "It's a different experience than church life. It really is. It's open to everybody, too. Anybody can come."

"You have to be Episcopalian, don't you?" Judy asked.

"I guess that's right," Richie said. "There are some rules. I don't think the Jewish folks would fit in. They won't understand. You have to be Episcopalian and pay a hundred dollars. But if times are lean the group will cover the cost."

Judy was curious about Cursillo because she was curious, now, about all things religious. Whatever it was that impelled her to church was boundless and insistent. She was still, as she had said, trying to figure out what was happening to her. She plunged into question and debate as she had in her first meetings with Stelk the year before. Her greatest frustration was that Stelk often seemed too busy for the questions that kept popping up, her own and the ones she kept hearing from her food pantry coworker, Susan Hafford.

"Everybody looks at Susan and sees this perfect, prim little Episcopalian lady," Judy said. "But we're sitting in a Chinese restaurant in Danbury at ten o'clock at night and she's asking these severe questions of faith. I don't even think it's questions of faith. I think she just needs something she's not getting, in terms of guidance. If she knew the answer, she might accept it, but she doesn't know what the answer is, and I'm not even sure she knows what the question is. And she's saying, 'I wish there was someone I could talk to. Someone like you.'

"Except I don't have the answers because I'm the new kid on the block. I think she wants the official answer."

One Friday after the food pantry distribution, Judy said, she and Susan had stayed at the parish hall talking until the middle of the afternoon. Finally, Judy had said, "Okay, pretend I'm Father Stelk. What do you want to ask me?"

"Okay. How do I know that Jesus Christ even existed? I never saw him."

"How do you know Napoleon existed? You never saw Napoleon."

Susan said she believed, not because she was convinced of the historical truth of Christ's existence, but because she needed to believe something. Judy had no such doubts. Her own questions had to do with the proper exercise of faith. They grew directly from her Catholic youth. Embracing religion anew, she could not embrace it casually. Her questions helped her test the validity of what she found herself doing. "This whole thing of Lent, for example," she said. "I'm still walking around with all this Catholic crap in my head. Twenty years of that kind of indoctrination is really hard to recuperate from.

"So Lent is coming. I have no idea how to deal with this. Stop eating chocolate for Lent? Why aren't we hearing about sacrifice? Or come up with some projects. I would much rather do something extra than pretend we're giving up something if we're giving up chocolate." Judy was frustrated by her inability to find the answers for such questions. "What is the forum for that?" she asked. "What's the company policy? Like when I see the services for Ash Wednesday, I don't see that you have the choice of having ashes imposed upon you or not. I make an intelligent decision whether I want this done to me based on what? Based on Catholic dogma? I'm not interested in that. Is there a different viewpoint? I'd like to know."

She had said just after we met, when she started attending St. Mary's, that she would not make a pledge to the church.

She said she didn't want the obligation and she didn't need the tax deduction since she didn't itemize. And then during the pledge drive Stelk had said, "You wouldn't work for somebody who said, 'I'll give you some money when I can afford it.' "

"I understood that," Judy said. "I could deal with it. You've got to know. This thing doesn't run itself. So I pledged. That's what I need about Lent and Ash Wednesday. Something I can relate to."

✢

Winter stretched on in a series of glum days. Snow plowed to the edges of St. Mary's parking lot stood in mounds that refused to melt and just got dirtier. Gerry Cousins hired a trapper to capture the fat raccoon that lived under the Pine Room, and took its leisure going through the garbage cans outside the kitchen. But somebody stole the traps.

"Probably an animal rights nut," Gerry said. He decided to build an enclosure for the garbage cans.

Air sorties continued in the Persian Gulf, along with missile attacks and counterattacks on Saudi Arabia and Israel. Oil continued to pour into the Gulf from sabotaged Kuwaiti oil terminals. The slick was easily the largest in history. The Cable News Network showed the queasy drama of Patriot missiles intercepting Scuds, exploding buildings as seen in phosphorescent green through Allied bombsights, bewildered cormorants trying to spread their oil-soaked wings, reporters ducking bombs in Baghdad and generals pointing to targets on maps. It was a gripping spectacle of destruction, and CNN saw its ratings rise. The candle flickered incessantly over the prayer scroll on St. Mary's altar.

Stelk spent much time at his desk. Often, he seemed weary, distracted by more than routine parish duties. There was a fey, neglected quality about him. He needed a haircut, and the hair on his neck looked like tangles of cobweb over his collar. He seemed caught in a trough of failed momentum.

I stopped in his office one afternoon as he was going over revisions of the prayers that supplemented the standard versions of the Prayers of the People. When he reached a stopping point, he gave vent to some of his frustrations.

"There are times when I wonder what the blazes I'm doing here," he said abruptly.

Several things were on his mind. The apparent failure of the parish hall expansion and his inability to arrange sessions with Cynthia Bondi and Alice Marwick were uppermost. But he was speaking generally as well. There had been times in his priesthood when, Stelk said, he felt "unable to be of any particular value or effect with regard to people's lives and problems." They had occurred at various times through the years. As he spoke one incident stood out. It clearly haunted him, almost as if he feared a repeat of the dissension that had doomed his tenure in Gambier, Ohio.

"Things are still going well here," he said. "But there was a period back in my former congregation where I was really getting burned out." The oblique reference to "my former congregation," the Harcourt Parish on the Kenyon College campus, was a way of saying he still wasn't comfortable talking about the rift between himself, Kenyon's president and his congregation. Stelk's forced resignation left him, for the first time in his priesthood, without a parish. He took on a term of service to the diocese as a supply priest, traveling from church to church and filling in where he could. He also worked as a substitute teacher. He enjoyed teaching, was good at it, although his level of patience was geared more to college than to high school students, and he had thought for a time of abandoning the priesthood and taking up teaching.

"I was really wondering why I was messing around with all this stuff anyhow," he said. "Nobody else seemed to care. At that time my friends in the Foreign Service and the Air Force were all beginning to retire, retiring and taking other well-paying jobs and doing all kinds of good things . . ." He paused and thought a moment. "But I don't want to get into all that. I don't want to dump on anybody."

Ginny had described Gambier obliquely as "more of a mistake."

Kirsten Stelk Byrne had been more direct. "It was a cloak-and-dagger affair," she said of the parish revolt that led to the call for her father's resignation. "It seemed like everyone was turning against him. It was a rough couple of years. He's still bruised. He's much too honest a person to survive in the political arena."

Kirsten added, "He tends to feel a lot of other people's pain and he tends to take that on himself. He's seen a lot of pain."

Stelk's father died at the end of 1987, of cancer at age eighty-one, and his mother died less than a year later, at eighty, just before the Stelks moved to Mohegan Lake. But the death that had most affected him occurred much earlier. When Stelk's younger sister died he was left an only child, angry and embittered.

Anne Stelk Worrell, recently married, had died in August 1977, of a rare form of leukemia which was diagnosed too late. She already had lapsed into a coma and was dying. She would have died in any case, but Stelk resented the late diagnosis for robbing his sister of precious months or years. Anne "had finally gotten her life together," is how Kirsten put it, and then she was dead and Stelk was supporting his parents emotionally and grieving at the same time, and the years had eased the memory only slightly.

The day was gray and close with fog that curtained the windows of Stelk's office and masked the trees in the picnic grove behind the parish hall. I expected to hear foghorns from the icebound lake behind the church, past the clustered condominiums built along its edge. Stelk made some final notes on his prayer sheets and looked at his watch. He said he was late for his Rotary Club meeting at the Imperial Wok in Yorktown Heights. The club was having its annual luau, and he had to find something colorful to wear.

He grabbed his black raincoat and was just rushing out of the office when the phone rang.

"Yes, yes," he said impatiently after the caller had identified herself. "Look, I've—" Then a look of concern crossed his face, and he said, "What's the trouble?" He sat down again, still in his raincoat, and listened.

"It's Mary Bohun," he mouthed, his hand over the receiver. He spent the next ten minutes with her on the phone, listening to her talk about problems she was having with her young son, Nicholas.

"There's another side of the coin," Stelk said when he hung up the phone. "There are times when there is a very profound kind of realization that I have been involved in something in a person's life which has been very important and deep and touching and helpful."

Then he bolted up and hurried to the rectory. He reappeared shortly wearing a shirt splashed with garish orange flowers under his black raincoat. He leaped to avoid puddles as he went running to the car.

✢

George Munroe's transformation after making his Cursillo was immediate. He put away the New York Giants sweatshirt he had worn to the parish meeting on Super Bowl Sunday and began wearing sweatshirts with religious motifs. With his grizzled beard and expression of pious contemplation, George resembled a biblical prophet.

Ash Wednesday came. Judy left the service with a smudge of charcoal on her forehead and washed it off immediately. She had sought out Stelk and insisted he give her the advice she needed. He had told her the point was not to parade her penitence:

"This is on your forehead, but that's not where it's going," he had said. "It's visible, but it's on your heart."

"I can relate to that," Judy said happily.

At that Friday's food pantry distribution, Judy received a note from one of the regular clients: "I miss Jones woud ask pormason for my mom tow peek up my food. Miss Jones." That set Judy to musing about the effects of the recession that she saw on St. Mary's doorstep each Friday. The numbers had declined since Thanksgiving and Christmas. Still, at least forty people were coming every week, double last summer's rate. Judy was beginning to believe that even a strong economy would not reduce the lines that much.

"Is it possible that this trend will continue at this pace? Or worse, escalate? I don't know," she said. "But I tend to think that a good portion of these people are hard-core unemployable.

"Take Mr. B. Mr. B. has a mental disability that does not seem obvious unless you say the wrong thing to him and he threatens to punch you out. Which he did last week when Mr. F. said he wasn't sure if Mr. B. was coming and didn't pick up his groceries like he was supposed to. You see Mr. B. and you see a white man, I assume he can sign his name and read and write and walk and chew gum, you say, here's a person who could have a job. Until the first day his boss tells him something he doesn't like. And that'll be the end of that.

"I'm getting to see more of who they are, but I don't have a whole lot of hope that many of them, short of winning the lottery, are going to succeed."

+

"I wish we could do it all again," said Lily Van Horne.

It was the first Sunday of Lent. The day before, nearly a hundred people had crowded St. Mary's for a memorial service for the church's rector for thirty-six years, the Rev. Canon Joseph Germeck, who had died. Germeck's tenure had been vigorous. He had led an effort to expand St. Mary's in 1959 and later tried to establish an outpost, a mission of St. Mary's, in Yorktown Heights. According to documents in the diocesan archives, the mission was viewed "with great alarm" by the struggling congregation of the Church of the Good Shepherd in nearby Granite Springs, which Germeck had headed as vicar from 1938 to 1953 in addition to his duties at St. Mary's. The prospective mission was eventually derailed. Germeck had served the parish until 1971, when he retired.

Stelk had just preached an eloquent sermon describing prayer as "a conversation, a dialogue, a two-way street. It means not only to speak, but also to listen, to be silent." In the parish hall after the service, Lily said she and Harold were about to celebrate their sixty-first wedding anniversary.

As she recalled their long life together, Lily was reminded of Harold's inability to master French despite their marriage in the French Evangelical Church in lower Manhattan on February 20, 1930. "In all these years, with all our family speaking French," she said. "But I would. I would do it all again."

Harold leaned close to hear what she was saying, then looked up with his bright-eyed smile. "That goes double for me," he said.

I asked how they were getting along, and Lily said she was having trouble with her vision. "Have you heard of macular degeneration?" she asked. "I can't see. I can't read." She was thinking of having an operation for cataracts, but wasn't sure. "I don't know," she said. "I'm pretty old." Shortly, however, she was reminiscing.

Lily had gone from her translator's job at the French consulate to Cartier, the jeweler. She and her boss, an American, were in charge of buying loose stones. She remembered the store's founder, Louis Cartier, fondly. "Mr. Cartier, oh, what a . . ." She stopped, groping for words as effusive as her adoration for Cartier's savoir faire. She described her work in a similar tone.

"Somebody might come in and want a two-carat diamond. We knew all the people in the market of New York City, and we'd say, 'We want a nice selection of two-carat stones.' And they'd all come in, very hush-hush, they had to ring a bell, we had to open a little window, let them in, just my boss and I. Oh, it was fun! Somebody wanted an emerald, a ruby, a sapphire, then we'd search the market. I remember one day a man came in, and he was opening his little papers—they carried them, you know, in little folded papers—and a diamond popped out, and we looked and looked and looked, and couldn't find it, and you know in those days, this was long ago, they had cuffs, and it was in the cuff of his trousers."

Harold interjected, "You know in those days, people were

more or less honest." Then he added, "You know, we've always had a good life."

But Lily wasn't finished with her story. "There were a lot of little small rooms where a customer would come in. And some of them were known. And through the building it would circulate: Mary Pickford's upstairs, buying, and everybody would go up to look. Oh, it was fun, a lot of fun.

"But anyway, so, then I met him." She nodded at Harold. "Then I had to speak English all the time."

They looked around at the emptying parish hall. "I wonder where Bob Lockhart is," Lily said. "He was going to take us home. I hope he didn't forget. Oh, it's just awful when you can't drive anymore."

They sat down to wait near the door, looking faintly bedraggled, like sparrows in the rain.

✛

Stelk again marked Lent with a series of healing services. This year he had the idea to make the service part of a Lenten evening that would continue with a light supper and videos tracing the history of Anglicanism and the Episcopal Church in the United States.

I joined a larger than average group on the night of the first service. George and Kathy Munroe were there. Ann Marwick brought Alice and David; her husband, Alan, a redheaded Scotsman who was a physicist with IBM, never came to church. Joyce Donovan, the new senior warden; the altar guild's Eleanor Arnold; choir member Joe De Domenico from Mohegan Manor; Bob Lockhart; new vestry member Beverly Harris; the reading teacher Barbara Miesch and Eugene Jackson were among the others. Ed Lumley was the lay reader. When it came time for the anointing, each of us was anointed in turn and stepped back from the altar to join a ring of people holding hands. Alice Marwick found her brother's hand and then David groped for Eugene's and Eugene found Barbara's and Barbara found Joe's, until the chain was finished.

The first night's supper was soup and bread and cheese.

Stelk insisted the meal be eaten in silence, according to Lenten tradition. But it was hard to get everybody to shut up. The videos followed a favorite theme of Stelk's: "We are not just another Protestant denomination," he said, adding, "and St. Mary's is not a typical Episcopal church."

"No, we're poor," said Kathy Munroe, enunciating her favorite theme.

Bill and Caryl Miller were absent from the healing service. They had been regulars the year before, but as the advance of her amyotrophic lateral sclerosis robbed Caryl of her movement, she got out less and less. She had trouble sleeping because it was difficult to find a comfortable position, and so she slept late in the morning after Bill had gotten up. When she awoke, the complications of dressing her began.

Bill continued to make their lives as normal as he could. He took Caryl away for weekends, with or without Justin, to break the monotony of her view from the living room. Many of her friends—or "people I thought were my friends," as Caryl put it—had dropped her since her illness. She, like Bill, was pained by the thought that the friendships had been such shallow ones. The best of their friendships remained constant.

One Sunday afternoon, I dropped in to find them entertaining their friends Paul and Toby, a couple from the neighborhood. They were wearing colorful warmup suits. Paul was on crutches. He said he'd torn tissue in one of his calves.

Caryl said she would have liked to be on crutches. She was seated in her chair, where she spent most of her time now. "My legs are at the end of their rope," she said. "And my hands are virtually useless. I'm getting weaker. I feel tired. But not sick." The slur in her voice had gotten worse, but she could still be understood.

Bill said Caryl had been taking Prozac for three weeks to fight depression.

"It helps," she said. "I used to cry. I was crying all the time. It got so when somebody said something nice to me, I would cry."

But Justin's behavior still bothered her. "He does his duty," she said, smiling bravely. "Last night, Bill went to a party in the city and Justin stayed home. I told him he had to mommy-sit. But he doesn't have any compassion. I don't feel that from him."

I was at the church the next time Stelk went to take her home Communion, but he said he wanted to go alone. Bill and Caryl's sixteenth wedding anniversary was approaching. Stelk wanted to focus on that without distractions. "There may not be another one," he said.

✢

Judy Salerno kept looking for arguments about the war. She was disappointed in Stelk's sermons on the subject. Although she was deciding—reluctantly—that there was a difference between the Persian Gulf War and the war in Vietnam, she still thought that it was too easy to justify war if all you had to do was struggle with your conscience. Had everything been done? Judy didn't think so. She argued that economic sanctions could have been given more time to work. "But that's not what George Bush wanted," she said. "He wanted a 'good' war to distract from the economy."

Bush also was an Episcopal president who was getting his spiritual advice from Billy Graham while the Episcopal bishop of Washington was picketing outside the White House.

The ground war in Kuwait came with fury and abruptness on February 24, a Sunday. It was a Normal People Sunday at St. Mary's. The local paper, the *Reporter Dispatch,* had described it unimaginatively in its Saturday church notes: "The choir will not sing. Instead, they will sit in the pews like regular churchgoers." Carol Obligado thought that was worth enlarging and pinning on the choir's bulletin board.

The morning news reports were full of Allied tank columns moving against Iraqi installations in Kuwait. The wholesale bombing of Iraq continued.

When John and Vincent arrived at church that morning, John was in a state. His discomfort was both painful and perplexing, and seemed to have no connection with the news. The pair were in their usual place in the front row on the left. John was wearing a dark blue shirt printed with large daisies. He knelt through the processional hymn and continued to kneel during the Lesson and Epistle. He murmured a prayer, and his hands moved to form a cross, over and over.

He still was kneeling when Kim Taylor moved to the middle of the chancel to hold the Bible for Stelk's reading of the Gospel. John stopped murmuring prayers and began making kissing noises, loud, smacking kisses. He was kissing his religious medals, fervently and repeatedly, first one, then another and another.

Stelk read from Mark. John kept kissing his medals. "If any man would come after [smack] me, let him deny himself [smack] and take up his cross and follow me [smack]. For whoever would save his life [smack] will lose it; and [smack] whoever loses his life for my sake and the gospel's [smack] will save it."

Stelk ignored John with an effort. John stayed on his knees and pressed the medals to his lips. Stelk finished the reading. He glanced down at John on his way to the pulpit and, once he got there, looked back with an air of patience tried. But John had finally satisfied his need for penance. He settled back as Stelk began his sermon.

Stelk did not preach about the war. Instead, he asked for prayer. He announced that the round-robin series of prayer vigils for peace in the Middle East would return to St. Mary's on Thursday. The prayer scroll on the altar had grown to twenty-four names.

"I bid your most intense prayers," Stelk said. "It will take, not just a minor miracle, but a pretty medium-sized one to make sure that all twenty-four come back. We're going to be burying some, friends, loved ones, whoever they may be. This is serious business. Prayer can be very serious, too. I commend all twenty-four to your prayers, daily."

Beverley Taylor had added a new name to the scroll. Her nephew, Bryan Dorsey, was on the ground in the fighting. "He's the one I worry most about," she said. "He's a Marine."

But by Wednesday, before the prayer vigil returned to St. Mary's, the Iraqis were being routed toward Baghdad. President Bush halted the hostilities at midnight. The news came on the radio after the healing service. The supper was over and the video rewound, and the choir was practicing its anthem for the following Sunday, "Righteous, O Lord, Art Thou," with music by Vivaldi.

"We've experienced a full-scale moderate miracle this week," Stelk said on Sunday. "We should spend the weekend giving thanks."

News about the twenty-four was slow to reach St. Mary's. It turned out that none of the men and women on St. Mary's prayer scroll had been killed or wounded.

But one hundred and forty-eight American troops were killed in the fighting, thirty-five by so-called friendly fire, and almost five hundred wounded. Their families could not rejoice in miracles. Iraqi casualties were estimated as high as one hundred thousand.

17

The Lenten healing services continued, but austerity gave way to competition in the postservice suppers. Each volunteer host tried to outdo the last. Beverly Harris followed Ann Marwick's noodle soups with vichyssoise. Judy Salerno followed Beverly's vichyssoise with a soup that incorporated potatoes, tomatoes, chives, broccoli and "a lot of cream." She laid out accompaniments of crackers and cheese, olives, grapes, orange slices, home-baked raisin bread and cookies.

More people were coming every week. Some twenty of us were seated at two tables, trying to follow Stelk's admonition against talking. There was the clink of spoons against soup bowls.

The silence ended, and Stelk was introducing the latest of the videos on Anglican Church history when Harold Van Horne spoke up. He wanted to know what had happened to St. Augustine. "As I recall from my school days, he was a very important man," Harold said.

"That was the first week," Stelk said.

Lily leaned to Harold. "We weren't here the first week. That's when they talked about that."

"But you talked about him, though? That's good."

Harold had strong ideas about Christian education. He objected to Normal People Sunday because it gave the church school classes one Sunday off a month. "I don't care at all about the color of the vestments. That's the minister's job," he said. "But the children need to learn the important things, like the catechism. And I'd put St. Augustine in that category, too."

The meeting was breaking up and the choir members arriving to begin their practice when a young couple entered the parish hall and stopped to look about. The man, wearing sweatclothes and athletic shoes, was burly, with curly hair a shade darker than his wife's. She was tall, with curly brown hair and light freckles across an upturned nose. She wore a loose sweater and stretch pants tucked into boots and was carrying a baby dressed in a blue bunny suit. Stelk greeted them and ushered them upstairs to his office. He said they had come for a baptismal counseling, and I asked if I might join them.

Stelk introduced the couple as Gregg and Sally Heineman. The boy, whose name was David Keith, was almost three months old.

Stelk settled into his squeaking, high-backed chair, fingered a flap of torn plastic on the arm and asked the Heinemans about themselves. They had been attending St. Mary's for several months, since returning to the Northeast from Texas.

"I had seen signs for the Church of the Good Shepherd," Sally said. She smiled easily. "I went there a couple times. I didn't know this church was here, but we drove by it one time, and I thought I'd like to try it. And I was so moved by your sermon . . ."

"Oh my," said Stelk, reddening and laughing to cover his embarrassment.

"I liked the church and the people. It was friendly, but I didn't find it real pushy. It had a warm, friendly atmosphere. I liked the fact that there were a lot of young people. And older people. It had a nice range. It was similar to the church I had grown up in in Rhode Island, where people are real friendly, but it's not pushy or overwhelming."

Gregg said, "My religious background has been, uh, getting married. It was never a big thing in my family. My mom had some when she was growing up, but my dad never did, and they never introduced any of that to us at all. The only times I've ever been in church is for weddings, and since we've been married I've gone at Easter and Christmas.

"As far as Sunday, I don't think you've seen me, have you?"

Stelk laughed and said he didn't think so. He had met Gregg when he visited Sally in the hospital after the Heinemans' son was born. He'd scheduled the baptism for April 28, when, the diocese had informed him, one of the bishops would be visiting St. Mary's. Stelk told the Heinemans he wanted to go over the service. He found prayer books for the couple, while David Keith grasped his mother's little finger with one hand and explored his mouth with the other.

Stelk traced Judaism's departure from other religions by its identification of one God. "And at a particular point," he said, "God focused on one individual. One human being, like all other human beings. But within the life of this human being something profound happened. Something that we really can't understand, that was validated at the execution of this individual and the resurrection of this individual. And this act of resurrection, testified to by numerous people and known and experienced by other millions over the years, made possible a new relationship in the created order. We didn't have to live the way we had been."

Stelk was wearing his dark shawl-collared sweater with the Snoopy pin in the lapel. A prayer book was open in his lap, but he spoke without referring to it as he looked over his half-glasses at the Heinemans sitting on his office couch.

He explained baptism as an act in which God, "in some way that we can't quantify, can't measure, can't analyze, can't put on a chart, is involved. What we are doing is celebrating a life, a new life. The human life is already present. In baptism, we are celebrating God's love for this human life." The little boy stirred and cooed. Gregg and Sally listened in postures of attention.

"That's what we mean when we say baptism is full initiation by water and the Holy Spirit. We add the water, God adds the spirit," Stelk said.

Stelk explained that the ceremony was a way of initiating a child into the continuity—"the family"—of the Church. "Later on, when David grows up and has a chance to think things through, he may say the whole thing's a bunch of hooey and live a very, very fine life without the Church." Gregg looked surprised that Stelk would suggest such a possibility. "What that means, God knows. I don't."

The boy sneezed, loudly. Stelk continued, "But he may, understanding the promises that were made for him at his baptism, choose to try to live this life on his own."

The continuity and shared responsibility was the heart of the baptismal process, more than the symbolic cleansing. Stelk ran through the questions put to the parents and godparents in the ceremony, beginning with, "Will you be responsible for seeing that the child you present is brought up in the Christian faith and life?"

"The response is, 'I will, with God's help.' Now, if you or any of your godparents have any trouble with any of these responses we need to deal with that ahead of time."

"I don't think we'll have any problem with that," Sally said.

Stelk spread his arms expansively. "I wouldn't anticipate any. But what we have here is a turnabout. Instead of going east you're going to go west. Instead of serving the forces of the world, which are self-destructive, which aggrandize Number One, and I want everything, and everything for me, what we're doing is turning away from this self-destructive behavior into a lifestyle that says this world is more than me. I am part of it, but what is really essential in my life is that I am able to help someone else."

The couple nodded.

Stelk described the rest of the ceremony and the child's introduction to the family of St. Mary's. "I will, as I always do at the end of the baptism, parade David up and down the aisle, so his new parents, that whole churchful of people who become his godparents in a sense, can see their new son and remember that they're responsible for the kind of world this kid grows up in."

Stelk explained that the child should be brought to the altar for Communion. He said, "I'll dip my little finger in the wine and put it on his lips, and I haven't seen a child yet who liked it, but it's part of the full ceremony of Christian initiation."

Gregg said, "I've never gone up for Communion. Would you like me to, on that particular day?"

"The only question I've got to ask is, Are you baptized?"

"No, I'm not."

"You're not. Then I can't give you Communion."

"Okay. That's fine. I just didn't . . ."

"I can baptize you," Stelk said.

Gregg was speechless for a second. Stelk laughed to help cover his embarrassment. "What do you think? It might seem a little unusual, but there's nothing unusual about it, really. Give it some thought."

Gregg looked helplessly at Sally.

"I can see this is going to be an interesting conversation," Stelk said.

Gregg changed the subject by asking if out-of-town guests could be accommodated at the service. Sally said David would wear her grandfather's baptismal gown for the ceremony.

+

Lent drew down to Palm Sunday, the Sunday of the Passion. St. Mary's readied the palms and bells and instruments that recalled Jesus' welcome to Jerusalem, where he would die. Its crosses were shrouded in red to symbolize his crucifixion. I entered the parish hall where the congregation was gathering, and Ed Lumley thrust a copy of the Passion, Mark's account of Christ's betrayal and crucifixion, at me.

"You read this part," he said.

Ed, the dean of the lay readers at St. Mary's, was around fifty. His features were ordinary, but his darting eyes were disconcerting. Ed had undergone a difficult divorce that forced many in St. Mary's to choose sides. It ended with his ex-wife, Joanne, leaving to attend another church when it was clear the parish wasn't big enough for both of them. Joanne was an enthusiastic Cursillista, while Ed had a dim view of Cursillo. Ed had worked on Wall Street until the pension fund he managed was closed down. Now, with two grown sons at home and enough money in the bank to stave off panic, Ed was testing gourmet recipes and considering new job opportunities. A nattily conservative dresser, Ed hid an acid wit under his gray suits and navy blazers.

I looked at the sheet he'd handed me. The part he wanted me to read was circled. It was the part of Judas. Ed grinned. Diane Cousins was standing nearby. "Talk about typecasting," she said.

The procession entered the church to the jangle of bells and the clack of castanets. Dick Tramonti, the General Foods sales manager, read the part of Jesus in the Passion. Judas had two lines. Stelk spoke in his sermon of reliving the walk to the cross with Jesus in order to grasp new life: "Experience the life of this week, walk with the Christ in these last days . . . until we burst out of here with the joy of the Resurrection on Easter Day, having shared the grief of the death. It is this passage that can lead us through into inward and spiritual grace."

It was an overcast day, muggy and mild for late March, a day that promised the rebirth of spring. Gerry Cousins went around with a pole, opening windows. The crowded church stirred when Stelk added his daughter Marla's name to the prayer list during the intercessions. People looked at each other with concern. Stelk explained during the announcements. He said, "I'll do it now so I won't have to do it a hundred times at the front door. We included our daughter Marla in the prayers today because she and three friends were in an accident in Colorado on Friday night."

They had been crossing the Rockies at Rabbit Ears Pass, on their way to Steamboat Springs for a concert by a band called Phish, when a snowstorm blew up suddenly. They lost control and the van plunged off the road and down a mountainside. There were murmurs in the church as Stelk described what happened next.

"Daniel O'Connor, who was in the back, was thrown out

and killed. The two girls up front, Megan Sherman and Laina Shill, were wearing seat belts. They had some scratches and bruises. Marla was tossed around in the interior as the van went down the mountain. The three of them are in good physical health, badly bruised and aching. But they will have the trauma of the death that they'll be dealing with.

"Not that this is more important than the others on the prayer list," Stelk added. "But I know you'll be asking . . ."

The accident had happened Friday night. A few small trees had stopped the van's plunge down the mountain, and Marla had been trapped inside. She remembered, she told me later, that it took a long time for help to come. She didn't remember praying, which she did (reciting the Lord's Prayer) when she felt the presence of a ghost in the haunted house she and her roommates occupied in Colorado Springs. She remembered that she thought about her friends and family. She could feel the van rocking as the wind blew, and she wondered if the trees would break, or if gas was leaking and the van would explode. Then help came, and she was lifted back up to the road on a stretcher.

She had called her parents from the hospital in Steamboat Springs. She told them she was being released, but Stelk and Ginny felt a turmoil of concern and anxiety all mixed up with happiness that she had survived. Stelk wondered what to do next. Don't come, Marla said. He thought of Delaware, Ohio, and the morning Marla, as an infant, clambered under all the pews of St. Peter's Church to visit him as he prepared the Sacraments.

Stelk didn't linger at the front door after the service. As soon as he could, without stopping to unrobe, he went to his office and got on the phone to Colorado.

Marla told him, again, that she was fine. She was surrounded by sympathetic, supportive people. Her parents had visited her in Colorado Springs just a few weeks earlier, and she repeated that there was no need for them to come again. It would distract from the shared grief that the survivors felt, the shadows of guilt and the comfort of empathy that no one who hadn't been there could really understand and share. Ginny felt guilty about not going out. Marla said it would have been just another strain.

Later, after the memorial service for Daniel in Washington, D.C., his family's home, Marla coped in terms of a faith she understood more loosely than her father.

"I don't know why things happen," she said. "I don't know. I really don't. It kind of confirmed my belief in fate. But things happen for a reason.

"I relied on the fact that I believe that everyone has their own energy, or soul, or whatever you want to call it, that determines your choices or your personality. And that means that when you die you don't just go away."

+

The anxieties of Marla's accident did not die, but rather were submerged for Stelk by the swelling tide of Easter. Holy Week pulled him into its momentum, and he began to feel a rising joy that he exhibited as energy and a bubbly kind of chatter with everyone he met. His Easter face replaced the drawn look of concern. Within, his faith conquered the skepticism he occasionally felt. And on Easter morning, when he gazed from the back of the church across the crowded sanctuary, with its families with organized mothers and harassed fathers and babies bundled in flannels in spring colors, and called out, "Alleluia. Christ is risen," his voice contained the excitement of fulfilled anticipation.

"The Lord is risen indeed. Alleluia," the congregation replied, the first of its Easter responses.

"Today is a day of joy," Stelk said from the pulpit, spreading his arms and surveying the house with a smile that was a benediction. Bright tulips filled the windowsills and the corners behind the altar. The pews rustled as the people settled in, and the church was filled with the small chortles and trills of children. "Celebrate. I want you to enjoy. Have fun. And don't sit on your children.

"God has progressed beyond simple justice to reconciliation, to the divine intent that is the purpose of all of human existence. Christ is a source of joy and celebration. The joy that flows through you and out of you, this whole world can use it. We've got it by the bucketfuls. Joy! I bid you joy.

"Alleluia. Christ is risen."

The congregation responded, and Stelk said, "That isn't good enough. Alleluia. Christ is risen."

The response came back, louder this time, "The Lord is risen indeed. Alleluia."

The littlest children celebrated by seeking out the mysteries of the forests of legs under the pews. One boy rolled happily among the kneeling cushions, then pressed his mouth against the vinyl surface, made a rude noise and laughed delightedly. It was easy to see Marla as a child, crawling among the shadowed tunnels underneath the pews on a quest to find her father.

A young father approached the altar for Communion, bearing his child in the crook of his left arm. He was a big man, and clearly strong, and he looked with adoration at the child he carried effortlessly. He knelt, and lifted his right hand to take the bread, and Stelk bent low to give the child his blessing.

✢

Spring splashed its paintbrush around Mohegan Lake. Crocus and daffodils pushed forth and bloomed. Forsythia blossomed in full yellow. Japanese magnolias slowly released their tight pink buds. Dun-colored grasses began greening, and weeping willow trees were frothy with new growth. On one odd day in early April the temperature pushed into the eighties.

The Harvest Fair committee met, a sure sign that the season was changing. Lowell, the husband of lay reader Chris Warnecke, was again in charge of planning the fall fund-raiser. Another sign of spring was the impending visit of a bishop. This year it was to be the suffragan, Walter Dennis. The assistant to the diocesan bishop was an imposing, spirited black man Stelk had met years before in Newport News, Virginia, and come away impressed. He looked forward to seeing him again.

A breakfast of the ushers intervened. The ushers did more than hand out bulletins, take up the collection and manage an orderly flow of worshipers to the altar for Communion. They counted the congregation, which let Stelk know how much bread and wine to consecrate. This was important. A priest who overconsecrated wine could ruin a Sunday afternoon for the lay readers and for himself, for all the overage had to be consumed. Stelk had worked with an overconsecrating priest in seminary and was often in a wine haze before noon. Leftover consecrated bread also had to be consumed. Since the ushers were the last to take Communion, Stelk could threaten them to get the count right.

"When I get to the end, if I have too much, it's either me or you," Stelk said. "I'm going to start handing out big chunks."

"It's when you get ham and cheese on it that you know there's too much left," Walt Decker said.

"The lay readers will thank you if you get the count right, too," Stelk said. "They'll be able to stay awake all afternoon."

Some priests demanded more precision than others. Marc Lee had told the ushers which collection plate to hand him first. Stelk was not so picky about that, but he wanted the kneelers and the prayer books and hymnals restored to order at the end of every service. If the ushers forgot to do it, you would find Stelk in the church after everybody had gone home, hurrying from pew to pew, lining up the kneelers and rearranging the books, red (the prayer book), blue (the hymnal), red, blue, red, right side up and front side out, in each of the wells on the backs of the pews.

"And save the inserts from the bulletins," Stelk instructed. "They can be reused."

Just then John entered the parish hall and stopped abruptly just inside the door. I was afraid Vincent, usually just a step or two behind, would crash into him and send them both tumbling down like tenpins. But John was alone. He hungrily eyed the tables laden with Dunkin' Donuts, bagels, rolls, orange juice and coffee.

"What's this?" John asked.

"This is a meeting," Stelk told him.

"Can I come to this meeting?"

"No, John."

"Can I have coffee, doughnuts?"

"No, John. This is a meeting."

"I can't come to this meeting?"

"No, John."

"I can't have coffee, doughnuts?"

"After church, John."

Stelk's mention of the service restored John's equilibrium. He said he had to use the bathroom and disappeared into the men's room. The sound of him urinating and then washing his hands came through the open door.

"Some of us communicate in different ways," Stelk said. I remembered the day John had kissed his medals through the Gospel up to the beginning of the sermon. "But it's a ministry. Just one of the ministries that we perform."

John emerged and asked if the church was open. He said he wanted to say a prayer for Vincent, who had been hospitalized after a sudden bout of uncontrollable shaking. Stelk had visited him in Peekskill Hospital, and Eleanor Arnold had taken flowers. The roommates were inseparable, and now John's devotion to his friend emerged as he mustered his courage to tell the ushers and the priest that he meant to go and pray.

"It's open. Go on in," Stelk said.

"I want to say a mass, a prayer for Vincent." John's huge eyes were pleading for assurance.

"That's good, John."

"Is it open? I want to say a prayer for Vincent."

"It's open. Go on in."

"Thank you, Father."

John disappeared toward the church. The ushers' watching faces hid their thoughts. Stelk stood up. He surveyed the tables and asked, "Is there one of those chocolate doughnuts left? Or are they all gone?"

✛

Stelk had an agenda for the bishop's visit. There was still the prospect for expansion. Stelk had not lost hope for that, even with the diverting possibilities presented by the FOR SALE sign on the house next door. The suffragan bishop could be a useful ally in either case. Bishop Dennis also would confirm Stelk's candidates for the Mature Profession of Faith and install a new class of candidates.

Stelk knew he had failed in his instructions to the candidates. More accurately, he had failed to solve the schedule problem. Neither Cynthia Bondi, with her after-school work at an orthodontist's office, nor Alice Marwick, with her band practices and debate meets, had found a time to meet with Stelk that he could manage. He had put off delegating responsibility for what he wanted them to know until at last it was too late.

"I bombed out on this last year," he confessed to the ushers at their breakfast. "But we're going to try it again." This year, he said, he had a new approach in mind. He planned to reduce dependence on his schedule by having the new crop of candidates choose mentors from the congregation. "This will be an adult they can talk to, someone to ask questions of, and who is involved with the church actively," he said. "Because part of what this means is to serve."

Alice and Cynthia would be confirmed in any case, he said. They had, after all, entered their candidacy with the best of intentions.

The breakfast wound down, and people began to drift into the parish hall before the ten-thirty service. The choir robed and began to sing, practicing the morning's anthem. The acolytes gathered in their hallway outside the sacristy. Alice and Cynthia were scheduled to serve, and when they came in, Stelk took them aside.

"Bishop Dennis is coming in two weeks, and I'd like to get you two confirmed," he said. "Is there a time between now and then that we can meet?" He pulled his overflowing address book from his shirt pocket and opened it.

The young women compared their schedules with Stelk's. Cynthia worked Mondays, Tuesdays and Thursdays from two-thirty to six-thirty. Alice said, "Monday I have debate. Tuesday I'm free. Wednesday I have debate. Thursday I have jazz band.

Friday I baby-sit until late every single week. And this weekend I have the state debate tournament."

"I have been trying to find a time for a year to meet with you two," Stelk said, exasperated.

"Two weeks?" said Alice. "What is it in two weeks?"

"That will be the twenty-eighth," Stelk said.

"Uh." Alice looked embarrassed. "I can't be here on the twenty-eighth. That's the state band competition in Virginia."

Stelk's face reddened. "Okay, I guess that means she's getting confirmed and you're not," he said to Alice. He turned on his heel and entered the sacristy to begin vesting for the service. His sour mood was apparent as he whipped a knot into the cords at the neck of his alb and then chased everybody from the room, saying, "I've got to think."

He still was furious when he emerged. He knew, rationally, that busy schedules were no one's fault. He felt thwarted nonetheless to have the journey he'd initiated with such hope, to such fanfare in front of Bishop Grein, fall victim to overcrowded datebooks. The lay readers, choir and acolytes were waiting. Stelk breathed deeply and ordered the procession to begin.

✛

As Stelk and the parish prepared for Bishop Dennis's visit, Bill Miller welcomed Caryl home from eleven days at Helen Hayes Hospital in Rockland County. She was being fitted for leg and ankle braces. Caryl, however, said mobility was not the most important thing.

"I don't care about walking," she told me one Sunday afternoon after Bill had helped her dress and moved her into her chair in the living room. She was neatly dressed in brown patterned slacks, a black sweater and sneakers. "I mean, I care. But the most terrifying thought to me is not speaking. Because if I lose my voice, I won't be able to communicate. That scares me more than dying."

Caryl had been working with Debra Zeitlin, an augmentative communications specialist at the hospital's Center for Rehabilitative Technology. She was excited about a computer she had tried that would allow her, when her speech inevitably was slurred beyond understanding, to put her thoughts in print or on a voice synthesizer. Bill's insurance company had agreed to provide Caryl with an electric wheelchair, but the Millers had asked, instead, for the computer.

"I want to keep a journal," Caryl said. "It's really bothering me because I have so much to say and I can't write and I can't really speak and that will let me have my outlet. You learn a lot by sitting and being an observer."

Caryl had retained extraordinary poise in the face of her deterioration. I was always impressed by her thoughtfulness and ability to articulate her feelings. She was more of a doer and an organizer than Bill, who was still on sick leave from American Express. She was more effectual. While he focused on gestures meant to ease her passage and re-create moments of their life together, and tried to cope with his own pain at the same time, she could see things he couldn't.

Bill shuffled in from the kitchen with a cup of tea. She could no longer sip from the cup, and he'd placed a drinking straw in the tea. He had changed from the casual clothes he wore to church to jeans and a pair of shapeless slippers. He was reminiscing, and he started Caryl laughing with his description of himself as a bank "liquidator" when they met. He talked about their cross-country elopement and Woodstock and his return to office work at American Express. It was a time of rapidly changing values, and Bill's changed as rapidly as anyone's. "You think my hair's long now?" he said. "You should have seen it then." His supervisor made him sit out of sight behind a coat rack. Then he challenged the company's dress code. "I used the Civil Rights Act of 1968 to get out of wearing a tie," he said. "It was passed for women, but I brought an equal treatment case and won."

"The apple doesn't fall far from the tree," Caryl said.

She explained that Justin had gotten into trouble at his junior high school for wearing a hat that was on a list of banned attire. "He told me, 'It's a stupid rule and I'm going to fight it,' " she said. "I didn't like it at first but then I thought he should stand up for his beliefs. I want to propose to him the proper way to fight it. If he really thinks it's a bad rule he should get a petition and get other kids to sign it and fight it in the proper way."

She looked at Bill. "It reminds me of you," she said.

Caryl spent much time thinking about Justin. His attitude still troubled her. His battle to accept his mother's illness seemed, at best, a stand-off.

"I just don't know," she said. "He seems fine on the surface. He just kind of ignores the whole situation. But I think he's accepting it. He brings friends home now. He and his friends came and sat with me one day, and I thought that was very good. We talked about records and the music he likes. He won't talk about my illness. He'll change the subject or just walk away. He says he understands. He'll say, 'I know you want to get up and walk up the stairs.' But he doesn't show me any compassion in any way, and that bothers me. I have to ask him, and he acts like it's a big deal. He never comes to ask me, 'Mom, do you need anything?' "

I asked Caryl, as I often did, whether she was closer to finding the inner peace she said she sought. She wrinkled her nose. "I think I'm learning to accept more," she said. "My sister has come to live here now. Rose is in denial about my illness, but because of that she's got a lot of positive thoughts. She makes me scream. We laugh a lot. She's giving me new hope.

"It's an ambiguous situation. I've learned to accept, and in acceptance you kind of lose hope. She's giving me new hope, so I have the best of both. If I could just get the body to follow the mind. I feel about ninety-eight years old, but that's only my body, not my mind."

Bill and Caryl said they were considering psychological counseling for themselves. But Caryl's near-desperation to be able to communicate was aimed primarily at Justin.

A knock sounded at the door. Bill opened it and Stelk strode into the living room carrying his home communion kit.

He stood for a moment, making uncomfortable small talk. As he readied the wafers and the small silver chalice, Bill called to Justin.

The teenager appeared at the head of the stairs. He was holding a portable telephone receiver. "Hold on just a minute," he said into the phone, then spoke to Bill. "Yeah?"

"He's got a phone attached to his ear," Caryl said.

"Do you want to partake in this?" Bill asked.

Justin looked at Stelk in his clericals. "No," he said, and disappeared into his bedroom.

"You never ask him, you tell him," Caryl said.

Bill followed Justin into his bedroom and closed the door. Stelk pretended nothing was happening. Caryl talked about the ceremony she and Bill had planned for the following month at St. Mary's, the renewal of their wedding vows. She said, "We had always planned to do it after twenty years. We've been married for sixteen. But I told Bill, 'We'd better not wait.' " She rolled her eyes and smiled.

"I'm looking forward to it," Stelk said.

Bill reappeared, but without Justin. "He won't come out," he said with a shrug of defeat and a look of puzzlement. "Let's go ahead."

Stelk said the brief communion service and administered the Sacraments. Caryl accepted the wafer with her eyes closed and allowed the priest to tip the wine into her mouth. She smiled until Stelk left. Then she looked toward Justin's bedroom door. "It's hard for me to discipline him now," she said. "But I still can make my feelings known."

+

A poet named Charlie Smith wrote, "It's too bad the way spring plays with us this year, waving a bright handkerchief out winter's window . . ." A hard rain driven by a raw cold wind raked a landscape filled with golden splashes of forsythia, pale blushing Japanese magnolias, purple wisteria and showy white cherry blossoms.

The bishop's visit was a week away, but Stelk had been thinking about Jonathan Daniels. More than a year earlier he had remembered his seminary classmate at a Lenten healing service. "Christianity should confront the status quo," he said, and told of Daniels's murder in Alabama in 1965 while working in the civil rights movement. Stelk had lamented then that the Gospel that stirred him to talk of Daniels was relegated to a Tuesday during Holy Week.

Today, the third Sunday after an early Easter, presented another possibility. John 10 described the good shepherd as one "who lays down his life for his sheep."

"Let me tell you a story today," Stelk began his sermon. Something in his voice, some portending quiet, said it would not be an ordinary sermon. Too much of Stelk was in it, of his values and his disappointments and of one unbalmed sore place at the center of his soul.

"Twenty-six years ago a young seminarian named Jonathan Daniels responded to a call for help after the debacle at the bridge at Selma. Jonathan got permission from the seminary and his bishop to go to Alabama. He suffered the slings and arrows of outrageous white folk when he tried to go to an Episcopal church with his black friends.

"He was arrested [along with a white Roman Catholic priest and two blacks, one a woman named Ruby Bales] . . . taken to the Lowndes County jail . . . and released without warning on the morning of August twentieth . . . There was nobody to meet them . . . They walked down the road to a country store . . . A deputy sheriff was standing on the porch. He leveled his shotgun at Ruby Bales. Jon shoved the gun down and took the charge full in the stomach. He died instantly. He acted as he knew he had to act.

"The shepherd lays down his life for the sheep.

"But the remarkable thing, my friends, is that Jon died, but Jon did not die. Jon lives." Stelk said a day in Daniels's memory in the cycle of prayer—August 14, the day he was arrested, since the day he died, August 20, was already taken—had been proposed to the Episcopal General Convention, and an icon memorializing him and other martyrs was being erected at the Episcopal Theological Seminary.

Then, his voice breaking at times, Stelk described his role in Daniels's life and death. Stelk had been chairman of the Social Action Committee that sent Daniels on his first trip south, to North Carolina in 1964. But he hadn't gone himself. When Daniels went to Alabama it was as a representative of the Episcopal Society for Cultural and Racial Unity, in which Stelk was also active. He seemed to be saying he had shirked a challenge that Daniels had accepted.

"I was invited on the trip," Stelk said. The Southern Christian Leadership Conference had called St. Thomas's Church to ask for reinforcements in the Selma to Montgomery march. "I couldn't go. Oh, there were all kinds of excuses for not going. I was married, we had a new baby, I had my duties as curate at St. Thomas's Church in Washington. The rector was gone, and I was supposed to be minding the shop. And I said no, maybe next time."

He recounted the parable of the wedding feast, from the Gospels, in which many are called and few are chosen. It teaches that a total commitment is required of disciples.

"So, you see," Stelk said, "Jon died for me."

The anguish in his voice riveted the congregation. Karin Efman brushed away a tear, and she was not the only one. The acolytes sat stock still, watching Stelk across the chancel. The church was absolutely quiet.

Stelk closed the sermon with a prayer that seemed to be for himself alone. "I do pray that we may know the shepherd when he calls us by name."

The Prayers of the People began reluctantly, with a sigh that sounded like regret at the passage of a special moment.

The congregation that passed from the church into the treacherous spring day looked at Stelk differently as they shook his hand and departed. He was a more vulnerable priest than they had known, a man who, in providing comfort, occasionally had need of it himself.

18

Stelk at last was talking to an actual confirmation class. This was a new crop of candidates for the Mature Profession of Faith, assembled in the church office with their parents, hearing what Stelk had in mind for them.

They looked bored.

Bobby Soso, accompanied by Bob Sr., who had shaved his beard, leaving a Fu Manchu mustache, had his glasses shoved onto his forehead and was staring into the middle distance. Morgan McCoy was squirming, while Marsha, his mother, listened. Justin Miller, as funky as possible in a sweatshirt, cutoff sweatpants and high-top Reeboks, was playing for laughs. The only girls in the group, Mia Malan and Suzanne Crew, were trying to ignore all this, and Barry Tucker was standing in for Barry Jr., who was absent.

"Are you ready to get married?" Stelk asked the teenagers. The boys rolled their eyes and suppressed giggles. "Hey, don't forget Romeo and Juliet were fourteen or fifteen." He spoke to Morgan and clapped Justin on the shoulder. The boys squirmed.

"I just want you to understand that this is a serious commitment," Stelk said. "And I plead that you deal with it seriously. It's not necessary to salvation. It ought not to be something you do because everybody else is doing it. It ought not to be something you do because your parents want you to."

Richard Malan, Mia's father, said, "It sounds like a pretty

heavy commitment, the way you present it." The Malans were ex-Catholics. Richard sounded worried that he was consigning his daughter, who at thirteen appeared to be going on eighteen, to a convent.

"We're trying to build disciples," Stelk said. He said he expected the candidates "to be part of our ongoing worship life, to serve as acolytes, ushers, even lectors. A Christian life is a life of service. Community service is included in that, too. I'd like to see a retreat built into this somewhere along the line. You can have some fun and games together, go away and get to know each other, relax a little bit."

The teenagers didn't seem thrilled at the prospect of spending a weekend with each other.

Stelk said he envisioned a September-to-June process, conforming to the school year. He told the young people they would choose mentors from within the congregation. "These will be people you can look to for guidance. Sometimes the priest can be intimidating, so this is to get away from that," he said.

"What's going to happen Sunday?" Richard Malan wanted to know.

"They'll be introduced as candidates and receive the bishop's blessing and ask for God's strength and guidance during the year ahead."

"If you don't do it Sunday, when could you start again?"

"The next time the bishop comes," Stelk said. "Which would be sometime next year."

The potential candidates went home to think it over until Sunday.

+

A long black Cadillac pulled into St. Mary's parking lot on Sunday morning, and an old black man in a black suit left the driver's seat to open a rear door. A large black man wearing the purple shirtfront of a bishop emerged from the backseat. The Right Reverend Walter D. Dennis, Jr., took the large valise his driver handed him and stepped toward the parish hall.

Moments later he and Stelk emerged together. They walked around the far end of the parish hall, Stelk gesticulating and the bishop nodding, then walked along the edge of the parking lot, looking off into the weeds.

Then they went back inside to get ready for the service.

Ed Lumley was briefing the acolytes outside the sacristy when Stelk appeared with the bishop, fully robed now and carrying his miter and the crozier with its silver head shaped like a question mark. Ed was talking about the bishop's throne-like chair, which would occupy the middle of the chancel.

"You'll have to either go over it or around it during the procession," Ed told the acolytes.

Bishop Dennis listened to all this wearing a broad, affable smile. He seemed a counterpoint to the austerity of the diocesan bishop, Grein. He had an easygoing manner and an enthusiasm for the proceedings that was infectious. He spoke with a Tidewater Virginia accent. "Whatever you call out, that's what I'm gonna do," Bishop Dennis said to Stelk. He repeated to the acolytes, "What the rector says, that's what we're gonna do."

Carol Obligado popped in from the Pine Room, where the choir had been practicing the anthem, and asked for "the real time."

"There's Standard Time, Daylight Time and Rector Time," Stelk said. "I'm going to go on Rector Time."

"Well, what time is it, Rector Time?"

"It's almost time to go." The sound of the church bell ringing came from the back of the church. "Oh God, we thank you for bringing us to this wonderful day . . ." the bishop began a prayer among the servers, and then they moved to the back of the church and waited for Carol to launch the processional hymn.

The procession managed to avoid the bishop's chair. Bishop Dennis's first words made clear what Stelk had had in mind when he walked the bishop around the boundaries of the property.

"I always enjoy being with this congregation," the bishop said. "It is responsive and vital. I look forward to the time when this place will be able to expand. I've always felt that there ought to be some degree of expansion here, because every time I've come, the place has been packed." He looked out upon a congregation that had overflowed into the reserve of folding chairs.

"Your rector walked me around this morning and told me that you had owned all that property next door in 1960 and sold it. I had a Maalox moment." He waited for a surge of laughter to subside and added, "I hope you will be able to expand commensurate with your growth."

Three baptisms, the Heinemans' and two others, were scheduled. He described them as "plugging these children into two thousand years of tradition. Everybody in this place who has been baptized has done the same thing that every Christian over all the years has done, I don't care if they have been baptized in the River Jordan, in a hippie bathtub or a punch bowl in an English manor house." He said, "The water of baptism is the amniotic fluid of the Kingdom of God. As the child emerges from the mother's womb into a totally different world, so now these children will emerge from the world of sin and death into a world of grace and truth."

Of the candidates for the Mature Profession of Faith, he said, "Their task is to be prepared."

Launching his sermon after those preliminaries, Bishop Dennis said he had not been at St. Mary's since 1985; a bout of hypertension-related seizures had interfered with his normal three-year visitation cycle. He promised, "I'm not going to preach forever. But a preacher who doesn't get around but every five years ought to say something." His sermon lasted the better part of a half hour. It was based on the confusing parable, from Matthew, of the landowner who pays the same wage to laborers who began work at the end of the day as those who worked all day long and then dismisses the complaints of those who worked longer. Bishop Dennis drew a lesson of generosity from the confusion.

"There is a vast difference between the standards of human beings and the standards of God," he preached. "God does not deal with men and women by logic alone, but by an overflowing generosity that is concerned only with what we need, not with what we have earned and deserve." Stelk's preaching tone was conversational, but the bishop's big voice rolled through the sanctuary. He spoke with the rhythms of a Southern preacher. He didn't pause when a child began wailing, just spoke a little louder. His gestures were broad and expansive; his hands dipped and swooped like sea gulls. "Now, most people want God to treat them that way. But, dear friends, most people are determined not to treat their neighbors that way."

Rather than interpret generosity to others as a wrong to themselves, Bishop Dennis said, "Members of the majority should rejoice that blacks and Mexican-Americans and Puerto Ricans and Dominicans and Orientals are getting a chance to enjoy the same rights and privileges that they do. Those who have enjoyed the privileges of living in a rich country like the United States should rejoice that immigrants from other countries are seeking the same benefits. Men should rejoice that women are entering the work force and on an equal footing. Those who possess financial security should welcome the fact that the government is trying hard to make life more secure for a great many people."

The bishop spoke of the Christian promise that all people shall be served. But you could close your eyes and hear the words in a different context. They sounded like policies generally attacked in political campaigns. His sermon seemed to be for dreamers, not for the hard-eyed realists who set the policies of government.

"People are not Christians," the bishop said, "if their first concern is, 'What do I get out of it?' The Christian works for the joy of working, the joy of serving God and his fellowmen and -women.

"And that is why the first will be last, and the last will be first," which was the punch line of the parable.

✣

It was an unusual morning, full of surprises. Judy Salerno had freed her hair from the ponytail, the only way anybody at St. Mary's had ever seen her, and wore it cascading over her shoulders. Not only that, she was wearing a dress. This redefined her from a large woman in jeans and sweater to something of a beauty. There was a serene, Madonnalike quality that had been invisible before, and it was a revelation.

Barry Tucker Jr. had chosen Ginny Stelk, his Spanish teacher, to be his mentor. The Tuckers were squeezed together in the crowded pews, and so the teenager sat with Ginny on the day he was to begin his journey toward confirmation. He surveyed the scene in front of him, the lavishly robed bishop resplendent on his throne, and Barry, who, like the man who occupied that throne, was black, asked a question.

"Where's the bishop?" he wanted to know.

Ginny was taken aback. "That's the bishop," she said.

Barry looked surprised, then thoughtful.

Bishop Dennis performed the baptisms with the same exuberance he had put into his sermon, ending each with a stentorian "Amen." Stelk left the fathers and mothers and godparents standing around the font, and made the recurrent triumphal procession of his priesthood. Carrying each child aloft, gentled by applause from his congregation, he marched down the aisle and back three times, proclaiming, "Greet your new daughter. Meet your new son."

Gregg Heineman had chosen not to be baptized with his son. Sally said later he had told her he would if she really wanted it. But she didn't press him. Six months before they were married, Gregg's older brother had died in a motorcycle accident. It left him with a skepticism that kept religion at arm's length, as if a worthy God would not have let his brother die.

Bishop Dennis sat in his throne in the middle of the chancel to perform the confirmations and accept the candidates who were embarking on their journey to a mature faith. Justin Miller knelt in his impertinent best before the imposing figure of the bishop. He had bleached the lock of hair at the nape of his neck. He wore an oversized white shirt outside the waist of baggy bleached jeans and, of all things, a tie. Bill said it was the first time he had worn one. Bill hadn't been able to persuade Justin to tuck in his shirt. Bobby Soso, keeping up the family tradition of neatness, wore a black-and-white houndstooth suit. Five candidates felt the bishop's hands upon their heads; Suzanne Crew had decided to wait another year.

Melanie Bussel, in her choir robe, was confirmed along with Cynthia Bondi. It was something she had never got around to doing and had decided, at age forty-four, that it made no sense to wait.

"Do you reaffirm your renunciation of evil?" asked the bishop of the assembled confirmands and candidates.

Melanie spoke up. "I do."

"Everybody," demanded the bishop, and the hesitant teenagers joined in.

✛

The bishop sat down to dinner in the rectory and rubbed his hands together. There was pleasure on his broad-browed face. His enthusiasms were prodigious. He beamed at the beef Stroganoff Ginny placed before him. Though his high blood pressure had made him bank his appetite for food somewhat, his appetite for conversation was undiminished. There were four of us around the table; the Stelks had invited me to join them. The bishop launched a story about the power of the laying on of hands that was part of the confirmation service.

"Anyone can tell you the bishop who confirmed them," he said. "It has nothing to do with theology. I saw a man ninety-one years old not so long ago, and he could remember who the bishop was who touched him. You can call that zapping or whatever, and I was moved by that. That was his connection to the episcopacy," by which Bishop Dennis meant the body of the Church. "That shouldn't be his only connection," he said, "but it's one of his primary connections."

As he talked, I groped for the name of my confirming bishop and was unable to remember it. I thought, however, that I would have remembered Bishop Dennis.

The bishop asked Stelk why he was so eager to reform confirmation. Stelk said, as he had told the youngsters and their parents, that he was trying to create disciples.

The conversation meandered, touching on one point of religion or another and stopping for a time on confirmation vows. Like the baptismal vows, they could be reaffirmed. There was a reaffirmation service in the prayer book, intended to welcome back to the Church those who had fallen away. But in the openness of the Episcopal Church, it could spur what the Baptists referred to as an altar call, when worshipers went to the altar to testify to their belief. Bishop Dennis had another story at the ready.

"One Sunday a priest just decided," he said, with a storyteller's cadence in his voice. "While I was there for confirmations. He just did it. He said, 'How many other people would like, on the basis of this spirit-filled morning, to reaffirm your Christian vows?' I thought, 'My God, please.' And about fifteen or twenty people came up, and there I was. You talk about spontaneous!"

"Wow," said Ginny. "Wow."

"That's where my conservatism comes in," said Stelk. It wasn't the kind of thing he would have done. Stelk would say he was old-fashioned or conservative, but his love of the Church was partly for its ceremony, its music and the elegant Liturgy that was like a conversation between the congregation and God, with him in between. His fondness for traditional ceremonies was so great that Ginny liked to say he would burn incense in St. Mary's if he thought he could get away with it, although he'd never tried.

"That caught me totally by surprise," the bishop was saying. "Here were people lining up on either side, coming up for reaffirmation. Oh my." He laughed with gusto and affection. "You don't ever know what's going to happen in the Episcopal

Church," he said, and used his napkin to dab tears of laughter from the corners of his eyes.

"And this was not Valdosta, Georgia, either," Stelk said. In Valdosta, a Pentecostal congregation had moved en masse to the Episcopal Church, making it the largest congregation in the South Georgia Baptist stronghold.

"The Episcopal Church is full of delights." Bishop Dennis chuckled heartily.

Stelk repeated his quote from Bishop Tutu. "I use it over and over again," he said. "The Anglican Communion is 'untidy, but oh so loveable.' "

Bishop Dennis said it was hard for a bishop to be humble. "When I go to a church, there's always a fuss," he said. "You could easily get to be, just triumphal. That's why I always wash feet on Maundy Thursday. It reminds me that in all the fussing around and all the splendor, I wear the marks of *diakonea.*" He was talking about the deacon's role of service.

Outside, the bishop's driver waited. Richard Benjamin had driven Bishop Dennis since the bishop's bout with seizures. He always insisted on skipping services and meals. Both, he said, were off his diet.

✛

Old issues nagged the vestry, even as its shift to portfolio management went smoothly. The prospects for expansion remained as unsettled as ever.

A number of vestry members had tromped through the mock Tudor house next door. It needed renovations, and an independent appraisal to determine its true value. Walt Decker, who retained the finance portfolio, was unenthusiastic. While Stelk had seen a potential for church school classrooms, meeting space and offices, Walt saw the house beside the rectory as more limited.

"It's worth exploring," he told the vestry as it convened on the last day of April, after the bishop's visitation. "But the only arguments for it that I see is that it will protect our flank on that side, and it could be a house for an assistant if we get to that point."

As an investment, he said, the asking price was too high and the rent potential too low.

David Odell, who still headed the parish expansion committee, was dead set against it. "I think it would be a millstone," he said. "Let's not get hung up on it. Let's not let it divert us from our real need, which is to expand. We are bursting at the seams."

Stelk listened to all this with his elbow resting on the table and one finger tapping at his chin. He had told me the last thing he wanted was to squander time and money on a stopgap purchase, which is what the house next door would be. But in the best of all possible worlds, he would have liked to do both.

"That's right," he said. "Let's keep the two things separate. It would be nice to have that. The bishop said, 'Buy the damn thing and protect yourself on that side.' But the main thing is expansion. We continue to grow. This vestry still needs to look at options for expansion."

John Harbeson, who recently had started lay reading and spent some Sunday mornings scuttling back and forth across the chancel, splitting his time between hymns and prayers, pointed out that recession lingered despite the buoyancy that followed victory in the Persian Gulf.

"This economy looks like it's going to turn around," said David. "If we're going to do fund-raising, we should catch it on the upswing."

There was a mime chorus of nodding heads around the table.

David stretched his long legs out underneath the table and continued. "This is the future of the parish. There's no way around it. I don't think there's anybody here, or even their parents, who have ever donated for a brick for this place. Everything we have now was done by people who came before. We're living with what they did for St. Mary's. It's time for us to create something to serve our children and grandchildren. It's our turn to stand up and be counted."

Stelk saw the phoenix rising.

"I think what's needed would be a clear-cut directive from this vestry," David said.

"There was no formal decision to table the expansion," Walt said. "It would just be a matter of rejuvenating the committee."

"Well," said Stelk, "I think it would be helpful if the vestry reaffirmed its commitment to expansion."

The motion passed without dissent, leaving Stelk to once again prepare the parish.

✢

Eight fourth-, fifth- and sixth-graders were sitting on the steps of the fire escape from Stelk's office. Their teacher, Karin Efman, was conducting Sunday school from the lawn below. It was a bright May morning, the sky a brilliant blue with puffs of cloud and the sun high and hot. Dandelions were blooming in the grass, and the trees were in full leaf. Karin had decided to free her students from the parish hall. I arrived late to church and stopped to listen. "God in the world today," was her topic for the morning.

"What did Jesus say?" she asked.

"I'll be back," one of the kids said.

"Well . . . that's right. But who did he say would be here?"

"The Holy Spirit."

"Yes, so God is with us because of the Holy Spirit."

The children, five boys and three girls, were seated two to a step, and the pair on the landing at the top leaned backward out of sight and turned their faces to the sun. All you could see were their legs dangling over the step.

"Okay," Karin said. "So where is God? Is he up there in that cloud? Is he in that tree? What about here, in this concrete? Michael, please sit down."

"He couldn't be in concrete," Michael said. "They didn't have it then, so he couldn't be in it. God's in everything he created."

"That's true," said Karin. "But God was before all else,

before the earth was formed. So you could say he created everything, even concrete."

"Yeah, but why did he make all this stuff?" said one of the kids on the top step. They were sitting up again. "Like grass. No one uses it."

"Why did he make mosquitoes?" came a voice from a lower step.

"Why did he make ticks?"

"To kill us," someone said.

"Do you think God made anything for no reason at all?" Karin offered.

"Why did he make us?"

"Why do you think he made us?"

"To blow up the earth."

"To save the earth."

"The earth would be better without us."

Strains of organ music and the voices of the choir came through the open windows of the church. It was not a day for strict attention. Somehow the subject got around to the Garden of Eden and the tree of the knowledge of good and evil. "How old was it?" one of the kids wanted to know.

"I don't know. I wasn't there," Karin said. "Although I might seem that old to you."

"How did God make electricity?"

"God gave people a brain, and some people became scientists, and that's how God created electricity."

"But how?"

"I'm not good at science," Karin said.

"How does coal turn into diamonds?"

"I told you, I'm no good at science." Karin looked at her watch.

"Immense pressure." Karin turned around to see Rebecca Munroe, who had come out to say that it was almost time for the offertory hymn. Rebecca was Kathy and George Munroe's thirteen-year-old daughter, a pretty redhead who had her hair pulled back this morning with a purple band. She was in the seventh grade—and *was* good at science. "It's time to go in," she said.

The children streamed into the church to the strains of the offertory hymn, greeted by the welcoming faces of the congregation. Parents and nonparents alike watched them fondly, for their presence signified new life and continuity. They were a promise. For all of the comfort that prayer brought to each worshiper, for all of the generosity and sharing preached in the Gospel, the children were the crux. They were hope. Given that hope, each generation that tried and failed to create a better world could go on trying.

That was why Stelk challenged the role as "designated prayer" when his clericals made him the choice to offer grace or say the invocation. "I am no more a priest than any one of you," he liked to say. He simply handed down the story "that enables the laity, ninety-nine percent of the church, to be the people of God."

When Stelk was ordained in 1965 the priest's role was to save people from "this naughty world," according to a phrase in his ordination ceremony. It changed with the 1979 prayer book.

"The priest recounts the story of God's relationship to humankind," Stelk said. "He keeps the people aware of who they are, so that as the people of God they can take that knowledge into their daily lives, their work, whatever relationships they have with other people."

The hope he saw in children was what made the tradition worth passing on.

✣

The first time Bill and Caryl Miller were married—February 16, 1975, on Whiteface Mountain in the Adirondacks—it was below zero. This time, mid-May, a high had broken a spell of hot, muggy weather, and the temperature was in the sixties.

Justin was standing outside the parish hall door in a rented tuxedo and patent leather shoes when I arrived. He looked pleased with himself, although he said he was uncomfortable. Bill said it was not only the first time he'd worn a tuxedo, but the first time he'd worn a sport or suit jacket of any kind. Justin looked good in the tuxedo, actually, even with the bleached lock hanging down his neck and a pair of gold chains decorating his chest outside his shirt. A cross hung from one of them and a twisted gold horn from the other.

Bill was pacing back and forth inside, looking very much the nervous bridegroom. "It's a different nervous from yesterday," he said. "I was having an anxiety attack. This is an excited nervous."

Justin blew off the whole thing.

"I think it's . . . dumb," he said. "You get married once. Why do it again?"

"It's the blessing of the Church that's the important thing," said Bill. He told Justin that renewing wedding vows was the kind of romantic gesture women liked. Justin was unconvinced. "I still think it's dumb," he said.

Caryl was sitting in her wheelchair at the back of the church. Her father, Nick Pisano, a short old man with intense dark eyes, was by her side. She was lovely in a high-necked white dress with all sorts of net and lace. She wore pearl earrings and a flowery white headpiece with a net pouf in back that looked as if someone had woven a wreath of baby's breath around her head. She looked as nervous as her husband. A bouquet of small white roses and white carnations lay in her lap between her withered hands. There was a touch of net at her wrists.

Forty or fifty people had come for the ceremony. The Millers' next-door neighbors, the Tuckers, were there, along with Ginny, Ann Marwick, Marilyn Trudeau, Joyce Donovan and a few others from St. Mary's. The rest were relatives and friends of the Millers from outside the church. They included Caryl's aunt, who had a softer version of her father's face; her brother, who looked like a stevedore, a big man with a graying pompadour and wearing a sport jacket over an open shirt; Bill's mother, whose eyes were watery behind thick glasses; Steve

Ziniti from the pilgrimage to Lourdes, still hairless, with a yellow carnation in the lapel of his tuxedo.

Stelk entered from the sacristy with Bill and Justin. He said the ceremony was officially the blessing of a civil marriage, but added, "This is a marriage since 1975 that has already been blessed by God. We're here to celebrate that blessing." Carol Obligado struck up the music.

Caryl's sister Rose was her bridesmaid. Rose the bridesmaid was different from the Rose in sweatshirt and slippers who was her sister's caretaker. Today she was stunning in a smart dress with a black skirt and black-and-white polka dot top and a black straw hat with a great wide brim that swooped down over her eyes. She walked down the aisle with a bouquet in her hands. Caryl followed, pushed by their father. At the front he stepped away, and Bill moved to Caryl's side, and she smiled up at him shyly.

Stelk read the Lesson from the Song of Solomon and an Epistle and Gospel that also had to do with love, glancing now and then at Caryl. Then he moved to stand before Bill and Caryl to lead the couple in the renewal of their vows and to clasp a hand in blessing over the ring that Bill placed on Caryl's finger.

Afterward, Caryl sat in a place of honor in the parish hall. Someone opened a bottle of champagne. Steve adjusted the carnation in his lapel, raised a glass and toasted twenty years of friendship. Rose fed Caryl a wedding cookie. Bill held a glass of champagne to her lips. Stelk brought the church wedding register and showed it to her, filled in her name and Bill's and signed it for her.

Someone tied a heart-shaped silvery balloon inscribed "On Your Wedding Day" to the arm of her wheelchair.

A photographer herded the wedding party outside to take pictures against the backdrop of the church. During a pause, Caryl said she had had no word about her computer. It was painful to hear the deterioration in her voice. "I hope I get it soon," she said. "I want to write."

The sun faded during the picture taking, and someone suggested that Justin put his jacket over Caryl's shoulders, which he did. By then his pockets were full of money, wedding presents, and he said he'd changed his mind about the wedding. It wasn't such a dumb idea after all.

The reception was at the Zinitis' on Long Island, a long trip for Caryl by car. Rose took off Caryl's wedding shoes, which were tied with netting at the ankles. She put on her right shoe with its separate plastic brace extending up the calf, and then the left, new white sneakers with pink laces. Dave Schecter, the Millers' neighbor from across the street, helped Caryl out of the wheelchair into the car. Justin sat in the backseat of the car and ignored it all.

Bill said he was taking Caryl on a honeymoon to Sanibel Island, Florida. "We're going to have the same room we always had when we went there," he said.

✣

The long season of Pentecost began. On the following Sunday, Trinity Sunday, at the end of May, the fluid strains of "Amazing Grace" flowed from the organ like a great and stately river.

Susan Efman, home from Oswego for the summer, sat with her head on Karin's shoulder, nodding, with heavy-lidded eyes. Ginny Stelk announced that she was organizing volunteers to begin needlepointing kneelers for the altar rail and, eventually, the pews. Bob Pierpont, the fund-raising guru, said the current economic situation was no deterrent to a fund-raising campaign. He pricked up Stelk's hopes by adding that it was a good time to build, with advantageous mortgages and a lot of builders looking for jobs. Judy Salerno brought her father, Tony, to church; her mother, like her husband, Dan, still refused to come. John Harbeson, who had been elected (as a Democrat) to the Croton town board in March and was ending a six-month sabbatical from City University, said he was being "a scholar by day and a pol by night."

The new crop of St. Mary's T-shirts was unveiled at the parish picnic in June. They were purple and showed a quivering church, bulging at the seams, above the legend, "Growing . . ."

Stretched over some of the generous midriffs on which they were displayed, the T-shirts were a source of amusement.

Stelk and Ginny found a house at last. It was a tiny place, less than a thousand square feet, near Lake Tonetta in southeast Putnam County. "We finally decided it didn't have to be our dream house," he said. "It may not be the house we retire to, but it's a house." This time the deal closed without complications.

Stelk gave the invocation and benediction at the Lakeland High School graduation. He and Ginny celebrated Sara's twenty-fifth birthday with her on Martha's Vineyard, a trip they made in Ginny's Fiesta with its bumper stickers that read, "I brake for Hobbits and unicorns" and "No, Virginia, the rest of the world doesn't speak English." Stelk still fretted that his middle daughter was in a holding pattern on the island and not getting on with her life, and he still bragged vigorously about the plays she was directing. He reported every favorable comment and full house. Marla stayed in Colorado Springs to nurse the psychic bruises from her accident and her friend Daniel's death. She said it was "a pretty terrible summer," since she was making barely the minimum wage at her two jobs waiting tables. She started getting letters from Bill Miller. "It's strange, but I don't mind too much," she said. "I think he's just lonely and sees a connection to his past. Everyone needs to reach out to someone." Kirsten helped Joe renovate the house in Throgs Neck between his few carpentry jobs during the recession. She enjoyed going places with his daughters, who liked to introduce her as their stepmother for the shock value; they, and she, felt she was more like an older sister.

✢

One hot, hazy Sunday in the deep heart of the summer, when St. Mary's had gone to its schedule of single services and the windows were tilted open for the breeze, worshipers looked up during the processional hymn to see their acolytes dressed like tennis players. Sans robes, they wore white T-shirts, shorts, socks and sneakers. They were an amazing sight. Stelk had looked at the weather forecast the night before, seen a heat wave and decreed a change to summer whites. Bobby Soso hadn't believed it; he showed up to serve in a striped dress shirt and tie. Stelk said he was overdressed, and Bobby went to sit alone in church.

On that day Stelk spoke of Christ's "preferential option for the poor." Honor and integrity are not related to economic status, he said. Financial assistance to the poor "is part of what we have to pay for being civilized, to be concerned . . . all having to do with who we are as human beings and who we are as Christians. As Christians we are concerned for the least among us." He wondered in his sermon why state budget cuts being debated in Albany were coming out of programs for the poor, programs "for housing and feeding those who have less voice and less clout. The voice of the church has been largely silent, and I wonder why. We should be saying, 'No, no, no!' "

Judy Salerno waited for him to announce a petition drive. She said it was what she would have done.

On that day, too, Stelk announced that Sultan and Elaine Jabbour were leaving the parish to move to North Carolina. Their journey at St. Mary's Church, which had begun when their wedding reception could not be rearranged and had extended through their confirmations and their son's baptism, was ending. "We'll miss you," Stelk said. The congregation applauded. I remembered the morning Nicholas Alexander was baptized and Sultan's mother unleashed her primal cheer of joy that galvanized the congregation. The couple presented the bread and wine together, Sultan holding Nicholas Alexander, much larger now, in the crook of his left arm. The boy looked about with unaffected curiosity at the church he was seeing for the last time.

The next month Stelk and Ginny went on vacation to Ireland. Ginny sent a postcard of Blarney Castle and warned the congregation to expect some interesting sermons, as Stelk had kissed the Blarney Stone. He followed Joe Byrne's directions but ignored his advice and led Ginny on a walking tour of Joe's old neighborhood, which Joe had warned him not to do, and they were almost mugged before being rescued by the civilian police and spirited to safety in a beat-up car. Gerry Cousins used their time away to convert Stelk's office to space split between a nursery and a library. The old nursery became Stelk's office. It was a nice room, with a view toward the church from the window behind his desk, but of course Stelk couldn't find anything, his books were out of order, and he complained for a month.

Marla drove home at the end of the summer. She stopped in Washington to see Daniel's parents. She spent just a few days in Mohegan Lake before returning to Colorado. Ginny drove with her. Gwynyd the sheepdog rode in the backseat.

The weight of summer finally was too much for the trees, and fall began.

19

"Hallelujah," said the vestry in a chorus.

Walt Decker was holding up a check he'd received from Grace Church in White Plains. The amount, $18,863.94, was the proceeds from the sale to Grace Church of the house in Somers that John Baynard had bequeathed to the two churches. It was hardly the foundation of a building fund; the outstanding mortgage and back taxes had seen to that. But it was a victory to conclude the deal at all. "We were up against a negotiator in a collar," Stelk said, referring to Grace Church's rector, Peter Larom. For seven years, St. Mary's would retain a share of the accompanying trust fund as well. Since the operating budget was safely balanced and newcomers continued to fill the collection plates each Sunday, the money could be set aside until expansion plans were laid.

But as Stelk looked ahead to the new parish hall he so badly wanted, he sometimes saw a self-satisfied parish that wasn't eager to expand except on those Sundays when an overflow of worshipers squeezed into the church.

"I think the parish still doesn't understand what we're talking about," Stelk said one Sunday after church. "The vestry understands, the finance committee understands. But I mean the parishioners at large, in spite of everything we've done so far, and I don't know why." He was restlessly searching the bookshelves in his new office, looking for titles he knew he had but couldn't locate. He sounded like a salesman facing a tough sell with an exhausted repertoire.

"I don't know how else to say it," he said. "We are just running out of room.

"We have picked up between a dozen and twenty children in families, a total of maybe thirty people, over the summer. If we're going to be effective in teaching these children, we've got to find space for them. We don't have it, it's just that simple, not when they're meeting downstairs on top of each other with those third-rate folding doors.

"The future of this parish depends on it. If it's going to continue to grow as it is, it needs more room. It's not just to have a building. This congregation, whether it likes it or not, is going to continue to grow. It's for the well-being of the congregation and its members to plan for that growth and look ahead to see what St. Mary's is going to do to serve the area."

I asked if he had a timetable in mind for a ground breaking.

"Not really," he said. He was bent double, head tilted oddly as he searched a lower shelf. His voice rose in a strange echo. "We had thought of tying it in with the anniversary of the parish and all, that would be next May, when St. Mary's is a hundred and twenty-five years old. Aha! Here it is. Why did he put it over here?" Stelk pulled a paperback copy of Teilhard de Chardin's *The Divine Milieu* from a row of books and brandished it triumphantly. "But we're more concerned with getting committees set up to begin the planning process. There was a structure set up a long time back, but it never really got going." He pulled out three more books, moved them over and up and patted them neatly into place.

I asked if he would define his success at St. Mary's by whether he built a new parish hall.

Stelk left the books for a moment and leaned back against the edge of his desk. Through the window behind him, traffic on Route 6 moved slowly and a few leaves fell from a sycamore tree in the yard of the apartment house across the road.

"Success isn't really what a rector does," he said. "You like to do things where you can see a result, stack them up and see how high it goes. But you never really know what success is, unless it's having a congregation and a budget that continually grow. The problem is, what does it grow in?

"I'd love to see in the parish an active spiritual growth group such as the Douglases were looking for. Cursillo is fine, but it's not the only possibility. We have people who have talents in that area. We have people who are active in community concerns and helping those in need and could find ways to offer this as a gift to the congregation. We could find ways to take seriously the need for Bible study, theological reflection, to think through and live out more fully the faith we profess . . ."

Stelk said it was all just part of being a church. All of the buildings that might rise, all of the people who might attend, all of the activities, programs and enterprises that might occur, all were to a single purpose: "What is success? Why, it's to help people to grow in the knowledge and love of the Lord. No?" He raised his eyebrows, setting off a chain reaction in the furrows of his forehead.

✣

Caryl Miller was limp, draped rather than seated in her wheelchair at the top of the stairs. She had lost thirty pounds. Bill lifted her into the stair chair and strapped her to it. Its machinery hummed, and she descended the six steps. Bill carried down the wheelchair, unstrapped her, lifted her into the wheelchair, pushed her across the room, then lifted her from the wheelchair into the lifting chair that she no longer could operate. Her voice was all but impossible to understand, and she had trouble swallowing.

She looked delicate and pretty for all of that. Her eyes were bright. Her permanent had grown out, and her hair was short and neat. The apparatus that allowed her to communicate occupied a table in front of her. There was a portable computer, a printer, and a yoke that went around her neck and held a wand that produced a beam of light. She sent commands to the computer by moving her head into the beam. It kept her from being mute, and that made her happy.

Caryl had used the machine to write a note to a new home health aide. The note was a window on her illness and also a testament to her thoughtfulness and generosity. "I am writing this to help you get acquainted with me," she wrote. "Since I can't talk, I will write down some things that might help.

"The first thing is that I am like a rag doll. I have no use of my arms or hands. I have no balance.

"When I eat, I cough a lot after a few bites. Don't get nervous. Sometimes I have to stop for a while and continue at a later time. It's a long process and the key to dealing with every aspect of my care is . . . patience. My life moves in slow motion. When transferring me, if I have my brace on, you can just guide me and I can walk. If I have no brace, just pivot me.

"As we go along I will try to help all I can."

I had learned to admire Caryl greatly. She seemed awfully brave. It was hard to imagine what she was enduring, yet she never seemed to fall into self-pity. For all of the gratuitous use of the word "hero," I thought Caryl was someone to whom it could be justifiably applied.

She looked through the window longingly—it was a brilliant day—and began moving her head as she watched the computer screen. After a time a mechanical voice from the machinery in front of her croaked, "I like to be outside now, especially in the autumn." Then the printer whirred and the words appeared across a page. Caryl looked up and smiled.

She told me she had started writing a journal. A typical entry read, "Mood swings abound. Hysterical crying to laughter." Since then Bill had taken her to Woodstock, the site of his defining moment, and Caryl had described the trip. She used her pet name, Will, for Bill:

"The weather was perfect. A crisp autumn day. I was so glad to be out with Will relaxed. We met people he knew. They knew my situation and . . . I felt at ease. Usually people are uncomfortable with illness and death, so we end up talking about anything else. I have a lot of things I wonder about and would like to get input on but I don't dare for being called a crepe hanger. We sat around yesterday and talked about mortality. We read the Bible, sang and left. I wish we could maintain this peace at home."

The things she wondered about, she said through the computer, were "death and fear, which no one alive would know."

They had driven home listening to the Moody Blues, and when Bill stopped in the driveway, he lifted Caryl from the car and danced with her.

"It felt good to be held," she wrote.

But she was mad as hell about Bill's infatuation with an out-of-state woman he'd met at his annual return to Woodstock in the summer. "The infatuation from Vermont," Caryl called it. "I thought we were past that," the entry read. She was "disturbed," and "deeply hurt."

Caryl still was worried about Justin. He brought friends to the house regularly, which was a step. But he still made no effort to help her. She jerked her head into the computer's beam and wrote, "I worry about his whole generation and their materialism."

Much had evolved for Caryl during the course of her illness. Her faith had changed. "I am more in tune with the nature of things than with church teachings," she wrote. Church teachings, she wrote, meant "a lot of the rules, especially in Catholicism. The natural order is what I feel inside.

"I would simply say slow down and get to what's real.

"I would certainly be more sensitive to suffering.

"I would not be so worried about unimportant things. We get so hung up on nonsense. Like losing ten pounds. There is so much it would take hours." She sat back, apparently exhausted.

Another of her journal entries began with a paraphrase of Hamlet's admonition to Horatio: "There is so much more to heaven and earth than you can ever dream of in your philosophy."

She related that a friend had taped two movies for her, *L.A. Story* and *Hamlet*. "The two stories couldn't be further apart in content, yet the above quote turned up in both, which I happened to watch on the same day," she wrote. "Profound revelation or God trying to comfort me?"

Comfort or not, she felt God's presence. She wrote, "He is close by."

Bill followed me outside as I was leaving. The sound of football on television came from Barry Tucker's house next door. It was sprinkling rain, and we got in my car to talk. Bill already had told me he had met a woman. He had talked about her excitedly. I thought it was a way of trying to cope with Caryl's illness, just as Justin's was to pretend to ignore it. It made sense that Caryl was angry, but it also made sense that Bill would need an outlet, someone to whom he could spill out what were surely pent-up emotions. To find someone who took an interest in him reaffirmed his own life; it was a tonic that had perked him up.

I asked him if he felt he'd betrayed Caryl.

"If something happened, maybe. But nothing happened," Bill said. "But it made me think what I could have in the future, what I could be. Right now, I'm never myself. I can't do what I want to do. I'm married. I couldn't have any relationship with anyone."

Just then Justin appeared at the rain-streaked window, worry on his face. "What are you doing?" he asked in a panicky voice.

"Just talking," said his father.

I had a glimmer then of the turmoil they were fighting, how closely it boiled beneath the surface. How harsh and unfair it seemed for all of them, Caryl most of all, but Bill and Justin, too.

Bill said he saw changes coming in his life. He said he thought he would stay in the house until Justin graduated from high school. Then again, he wasn't sure. He talked about what he would do "when this is over."

✢

Coleman Hill said he was looking at another rough winter. He hadn't shown up at St. Mary's for a long stretch. When I finally caught up with him by phone, he told me his job at Palisades Fuel had gone from bad to worse. "There were four of us working, and three wanted the union, for benefits and all," he said. Coleman was the fourth. "The boss said he didn't care. So they went down to the local. Up until then it was pretty steady.

"I was doing service for the whole region, Rye to Putnam to Mt. Kisco. My time got cut down to thirty hours a week, but it never even got to that, because that's when the boss started playing games. He was sneaky about it. He started laying us off, one by one. I got a day here and a day there. It turned out the dispatcher was calling some guy from Mahopac.

"About that time the rent came due. I got two months behind, so we had to move. The landlady said she needed the house for her daughter."

Coleman said he'd moved his family to a smaller house. It had two bedrooms, not three, and his son and younger daughter were sleeping on couches in the living room. Coleman scraped through, occasionally driving a dump truck for a local construction company.

His construction and painting venture with his son, the business he called C & C, had ended up costing more money than it made, he said. He had been dunned for $2,000 in Social Security taxes that he couldn't pay. "I was working for myself, one person working with me. I didn't know. So I lost my shirt on that," he said.

The tide of bad luck even had engulfed a car he'd bought after earning a $500 discount by doing a paint job for the seller. "That car lasted two weeks and quit," he said. "It wasn't covered by the lemon law."

Coleman had filled out some job applications. He'd applied to another oil company, to a septic tank cleaning service called Honey Dippers, to the Field Home and to a group home down in Croton. "But they hired a guy. I got a letter saying thanks very much for my application. And they got somebody doing painting at the Field Home, too." He still was hoping something would come through. The family was in dire straits. He was behind on his rent, and the landlord was getting impatient. "I've been giving him a hundred, five hundred, but I don't catch up," he said.

Coleman said he had grown discouraged and hardly knew where to turn for help. The food pantry, he said, "is like a grain of sand on a beach. You get a little bag of groceries. It's not like food for a week."

He'd asked for help around the church. Stelk said the church had given to its limit. "If they say no, they say no, even if I know they've got it," Coleman said. "Christianity. It makes you feel funny." He'd stayed away from church because he owed money there, too. "I feel bad when I go," he said. Still, he relied on the Bible, which he said he'd read three times. "My mind speaks to me," he said. "It's there all the time."

✢

November came, cool and damp with days that kissed the face with mist and made leaves sticky underfoot. Karin Efman looked at her calendar and understood that Laurie would be away at school next year. She wondered how she still could feel the same, how Sue's leaving had changed nothing. She would cry next spring at the thought of Laurie's leaving for college and then would have several years to store her tears for Kristen.

No members of St. Mary's had attended a Cursillo since Jan Miller, a member of the choir, had gone to one in the spring. Karin and Kathy Munroe had felt unsupported in the absence of activities among St. Mary's Cursillistas. Ann Marwick, on the other hand, felt the pressure to gather as a Cursillo group on weekends was just too much. She declared that her weekends were for her family and said she didn't think the Cursillistas were bringing enough back into the parish.

Karin, too, was changing in her attitude about Cursillo. She had begun a two-year program of education for the ministry, and Cursillo had diminished in importance. She described it as "kind of a doorbell ringing, the beginning of a progression of steps." The education for the ministry program was further up the ladder. A group of eleven met weekly at St. Stephen's Church in Armonk to study Hebrew Scripture and engage in theological reflection under the leadership of Bob Dresser, the rector of the Church of the Good Shepherd in Granite Springs.

"I was struggling with what I was meant to do," Karin said. "This has meant a tremendous amount to me. It really saved me. I'm not sure I'm any closer to what I was meant to do," she added. "But now I don't worry about it."

The program was not a means to an end; Karin would not become a minister. "It's just to help you in your Christianity," she said. "And in your knowledge. It's very exciting."

Lily and Harold Van Horne applied to move into a home that would free them of the chores of housekeeping.

"The Andress Home. It's very nice. I don't know who Andress was. Some multimillionaire," Lily said.

"One of the millionaires of New York, long ago," said Harold. "It was originally a children's home, but now it's for adults. It's one of the nicest places I can think of. Right on the river. A real hotel atmosphere. Three meals a day right there in the dining room. Five stories, and the top floor has an infirmary, so if you get sick or break a leg, into the infirmary you go. It's perpetual care. The idea is that you go there for life."

Lily was concerned that they might have waited too long. "I don't know if they'll take us," she said. "We're very old. You have to be in good shape."

"You have to get letters from doctors, from ministers, from just about everybody," Harold said. "I've filled out pages and pages of application forms. Oh my. It takes months."

"Oh, forever," Lily chimed in. "If they accept us, we'll try to sell our place. We don't know. It's in the hands of the Lord. Oh, we'll miss it here. It's in Hastings-on-Hudson, you know."

Stelk said the Lord had spoken to the vestry, telling it to build a larger parish hall. He said, in a sermon that was also a sales pitch, "We are starting the expansion program once again."

He listed his reasons from the pulpit. "We are growing!" he declared, and begged the congregation, "Do not tell the fire marshal what we do on crowded Sundays with those wooden folding chairs. It is dangerous and illegal." He said the vestry planned to schedule by September 1992 a third service to relieve the crush. The issue hinged on whether St. Mary's could afford an assistant priest, someone who would also devote time to Christian education and youth programs.

"The food pantry demand has doubled," Stelk added. "It is not just the poor and the destitute. It is the middle class. We're facing a crisis in this country. Until we have the guts to deal with it in our political system, we'll have to keep offering Band-Aids."

He told the congregation that it could wait no longer. "This place and this time is every bit as sacred as Jesus walking in Galilee and Judea," he said. "This is the time and the place where God is present. This is the opportunity to be someone for God and to be God for someone. We must seize this opportunity. *Carpe diem.* Seize the day. This is the time and this is the place to fulfill the sacred trust. I believe this place, this parish will respond, preparing us for this time and this opportunity."

The challenge was effective. Pledges began pouring in, and Walt Decker estimated an $11,000 increase over projections. The vestry decided at its November meeting to announce the expansion drive at the parish meeting in January.

Stelk said that his candidates for the Mature Profession of Faith would begin their formal program in December. Four young people were embarking on the journey. Barry Tucker Jr. already had begun to meet with Ginny. Mia Malan had chosen vestry member Bev Harris as her mentor; Morgan McCoy had picked Frank Doyle, the church school superintendent; Bobby Soso had chosen Barry Tucker Sr. Stelk now called the program the "Journey to Discipleship."

Justin Miller had abandoned the journey for the time. Justin's life was profoundly more complicated than that of the other adolescents. They were struggling with hormones and pimples, while he was struggling with his mother's dying, slowly, before his eyes. They were embarking on a journey that required faith, and Justin's was shattered. As Caryl declined, Justin felt helpless, and the more helpless he felt, the more he began to act on his own to feel in control. He began to act recklessly, in ways that put him in danger.

A window of Justin's room opened over a small roof extension that he used for sunning and listening to the radio or just sitting, when he wanted privacy. It was also an escape route, low enough to the ground for Justin to climb down to some stacked-up concrete blocks and climb back up again. He started sneaking out at night. Bill said he was hanging out with teens from the city who were living in a group home near Peekskill, boys whose lives also were shattered, whose parents also were lost to them in some way, boys who, like Justin, were depressed and angry and on the edge of control. Soon he was following them into the city. The police picked him up in the South Bronx, and Bill had to go get him. Bill caught him stealing.

"I think he's stealing because he thinks his mother's being stolen from him," Bill said. "I don't know what to do. He doesn't listen to me."

The doctors told Bill later that Justin found glamour in his reckless life. It was a way of fighting the hopelessness he felt, of making him feel he was in control even as he watched the horrible thing that was happening to his mother, and in effect, to him. Sometime during the Thanksgiving weekend, Justin brought home a 9-mm pistol. Bill and Caryl awoke to the sound of a gunshot in the night.

Bill rationalized Justin's possession of the pistol in all sorts of ways, saying the other boys were using Justin, that he didn't know what he was doing. Justin hadn't hurt himself, but Caryl by then had seen enough to know that Justin needed what psychiatrists might call a cooling-off period. He needed time to regain control of himself and to understand what was happening to him. She told her health care worker what had happened and started a chain of events that ended with Justin hospitalized for a term of psychiatric treatment.

✢

Six candidates, a bumper crop, agreed to be nominated for the vestry. They included Bob Pierpont, the fund-raiser; Barbara Miesch, the reading teacher; Carol Obligado's husband, Fred; Betsy True from the choir; former vestry member John Tomadelli; and Keith McKenna, who was interested in finally getting a strong youth program going at St. Mary's. Ann Marwick, after just a year off the vestry, said she would run against Joyce Donovan for senior warden. Kathy Munroe put her name in for junior warden against Gerry Cousins, although Gerry still had his list of projects and had almost badgered the reluctant roofer into putting a new roof on the church.

Judy Salerno and Susan Hafford and the new host of volunteers gave out fifty-three turkeys among the sixty-seven bags of food at the Thanksgiving food pantry.

✢

On the day after Thanksgiving, my wife, Barbara, and I took the boxes that contained my parents' ashes from their empty apartment in Ft. Myers. We loaded them in a duffel bag with some sailing gear and drove to a marina near the causeway to Sanibel Island.

Mom and Dad had specified cremation but left no instructions for disposing of the ashes. I had decided to scatter them in the Gulf of Mexico. There they could lie among memories of our family. They had loved the Gulf coast, where I grew up. My mother had never stopped loving it, and my father, before he took a curmudgeon's attitude about the ever-increasing influx from the North, had built a sailboat to explore the waters around Ft. Myers Beach. She had scoured the area for stories, and he had pictured it in dozens of fine woodcuts. It would be a fitting resting place.

We took our gear, the ashes and a handful of flowers—red hibiscus and purple bougainvillea, clipped along the roadside—aboard a thirty-foot sloop. We motored into the channel that would take us through the Sanibel bridge and into the Gulf. The day was sunny, and a good breeze was kicking when we emerged into the pass between Sanibel and Ft. Myers Beach. We unfurled the genoa and sailed with it alone toward open water. We had a broad reach down the island, past the fishing pier. The island bristled with new hotels and condominiums. Speedboats towed brightly colored para-sails, another new addition to the quiet island I remembered.

I retrieved the ashes from below when I could see the south end of the island and the bridge over Big Carlos Pass. I brought the flowers up, too, and it was then that I realized I had forgotten to bring the Book of Common Prayer.

Both my parents loved the One Hundred and Twenty-first Psalm. They would have liked the old version, preferring the cadences of the 1928 prayer book to the sprightly modern language of the 1979 version. But I was without either version, and helpless.

So I reached into the ashes and sprinkled them, one after the other, and said halting words of love and prayer, and sent the flowers after them. The ashes were milky in the water, the flowers bright against their stain. Then the wind filled the sail again and bore us away. We were sailing fast, and my parents' resting place was quickly out of sight.

They would have wanted me to say the Psalm:

> I will lift up mine eyes unto the hills; from whence cometh my help?
>
> My help cometh from the Lord, who hath made heaven and earth.
>
> He will not suffer thy foot to be moved; and he that keepeth thee will not sleep.
>
> Behold, he that keepeth Israel shall neither slumber nor sleep.
>
> The Lord himself is thy keeper; the Lord is thy defence upon thy right hand;
>
> So that the sun shall not burn thee by day, neither the moon by night.

> The Lord shall preserve thee from all evil; yea, it is even he that shall keep thy soul.
>
> The Lord shall preserve thy going out, and thy coming in, from this time forth for evermore.

They would have liked that, and as hard as it may be to believe, a rainbow arced over Ft. Myers Beach as we came about and headed north along the shore again. It was a scrap of a rainbow, thin and very light. But it was enough of a rainbow to convince me, with all I had relearned of faith from the people of St. Mary's, that my parents were raised up among angels.

And more, that in a small church at Mohegan Lake, New York, and wherever people gather in humility to worship God, to forget themselves and offer some small portion of their lives and work to others, to speak and, more importantly, to listen; when they remember that what connects human beings to God is generosity and sharing, where and when that happens, we exist again as a community of people and divine work is being done.

✢

The community of St. Mary's gathered at the end of January for the parish meeting that would close out the old year and begin the new. There were the usual reports, the balloting for vestry members, the business of projection and review. All agreed that much had been accomplished, and much was left to do.

Stelk brought the small assembly to its feet when the business was all finished and closed the meeting with a prayer:

"Go forth into the world in peace," he said. "Be of good courage. Hold fast that which is good. Render to no one evil for evil. Strengthen the fainthearted. Support the weak. Help the afflicted. Honor all persons. Love and serve the Lord, rejoicing in the power of the Holy Spirit; and the blessing of God Almighty, the Father, the Son and the Holy Spirit be upon you and remain with you forever.

"Amen."

EPILOGUE

Barbara Miesch, Keith McKenna and Fred Obligado were the lucky candidates elected to three-year vestry terms as 1992 began, and Betsy True was elected to fill an unexpired term. Ann Marwick was elected senior warden and said she had missed vestry service more than she had thought. Gerry Cousins remained as junior warden to pursue his projects.

Within the new vestry and elsewhere in the congregation lay new seeds of activism.

Barbara Miesch, handed the portfolio for Christian education, went to work immediately. The new members and wardens were commissioned at the ten-thirty service the next Sunday, and Barbara announced that a discussion group would meet after the service in the Pine Room. "We're going to talk about the Gospel, what it is and how it works in our lives," she said. She soon announced a list of topics and speakers into 1993.

An Outreach Fair, advertising programs that needed volunteers, drew dozens of prospects after church one Sunday. The programs ranged from a battered women's center in Putnam County to Mi Tía, which funnels aid to women and children in Costa Rica. The big beneficiary was Midnight Run, the nighttime trips that carry food and clothing from the suburbs to New York City's homeless. Barry Tucker organized collections of men's clothing and assembled a group that agreed to meet monthly to make sandwiches.

Keith McKenna took over the portfolio for youth activities, and began planning a program of AIDS education to start in the fall.

Amelia Schultz, a willowy, intense young woman with boundless energy—she and her husband, Jeff, relatively new arrivals to the parish, were both choir members and lay readers—helped begin a revival of the Episcopal Church Women at St. Mary's.

Judy Salerno started editing the parish newsletter in addition to running the food pantry. Always scheming to produce something special for holidays, she bought some inexpensive Easter baskets and asked the congregation to adopt them. "You can take them home and add some goodies, like chocolate bunnies and jelly beans, for the Easter food pantry."

Stelk, everywhere he looked, suddenly found projects sprouting that he hadn't had to conceive and nurture.

+

Harold and Lily Van Horne were rejected by the Andress Home. Harold thought it was because of their failing eyesight. Lily was secretly pleased; neither of them wanted to leave Yorktown Heights and St. Mary's. Soon afterward, Lily fell and broke her hip, and began a long period of recuperation in Peekskill Hospital.

Harold fell not long afterward. His injuries weren't as serious as Lily's, and he was hospitalized only briefly. He and Lily, still recovering from her broken hip, received the services of a home health aide. But Joan, their daughter, said she didn't know what she was going to do.

"He's going to be ninety-four," she said. "How long can they go on?"

Coleman Hill landed the job he'd applied for with Honey Dippers. He described the job of cleaning septic tanks as "going down low." It paid enough to keep groceries on the table, keep the lights on and keep the rent current. The back rent was something else. He hoped, as summer neared its midpoint, that people would soon be thinking about their winter heating needs, and he'd be able to pick up some money cleaning oil-burning furnaces.

Justin Miller returned home a few weeks after his fifteenth birthday. Stelk, who had visited him during his hospitalization, saw a new young man. He said, "I've had the first real conversations I've ever had with him. I think he's going to be fine." Justin went on to make the spring honor roll in his class at Walter Panas High School.

Bill continued to try to give Caryl a world beyond her illness. He threw two birthday parties for her in February. He took her to Lake Placid at the beginning of the summer, and in August they made their annual pilgrimage to Woodstock. He also continued to grope toward a life after Caryl, which made her furious. She was on a feeding tube, sometimes she could hardly breathe, but she was still very much alive, as she described in a journal entry made on her computer.

ALS, she wrote, "takes your entire body away and leaves you with a brain that is fully cognizant and so much life left inside that you want to explode."

Her insistence on life wouldn't accept Bill's looking beyond her. "I am very aware of the psychology involving death and the way it affects the people around us." she wrote me during the summer in an angry and extraordinary letter. "The fact remains that I am still alive and alert mentally. All my senses are intact and I go out every day. I laugh a lot and tell jokes, play games and can still make love (with some modifications). And my heart still breaks."

Bill, she told me in the letter, was interested in a woman at the church. The fact that she was a psychologist Bill might have wanted to talk to didn't alleviate her anger. "Just because you know the subconscious reasons why you do things doesn't mean it's alright to go on doing them. There is still right and wrong," she wrote. "This is not the only girl he's been calling and seeing. There's one that's only half his age who he's been taking to dinner and talking to on the phone regularly. I could go on but I won't."

She considered it adultery and wished Bill felt the constraints of Roman Catholic guilt. "I'm not sure the Catholic Church was so wrong with its rules," she wrote. "My husband is sinning. I am profoundly sad and profusely angered and so deeply hurt there are no words to express the way I feel. I guess I feel betrayed, like Jesus."

She wrote other, more upbeat, letters, too, praising the nurses with whom she spent each day, recounting with delight their bargain-hunting shopping trips and crediting her computer, which she named Matilda, for enhancing her ability to pray.

"When I pray," she wrote, "it's usually done in silence. But sometimes prayers have to be spoken: those rare times when you're alone and you just need to talk to God one on one. Matilda makes that possible for me."

Bill, of course, maintained his view of betrayal as a physical act. As summer ended, he started a petition drive to make the Woodstock site a national historic site, which filled his time and helped take his mind off Caryl's deterioration. Justin took an after-school job bagging groceries and aimed for the fall honor roll.

✢

Stelk and the vestry clashed over hiring an assistant, and the divisions weren't easily erased. The issue wasn't the assistant, the Rev. Lisa Keppeler, who was ending a term as an assistant at St. Mark's in Mt. Kisco. Rather, it was Stelk's insistence that, although a part-time employee, she be given a pension, housing allowance, travel expenses and other benefits.

Gerry Cousins described it as a clash between the spiritualists and the realists on the vestry. He counted himself among the latter. "The spiritualists say leave it in the hands of the Lord and he'll provide," Gerry said. "We're saying, if the Lord wants to increase his pledge by twenty percent, we'll be glad to accept it because we're going to need it."

Stelk said that it was simply a question of doing the right thing.

Nonetheless, Keppeler was hired, beginning in September, to share Sunday services, work with youth and Christian education, and organize new pastoral care ministries, such as a calling committee to visit the sick and homebound.

Stelk announced a shakeup in the worship schedule coinciding with her arrival. He planned three Sunday services, at eight, nine and eleven. Church school for children and adults would fall between the later services.

The new schedule left the choir in a tizzy. Carol Obligado didn't know which service was supposed to feature music. She expected to alternate between the nine and eleven, but maybe she would have to split the choir. The confusion continued into the summer.

Hiring an assistant was theoretically a step needed to proceed with an expansion of the parish hall. But with the so-called realists on the vestry predicting a $20,000 budget increase, to $140,000 in 1993, and looming deficits, Stelk wasn't sanguine about the prospects for building. He sent prospectuses to eight architects, but the fund-raising committees were dormant, and he didn't know when, or if, work would begin on a new parish hall.

✢

These pressures seemed to wear on Stelk. He nearly collapsed during the evening service on Good Friday as the horrified congregation watched. He first lost his place during the Gospel and had to sit down. Then, as he was crossing the chancel to the pulpit for his sermon, he started to fall and was caught by someone in the choir.

Stelk refused to leave in the ambulance that arrived soon afterward. He insisted on returning to finish the service, signing a waiver before the ambulance crew would release him.

Stelk said it was a virus, or something he ate. Members of the vestry wondered if it wasn't something more serious, something Stelk was hiding for reasons that had to do with his need to be always in control. The question hung there, adding to the aura of uncertainty the budget and the new service schedule were creating.

Ginny faced the loss of her Spanish teaching job. The Lakeland School District told her she wouldn't be needed in the upcoming school year because enrollments had declined. By the time school opened in the fall, however, with a class here and a class there she was teaching virtually full time.

Stelk appeared healthy enough on the morning of May 3. It was a bright spring day, delicate with new green across the countryside that belied a poisonous atmosphere of riot and disgust. The Rodney King verdict, in which four white Los Angeles policemen were found innocent of assault in a beating that was caught on videotape, had set off a paroxysm of arson, looting, assault and shooting. It was an expression not only of criminality but of deep and profound anger. The rioting spread within Los Angeles and to other cities. By Sunday morning nearly fifty people had been killed. Virtually everybody with a pulpit of any kind spoke out for justice, for calm and for attention to the problems of the inner cities.

Stelk gave a post-Easter sermon about the disillusionment of the disciples after the crucifixion. The riots, the verdict, the neglect, all were absent from his sermon.

Afterward, he announced inquirers' classes preparatory to the bishop's June visitation. He announced a meeting of the Harvest Fair planning committee, and asked if there were other announcements, at which Barry Tucker rose and thanked the congregation for the hundred and fifty-two bag lunches volunteers had made the day before for Saturday's Midnight Run.

Finally, Stelk said he'd given the same sermon at eight o'clock and received two responses. "One person said it was very moving," he said. "The other said, 'I don't see how you can ignore the chaos in this country.' "

Then he called the verdict "one of the most stinking travesties of justice since my friend Jonathan Daniels was shot down in Alabama and his killer was set free." Stelk said he was less inclined than in the past to preach a social gospel. "My function is as a proclaimer of the Gospel. I've mellowed over the years," he said. "If this had been fifteen years ago . . ."

Stelk said, "I'm not unwilling to talk about these issues. The return of racism in this country appalls me. I'm not sure it's my function at this point. But if you want that kind of sermon I'm prepared to talk about that. Come and talk to me afterward. I can be converted."

Later he offered the Eucharist—a kind of dedication—"for those killed, injured or whose lives were disrupted this last week, and for the restoration of love, harmony and justice."

Judy Salerno said, "He gave a sermon about Doogie Howser sleeping with his girlfriend, for God's sake."

✢

St. Mary's celebrated the one hundred and twenty-fifth anniversary of its founding at the end of May. Marla Stelk graduated from Colorado College. At the same time Stelk's old outfit, the Strategic Air Command, stood down, its nuclear bombs declared irrelevant in the Cold War's aftermath.

"I thought, it's the end of an era," Stelk said. "Part of my life was closed out. Thank God, the whole reason for it disappeared."

Laurie Efman graduated from Lakeland High School and prepared to attend the State University at Oswego, where her sister Susan was a rising junior. Karin, to her surprise, found that she was crying less. She was becoming accustomed to the idea that her children were growing up. Matt Harris, the son of vestry member Beverly Harris, also graduated and prepared for college. Stelk said of the two acolytes, "I hope they go to church. But I only went five times in college."

Ginny said, "I think that's an exaggeration. He went less."

The year's episcopal visitation came on Pentecost, the day traditionally called Whitsunday that celebrates the descent, in tongues of fire, of the Holy Spirit upon the Apostles. For the occasion, Ginny had made for Stelk a bright red chasuble with yellow and orange flames, outlined in gold, climbing the chest of the short outer vestment.

It was the first Sunday of June—Pentecost falls on the fiftieth day after Easter—a mild, muggy day with a haze softening the new green of the countryside. The four young people whose journeys to discipleship were culminating in confirmation gathered in the parish hall before the service. Mia Malan and Morgan McCoy were unfolding banners they would carry as part of the procession. Bobby Soso was sitting on the staircase looking inscrutable. Barry Tucker Jr., wearing a dark suit, was bustling around nervously.

Outside the sacristy, acolyte David Marwick eyed Ed Lumley's outfit as the lay reader arrived to put on his vestments. Ed was wearing a navy blazer over a flashy pair of wide-striped blue and white pants. He needed only a straw boater on his head to complete the twenties look. I asked David if he thought Ed was planning to juggle or do a soft-shoe routine. "I thought maybe play baseball," said David with a grin.

Ed smiled thinly and retreated to the sacristy.

There were two other confirmands. One was an adult, Francine Herrmann, who was raised an Episcopalian but hadn't gotten around to confirmation. The other was Alice Marwick, who had begun to wear a new look of teenage melancholy. After missing last year's visitation because of her band trip, and looking ahead at a crowded high school schedule, Alice said, "I just didn't know if I was ever going to have the time again. I thought I just ought to go ahead and do it."

Judy Salerno had considered being received into the Episcopal Church and then backed off. She said, "I still had too many questions."

Like what, I asked.

She thought a minute. "Like, well, what is the Episcopal Church, really? What is my relationship with God supposed to be if I'm an Episcopalian?" She paused, turning her dark eyes to the ceiling. "And why would I want to join any club that would want me as a member?"

Stelk had designed a service complete with medieval pageantry to introduce the younger confirmands, the first real products of his dream of a maturely professed faith. Their banners—one showed doves of peace, another rays of joy, love and hope, the third candles and the fourth a cross—added bright splashes of color to the processional.

The visiting bishop was gaunt and frail, with a gray beard

that gave him the look of a wandering prophet. The Rt. Rev. J. Stuart Wetmore was the retired suffragan of the New York diocese, but he had another title, too, by virtue of being vestry member Mary Bohun's father and having a long association with St. Mary's. He was, Stelk announced, "the Bishop of Mohegan Lake."

Bishop Wetmore laid his hands upon the confirmands, but it was Stelk who performed the three baptisms that also were part of the service. He baptized the children with a zest and an enthusiasm that renewed him, as if he drew life from the water into which he dipped their heads.

And when he paraded them along the aisle to the applause of the congregation, when he said, "People of St. Mary's, greet your new son. People of St. Mary's, greet your new daughter," his eyes gleamed with a light that outshone the questions of the future and placed St. Mary's in the cradle of his faith.